1866-1991

125th

ANNIVERSARY

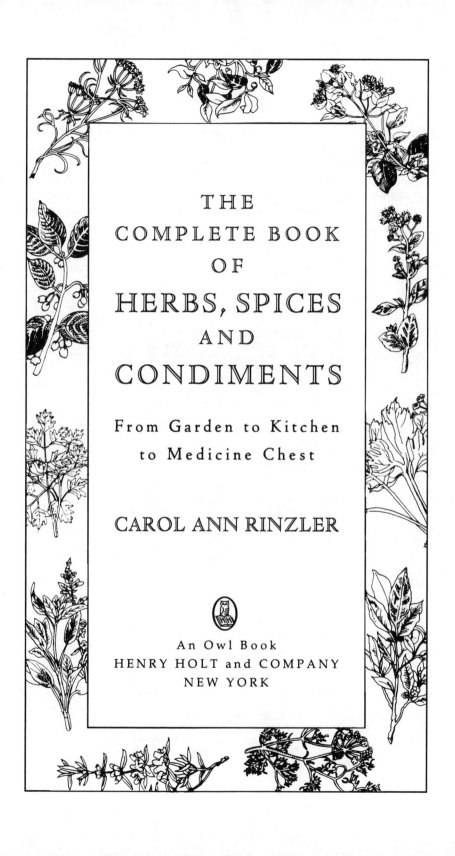

THE
COMPLETE BOOK
OF
HERBS, SPICES
AND
CONDIMENTS

From Garden to Kitchen
to Medicine Chest

CAROL ANN RINZLER

An Owl Book
HENRY HOLT and COMPANY
NEW YORK

Acknowledgments

Authors who write about scientific subjects are always appreciative of experts who are willing to take the time to discuss and explain their subjects. In writing this book, I am grateful to have had the chance to talk with James A. Duke, Walter H. Lewis and Varro E. Tyler, each of whom was kind enough to share with me information about the medical effects of plants. Without their gracious comments and assistance, I could not have hoped to tackle this job.

Library of Congress Cataloging-in-Publication Data
Rinzler, Carol Ann.
The complete book of herbs, spices and condiments : from garden
to kitchen to medicine chest / Carol Ann Rinzler. — 1st Owl Book ed.
p. cm.
"An Owl book."
Reprint: Originally published: New York : Facts on File, © 1990.
Includes bibliographical references and index.
ISBN 0-8050-1618-X
1. Herbs. 2. Spices. 3. Condiments. I. Title.
TX406.R56 1991
641.3'57—dc20 91-2016
CIP

Henry Holt books are available at special discounts
for bulk purchases for sales promotions, premiums,
fund-raising, or educational use. Special editions
or book excerpts can also be created to specification.
For details contact:
Special Sales Director, Henry Holt and Company, Inc.,
115 West 18th Street, New York, New York 10011.

First published in hardcover by Facts on File, Inc., in 1990.

First Owl Book Edition—1991

Printed in the United States of America
Recognizing the importance of preserving the written word,
Henry Holt and Company, Inc., by policy, prints all of its
first editions on acid-free paper. ∞

1 3 5 7 9 10 8 6 4 2

CONTENTS

A Note to the Reader

The information in this book regarding the medical benefits or side effects of condiments, herbs and spices, as well as their possible interactions with specific drugs or medical tests, is drawn from sources current as the book was written. It is for your information only and should never be used in place of your own doctor's advice or without his or her consent. Because your doctor is familiar with your personal medical history, he or she is best qualified to advise you on medical matters.

Please note that the effects attributed to some of the seasonings listed here may not happen to everyone who uses the seasonings or every time the seasoning is served.

CAUTION: All plants contain oils whose constitutents give the plant its flavor and aroma. Although many of the chemicals that give plants their flavor and aroma are potentially hazardous, there is usually proportionally so little oil in the plants that the majority of herbs and spices are generally considered safe in the amounts used in food. HOWEVER, SOME PLANT OILS ARE AVAILABLE IN CONCENTRATED FORM FOR USE IN MAKING YOUR OWN PERFUMES AT HOME. UNLIKE THE FLAVORING LIQUIDS SOLD AT THE GROCERY STORE, THESE OILS ARE NOT SAFE FOR USE IN FOOD. THEY ARE POTENTIALLY POISONOUS AND MAY PROVE FATAL IF INGESTED. THEY MAY ALSO BE HAZARDOUS IF APPLIED DIRECTLY TO YOUR SKIN IN CONCENTRATED FORM.

Before using any herbs from the garden, wash thoroughly to remove dirt and debris. Many insecticidal products are poisonous. NEVER USE ANY PLANT AS FOOD UNLESS YOU ARE ABSOLUTELY CERTAIN IT HAS NOT BEEN TREATED WITH AN INSECTICIDE. THIS INCLUDES PLANTS GROWING WILD.

INTRODUCTION

THIS IS A DIFFERENT KIND OF HERB BOOK.

It's not a cookbook or a guide to gardening or a collection of cosmetic tips. Instead, *The Complete Book of Herbs, Spices and Condiments* presents the seasonings as individual health products, each one complete with the same kinds of nutritional, chemical and medical benefits and side effects you expect to find in any vitamin supplement, prescription drug or over-the-counter product. Throughout, the emphasis is squarely on science, not magic.

The information is organized into entries, arranged alphabetically from alfalfa to yeast. Sometimes the name I use for the condiment, herb or spice may not be the one you use. For example, there is an entry for Marigold, but you may know these golden yellow flowers as "calendula," and what I call "black pepper," you may simply call "pepper." If you can't find the seasoning you're looking for by thumbing through the book, check the index. I have listed most of the common alternative names there to make it easy for you to find precisely what you're looking for.

Each entry begins with an easy-to-read chart that gives you the basics ABOUT THIS PLANT from which the seasoning comes. First on the list: the plant's botanical name. Since so many common names for herbs and spices sound or look alike, it's important to be sure you're talking about the right plant; if you know the botanical name, you're on certain ground. Next come the other common names (such as "green onions" for "scallions"), then its native habitat, the parts of the plant that are used in food, its medicinal properties and, finally, any alternative uses.

In the next section, ABOUT THIS CONDIMENT, HERB OR SPICE AS FOOD AND FLAVORING, you will find information about how the seasoning is grown or manufactured, how it is commonly used in cooking or food preparation, and a description of the specific chemicals that give the condiment, herb or spice its distinctive flavor and aroma. This section ends with a *Nutritional profile*, listing the amounts of vitamins, minerals and other nutrients you can expect to find in a common serving of each seasoning. Since we ordinarily use such small amounts of herbs and spices in our cooking, you may be wondering whether we can really expect seasonings to contribute significant amounts of nutrients to our diet. In many cases, the answer is definitely yes. Just one teaspoon of paprika has 1,200 IU vitamin A, 24% to 30% of the day's recommended daily dietary allowance (RDA) for a healthy adult. One teaspoon of dill seed has 32 mg calcium, which is 4% of the RDA for a healthy man or woman. This is twice the amount of calcium in half a medium grapefruit and 50% more than one cup of canned peas. One-half cup chopped fresh parsley has 27 mg vitamin C, 45% of the RDA for a healthy adult.

The numbers in the nutritional profiles come chiefly from publications of the U.S. Department of Agriculture. Because the USDA has not yet put together nutritional listings for every herb, spice and condiment you will sometimes find the symbol (—). This symbol does not mean that the seasoning has no nutrients, only that no authoritative nutritional analysis is currently available.

Next, you will find a section dealing with information about How This Condiment, Herb or Spice Affects Your Body. This section begins with a description of the physical effects of the active chemicals in the seasoning and continues with a summary of the medical *Benefits* and *Adverse effects* of the condiment, herb or spice in the amounts commonly used in food or food preparation or when you are gardening.

Once again, you may be wondering whether the small amounts of seasonings in your food can actually have beneficial or adverse effects. Once again, the answer is yes. Often the medical effects producted by seasonings occur at very low doses (a higher dose obviously makes the effect stronger). For example, an ordinary dusting of black or red pepper can irritate anybody's stomach lining. Pepper can also irritate the skin (which is why it is sometimes used as a "warming" poultice) and the urinary tract (which is why it is sometimes mistakenly regarded as an aphrodisiac). Even one cup of chamomile tea may trigger an allergic reaction in people sensitive to ragweed. "Normal" servings of salt, MSG (monosodium glutamate) and soy sauce may be hazardous for people on low sodium diets.

Sometimes you will find the symbol (—) after these headings. Remember, the symbol doesn't necessarily mean that there are no benefits or adverse effects, only that right now there is no precise information available either way.

Each entry ends with a section on How to Use This Condiment, Herb or Spice, a short list of practical ways to employ seasonings in cooking, around the house, as a home remedy, as a cosmetic or in the garden.

Finally, a word about how to tell an herb from a spice and vice versa. In general, the word *herb* is used to describe flavoring agents, such as marjoram and thyme, that come from a nonwoody plant, usually one that grows in temperate regions. The word *spice* is usually used to describe seasonings, such as cinnamon and pepper, that come from woody plants, usually those that grow in tropical areas. You can call any seasoning a condiment, but I use the word *condiment* to describe a prepared product, such as catsup, mayonnaise or Worcestershire sauce.

Carol Ann Rinzler

ALFALFA

About This Plant

Botanical name: *Medicago sativa*
Also known as: Lucerne
Native to: Europe
Parts used as herb: Sprouted seeds
Medicinal properties: (—)
Other uses: Animal feed

About This Herb as Food Flavoring

Alfalfa is a perennial plant, a member of the pea family widely used as cattle feed. Its leaves (available only from your own plants) and fresh sprouts (from your grocery or prepared at home) are used around the world as vegetables. Alfalfa is also sold in health food stores as a tea or in tablets or capsules of dried alfalfa.

Commercially, alfalfa fiber has been used in making paper, and alfalfa itself has been used as a source of carotene and chlorophyll.

Nutritional profile. One-half cup raw, sprouted alfalfa seeds has 5 calories. It provides 0.5 g protein, a trace of fat, 0.5 g carbohydrates, 5.5 mg calcium, 0.2 mg iron, 25 IU vitamin A and 1.5 mg vitamin C.

How This Herb Affects Your Body

Alfalfa contains *coumestrol*, a chemical whose effects are similar to those of estrogen. Coumestrol, which is also found in soybean sprouts, is about 3,000 times weaker than the synthetic estrogen DES (diethylstilbestrol). There is no proof that coumestrol has any effect on human beings. However, *zearalenone*, a similar chemical produced by moldy grain, has been an effective DES substitute in cattle feed designed to increase the weight of cattle, and changes in ovarian, cervical and breast tissue have been seen in rats, sheep, pigs and cattle fed foods containing these compounds.

Extracts of alfalfa appear to have antibiotic activity, but there are no scientific studies showing that alfalfa itself is useful. To date no scientific evidence backs up claims that alfalfa sprouts, tablets, capsules or teas are useful in preventing or treating such conditions as arthritis, scurvy, kidney disease or intestinal disorders.

Benefits. (—)

Adverse effects.   Alfalfa is a potential allergen: Animals that forage on it may develop photosensitivity (an allergic sensitivity to sunlight), and many people are allergic to the dust produced when alfalfa is milled.

A 1981 article in the British medical journal *Lancet* reported that people who eat large quantities of alfalfa seeds every day often develop a blood disorder called pancytopenia (a reduction in the number of red cells, white cells and platelets circulating in the blood). This condition disappeared when they stopped eating the seeds. In addition, when laboratory monkeys are fed alfalfa seeds and sprouts, they develop symptoms similar to those in people with systemic lupus erythematosus (SLE), an inflammatory immune disorder of the connective tissue in which the body seems to attack itself. People whose SLE is in remission may sufffer a relapse after taking alfalfa tablets or capsules. The culprit in both the blood disorder and the SLE cases may be *canavarine*, a chemical in alfalfa seed and sprouts that is similar to *arginine*, a nonessential amino acid.

How to Use This Herb

In cooking: To sprout alfalfa seeds, soak ¼ cup of seeds overnight in one cup of water. In the morning drain the seeds and discard any that are moldy. Then put the seeds in a wide-mouthed jar covered with cheesecloth (which will let air circulate among the seeds). Put the jar in a dark but airy cupboard, and rinse and drain the seeds two or three times a day, always checking for any signs of mold. (If any mold develops, throw out all the seeds and start again.) When the seeds develop sprouts at least an inch or two long, either use them right away or refrigerate them for a day or two. Use only in moderation to add crunch to your salads, soups or sandwiches.

ALLSPICE

About This Plant

Botanical name:	*Pimenta dioica,* *Pimenta officinalis*
Also known as:	Clove pepper, Jamaica pepper, pimento
Native to:	West Indies, Latin America
Parts used as herb:	Fruit

Medicinal properties: Antiseptic
Other uses: (—)

About This Herb as Food and Flavoring

Allspice is the dried, nearly ripe fruit of an evergreen tree that grows in Jamaica, Mexico, Guatemala and Honduras. It is called allspice because it tastes like a natural combination of cinnamon, nutmeg and cloves; up to 70% of the oil extracted from allspice is *eugenol*, the spicy smelling oil that gives cloves their characteristic taste and is also found in cinnamon and nutmeg. Outside the United States allspice is commonly known as *pimento* (which is not the same as *pimiento*, another name for some sweet red peppers).

Allspice is used in liqueurs (notably Benedictine and Chartreuse) and as a flavoring for ice cream, candy, baked goods and chewing gum. Allspice oleoresin (a combination of its resins and oils) is used in sausages. Commercially, allspice is used as a source of eugenol and vanillin.

Allspice is available as whole, small reddish brown berries or as a powder.

Nutritional profile. One teaspoon (1.9 g) ground allspice has 5 calories and provides 0.1 g protein, 0.2 g fats, 1.4 g carbohydrates, 13 mg calcium, 0.8 mg vitamin C and 10 IU vitamin A.

How This Herb Affects Your Body

Eugenol, the flavoring oil in allspice, is an irritant and an allergen. It is also an antiseptic and a fungicide (a chemical that kills fungi and mold).

Benefits. Like pepper and mustard, allspice can irritate your skin, causing the small blood vessels underneath to expand; the flow of blood to the skin increases making the skin feel warm. Because it contains tannins, which have a mild effect as a local anesthetic, it is sometimes used in folk medicine as a poultice or "plaster" to relieve the pain of arthritis, but it has no lasting medical value.

Adverse effects. Handling allspice may cause contact dermatitis (itching, burning, stinging, and reddened or blistered skin). In a 1979 Canadian study of 408 patients with eczema on their hands, 19 had a positive reaction to a patch test with allspice.

How to Use This Herb

In cooking: So long as you use the same *form* of the spice (that is, whole allspice for whole cloves, ground allspice for ground cloves), you can use allspice measure for measure as a substitute for cinnamon, cloves or nutmeg. To make a substitute for allspice, combine one part nutmeg with two parts each cinnamon and cloves (again using the same form and of the spice and *the same amount*).

Around the house: Allspice makes a wonderful air freshener. To mask kitchen odors, boil one teaspoon whole or ground allspice in two cups water on top of the stove, and let the aroma drift pleasantly.

ALOE

ABOUT THIS PLANT

Botanical name:	*Aloe barbadensis*
Also known as:	Aloe vera, Barbados aloe, Curacao aloe
Native to:	Africa, the Mediterranean
Parts used as herb:	Leaf (extract)
Medicinal properties:	Emollient, laxative
Other Uses:	(—)

ABOUT THIS HERB AS FOOD AND FLAVORING

The aloe plant is a member of the lily family, a succulent with narrow, prickly edged leaves that is native to Africa and the Mediterranean and is now cultivated in Florida and the American southwest.

Aloe is not an herb used in home cooking, but an extract of the leaf is used commercially to flavor alcoholic beverages such as bitters, vermouth and various cordials, as well as candies, baked goods and gelatins.

Nutritional profile. (—)

HOW THIS HERB AFFECTS YOUR BODY

The bitter yellow liquid that comes from the cells just under the skin of the aloe leaf contains the anthraquinone derivatives *aloin, isobarbaloin* and *aloe emodin*. Anthraquinones are cathartics (strong laxatives) that work by irritating the lining of the large intestine. Aloe juice or latex was once dried to a yellow powder that could be used as a laxative, but it is now considered too strong to be safe. Aloe gel, the clear, slippery liquid that comes from cells in the center of the leaf, is free of these carthartic chemicals. As a rule, when whole leaves are processed to obtain aloe for commercial skin lotions and shampoos, the gel is treated to remove the cathartic latex. However, some commercial gels may still contain some anthraquinones.

Benefits.   The fresh gel of the aloe plant is one of those folk remedies that works even though nobody knows exactly why. Aloe gel's ability to soothe small cuts and burns has been proved in laboratory experiments, but exactly which chemical in the gel gives it these healing properties is still a mystery. There is no proof that the processed, purified gel used in commercial skin lotions and shampoos has the same effects as the fresh juice.

Adverse effects.   Anthraquinone derivatives, such as those found in the aloe, trigger strong contractions and have been reported to cause severe intestinal cramps. Large doses have been linked to kidney damage.

How to Use This Herb

As a home remedy: Keeping an aloe plant in your kitchen gives you a cheap and effective remedy for *minor* burns and scrapes. But remember, as with any other home remedy, aloe gel must be used *only* for truly minor burns or cuts. **Serious injuries, especially burns, should always be treated by your doctor.**

As a cosmetic: Fresh aloe gel is a useful emollient hair conditioner. Break open the leaf, rub the gel through your hair, wait 15 minutes, then shampoo thoroughly. **If you are allergic to any plants, check with your doctor before using this or any other plant on your skin.**

ANGELICA

About This Plant

Botanical name:	*Angelica archangelica*
Also known as:	Archangel, European angelica, garden angelica
Native to:	Northern Europe
Parts used as herb:	Root, seeds
Medicine properties:	(—)
Other uses:	Perfumery

About This Herb as Food and Flavoring

Angelica, a large plant with fragrant leaves, is a member of the carrot family, native to Northern Europe and related to the American angelica (*Angelica atropurpurea*). The plant is a biennial, meaning that it lives for two years.

Angelica's leaves, stems and roots contain an essential oil with a faint licorice flavor that is used in liqueurs such as Benedictine and Chartreuse. Its leafstalks (which resemble celery stalks) are sometimes used as a vegetable. The leaves and hollow stems may be candied and used as a garnish, and the seeds are used in cookies and cakes. Its essential oil is also used in perfumery and as a flavoring in cigarettes.

Angelica's characteristic aroma comes from *angelica lactone* plus *angelic acid* and several chemicals related to *phellandrene*. Angelica is available only from your own garden. **Do not gather angelica growing wild. Water hemlock (*Cicuta maculata*), a deadly poisonous plant, has leaves that look like and may be mistaken for angelica.**

Nutritional profile. (—)

How This Herb Affects Your Body

Angelica contains the furocoumarins *angelicin, bergapten* and *xanthotoxin*. Furocoumarins are photosensitizers (chemicals that make your skin more sensitive to sunlight), mutagens (chemicals that cause genetic changes in cells) and carcinogens (chemicals that cause cancer). Angelica lactone, the most important aroma chemical in angelica, is an irritant that can be absorbed through the skin.

Benefits. (—)

Adverse effects. Handling the angelica plant may make your skin very sensitive to sunlight (photosensitivity) or cause contact dermatitis (itching, burning, stinging, reddened or blistered skin), a reaction most commonly seen in food workers who handle the angelica plant. To avoid this, always wear protective gloves when handling angelica plants in the garden and wash your hands thoroughly after handling the herb.

The small amounts of angelica seeds and stems used in food are considered safe, but large quantities of the root are poisonous.

How to Use This Herb

In cooking:

Candied angelica stems

1 cup fresh angelica stems
¼ cup salt dissolved in 1 cup boiling water

1 cup sugar
1 cup water

Wash the angelica stems and cut them into 2-inch lengths. Put them in a bowl or glass bottle and cover them with the hot saltwater, then let them sit overnight in a cool place (the refrigerator is fine).

In the morning drain the stems, peel, and wash once more in cold water to get rid of all the salt. Cook one cup sugar in one cup water until it makes a syrup, then add the angelica stems and cook for 15 minutes. Drain the stems in a colander or sieve, saving the syrup. Store the syrup in the refrigerator and the stems on a wire rack in a cool place for three days.

On the third day put the stems and the syrup into a saucepan, bring to a boil and then simmer for 15 minutes. Drain the stems once more, discard the syrup and store the candied stems in a tightly covered container in a cool place. Use the stems as needed for garnishing. (If you keep them longer than a day or two, always check for mold before using them. If you find any, discard *all* the stems.)

ANISE

ABOUT THIS PLANT

Botanical name: *Pimpinella anisum*
Also known as: Aniseed, sweet cumin
Native to: Egypt, western Asia
Parts used as herb: Fresh leaves, dried fruit
Medicinal properies: Carminative
Other uses: Pharmaceutical flavoring agent, cosmetic scent, rodent bait

ABOUT THIS HERB AS FOOD AND FLAVORING

Anise is a member of the carrot family, an annual plant that is native to western Asia and Egypt and widely cultivated in southern Europe, India and the United States. Anise "seeds" (the ripe fruit of the plant) have a faint licorice flavor when you chew them.

Oil of anise is widely used in commercial baked goods; as a flavoring in cough syrups, cough drops and tooth pastes and powders; as a scent in soaps; and in the licorice-flavored liqueurs ouzo and anisette. Anisette is a safe substitute for absinthe, the original licorice-flavored liqueur whose flavor came from oil of wormwood (*Artemisia absinthium*) (see p. 189.)

The licorice flavor of anise comes from *anethole, methylchavicol* (a chemical related to *chavicol,* one of the flavoring agents that gives black pepper its bite), and *anisaldehyde,* a chemical with a faintly vanilla flavor.

Anise is available at the grocery store as "seeds" (the fruit) and as an extract (typically, 70% alcohol plus water and oil of anise). Both are used to flavor cookies, candies and cakes. Licorice-flavored anise leaves, available only from your own garden, can be used fresh in salads and as a garnish.

Nutritional profile. One tablespoon (6.7 grams) of anise seeds has 23 calories. It provides 1.2 g protein, 1 g fat, 3.4 g carbohydrates (including 1 g fiber), 43 mg calcium, 2.5 mg iron and 11 mg magnesium.

How This Herb Affects Your Body

Anethole, which is also known as *anise camphor,* is an irritant found in basil as well as in anise. It can cause redness, scaling and blistering if applied directly to the skin. In laboratory animals anethole is poisonous when absorbed through the skin.

Benefits. Anise is a carminative, an agent that helps expel gas from the intestines. It is also a good source of iron. One tablespoon of anise seeds sprinkled on cookies, bread or cake provides 16% of the RDA (15 mg) for a woman and 25% of the RDA (10 mg) for a man.

Adverse effects. Anise seeds and toothpastes flavored with anethole have both been reported to cause cheilitis, a peeling and bleeding of the lips sometimes mistaken for the simple chapping caused by cold weather.

How to Use This Herb

In cooking: To make an anise-flavored vodka or brandy, add ¼ cup fresh leaves or 2 tablespoons crushed anise seeds to 1 quart plain, unflavored vodka or 1 quart brandy. Close the bottle tightly and let it steep for 24 to 48 hours, then strain and taste a sample of the vodka or brandy. If it is strong enough, strain to remove the herb, then store the flavored liquor.

As a home remedy: To make a carminative tea that may relieve intestinal gas, boil ½ teaspoon anise seeds in a pint of water, strain and drink. Some people simply chew the anise seeds.

Around the house: The scent of anise is attractive to mice and rats. Add anise seeds or fresh leaves to your rodent traps to make them more effective.

ANISE HYSSOP

ABOUT THIS PLANT

Botanical name: *Agastache foeniculum*
Native to: North America
Also known as: Blue giant hyssop, fragrant giant hyssop
Parts used as herb: Leaves
Medicinal properties: (—)
Other uses: (—)

ABOUT THIS HERB AS FOOD AND FLAVORING

Anise hyssop is a member of the mint family, related to basil, lavender, rosemary, sage and thyme. Its anise-scented leaves, available only from plants grown from seed or added to your own garden, can be used for teas and seasoning.

Like anise, anise hyssop contains *anisaldehyde*, a chemical with a faint vanilla scent used in perfumes and toilet soaps. Anise hyssop also contains *pulegone*, whose odor is sharp and spicy, between that of peppermint and that of camphor.

Nutritional profile. (—)

HOW THIS HERB AFFECTS YOUR BODY

Because anise hyssop is a garden plant with no discernible history of use in folk medicine, there appears to be no scientific evidence of its effects on the human body.

Benefits. (—)

Adverse effects. (—)

How to Use This Herb

In cooking: For a licorice-flavored tea, steep anise hyssop leaves in boiling water.

Anise hyssop's violet blue flowers, which bloom from late summer through fall, can be used—fresh or dried—to garnish fruit dishes or desserts.

In the garden: Anise hyssop is a favorite with bees, and because of its height (up to 4 feet), it is a fine landscape plant. An added benefit—it makes it own insecticide; anisaldehyde.

ANNATTO

About This Plant

Botanical name:	*Bixa orellana*
Also known as:	Achiote, arnotta, annotta
Native to:	The Caribbean
Parts used as herb:	Seed
Medicinal properties:	(—)
Other uses:	Fabric dye

About This Herb as Food and Flavoring

Annatto is the spice obtained from the seeds and seedcoats of *Bixa orellana*, a tree native to the Caribbean and cultivated in Brazil, Mexico and India.

Annato is a source of the carotenoid pigments *bixin* and *norbixin*, which are extracted from the seed and used as natural food coloring agents. Concentrated annatto pigments are red. Diluted for use in food processing, they make a peachy- to buttery-yellow dye once used to standardize the color of commercial butters. Today annatto pigments are used commercially in a variety of dairy products, including cheese, ice cream, imitation creams and whipped toppings, as a coloring in some mixed seasonings, and to color frankfurters and other sausages. It is also used to dye silk fabrics and in the manufacture of wood stains and varnishes.

Despite its versatility and the fact that it turns up in recipes in many well-known cookbooks, annatto is not widely available. That's a pity, because it is a cheap substitute for saffron, the world's most expensive seasoning. You are most likely to find annatto powder in Latin American

grocery stores, particularly in Puerto Rican neighborhoods, where it is sold under the name "achiote."
Nutritional profile. (—)

How This Herb Affects Your Body

Carotenes are yellow, orange and red pigments that occur naturally in fruits and vegetables. A few carotenoid pigments, most notably *beta-carotene*, the yellow pigment in carrots, sweet potatoes and squashes, are converted to vitamin A in your body. Bixin and norbixin, the carotenoids in annatto, are not, so annatto, despite its rich yellow color, is not a source of vitamin A.
Benefits. (—)
Adverse effects. (—)

How to Use This Herb

In cooking: If you use annatto as a substitute for saffron, add it sparingly. Annatto's bitter flavor can overwhelm a dish. As a rule, to maintain the proper flavor, commercial food processors use no more than one part annatto to every 400 parts of food.

ARROWROOT

About This Plant

Botanical name:	*Maranta arundinacea*
Also known as:	Bermuda arrowroot
Native to:	The West Indies
Parts used as herb:	Root
Medical properties:	Demulcent
Other uses:	Cosmetic base, glue base

About This Herb as Food and Flavoring

Arrowroot is a starch made from the rhizomes (underground stems) of *Maranta arundinacea*, a plant that grows on St. Vincent's Island in the West Indies.

All starches, including arrowroot, consist of molecules of complex carbohydrates packed into bundles called starch granules. The carbohydrates inside the starch granule are *amylose* (a long, straight molecule) and *amylopectin* (a short, branched molecule). When you heat a starch in liquid, its granules absorb the heated water. The amylose and amylopectin molecules inside relax, breaking some of their internal bonds (bonds between atoms on the same molecules) and forming new bonds between atoms on different molecules. The result is a network of carbohydrate molecules that traps and holds water molecules, immobilizing them and thus thickening the liquid.

It takes less energy (heat) to break and re-form bonds between the long, straight amylose molecules than it takes to do the same thing with the short, branched amylopectin molecules. Starches such as arrowroot, which have a higher proportion of amylose molecules, "cook" at a lower temperature than starches such as cornstarch and wheat starch, which are higher in amylopectin. This means you are much less likely to burn a sauce made with arrowroot. Arrowroot also has less protein than cornstarch and wheat starch, which is why it makes a clear sauce rather than a protein-clouded one. Finally, because it has virtually no flavor of its own, arrowroot is particularly useful for delicate fruit sauces.

Nutritional profile. One ounce (28 grams) of arrowroot has 45 calories. It provides 0.7 g protein, a trace of fat, 11 g carbohydrates (including 0.5 g crude fiber), 6 mg calcium, 1 mg iron and 3 mg vitamin C.

How This Herb Affects Your Body

Benefits. Like other starches, arrowroot soothes the skin. It can be used as a dressing powder to reduce friction and prevent irritation, and it keeps skin dry by absorbing water. More, though, isn't better: Too much powdered starch will make a sticky paste on the skin.

Adverse effects. Arrowroot is a potential allergen that may cause skin rashes, stuffy nose and reddened eyes in sensitive people.

How to Use This Herb

In cooking: As a thickener
                  1½ teaspoon arrowroot
                  equals 1½ teaspoon cornstarch
                  equals 1 tablespoon wheat flour
The arrowroot thickens at a lower temperature.

Although arrowroot is most familiar as a powdered starch, the plant's root can be boiled and served as a vegetable.

As a home remedy: Provided you are not sensitive to arrowroot, you can add ¼ cup of the powdered starch to a warm bath to soothe irritated skin.

As a cosmetic: Provided you are not sensitive to arrowroot, in a pinch you can use the powdered starch as a substitute for an adult's dusting powder. (Don't use it for children or babies: They may have allergies you don't yet know about.)

Asafetida

About This Plant

Botanical name:	*Ferula assafoetida*
Also known as:	Assafoetida, asant, Devil's dung
Native to:	Asia
Parts used as herb:	Roots and rhizomes
Medicinal properties:	Carminative, expectorant
Other uses:	Animal repellent

About This Herb as Food and Flavoring

Asafetida is a member of the carrot family, a foul-smelling plant native to Afghanistan, Iran and Turkistan (a region of Asia now divided among China, Russia and Afghanistan). Its odor comes from acrid sulfur compounds called *mercaptans,* the chemicals that give onions and garlic their characteristic odors. Asafetida tastes something like onions and garlic, only stronger.

Gum from its root and rhizomes (underground stem) is used as an ingredient in Worcestershire sauce, and small quantities are used as a condiment and flavoring in Indian and Iranian cooking. In the United States, asafetida may occasionally be found in Indian grocery stores, where it is sold either as a solid lump or as a grainy powder.

Nutritional profile. (—)

How This Herb Affects Your Body

Asafetida is a carminative (a substance that helps break up and expel intestinal gas). Like other plant resins, it may also be useful as an expectorant (an agent that causes the lining of the respiratory tract to weep watery secretions that make it easier for you to cough up mucus).

Some researchers have suggested that asafetida, like oil of garlic, may help lower blood pressure and increase the amount of time it takes for blood to clot. Like garlic, asafetida has been hung around the neck to ward off colds and other infectious diseases, but its only real effect seems to be its ability to keep other people (and their colds) at arm's length.

Benefits. (—)

Adverse effects. Like *urushiol,* the irritating chemical in poison ivy, the oils and resins (oleoresins) in asafetida gum may cause contact dermatitis in people who have been sensitized to it, but the reaction does not occur as frequently nor is it likely to be as severe as the reaction to poison ivy.

How to Use This Herb

In cooking: If you come across an Indian grocery that sells asafetida, you should know that the lump form is thought to have a purer flavor. To use the asafetida, break off a small chip with a hammer or meat-tenderizing mallet and pound it to a powder between two sheets of waxed paper. Then use as your recipe directs.

In the garden: Two of the sulfur compounds isolated from asafetida are natural pesticides similar to those in marigolds (calendula) and nasturtiums. To make a 2% asafetida solution for use in your garden, crush a chip of the resinous lump, then mix 1 oz of the powdered asafetida with 1 ½ quarts water and shake hard. Use the solution around your garden plants to ward off deer and rabbits.

ASPARTAME

About This Condiment

Chemical name:	N-L-*alpha*-Aspartyl-L-phenylalanine 1-methyl ester
Also known as:	Nutrasweet
Native to:	(—)
Parts used as condiment:	(—)
Medicinal properties:	Diet aid
Other uses:	(—)

About This Condiment as Food and Flavoring

Aspartame is a white, odorless, crystalline powder made from two commercially produced amino acids, L- *phenylalanine* and L-*aspartic acid.* Aspartic acid is a nonessential amino acid (one that can be made in your body) found in animals and in plants, especially young sugar cane and sugar beet molasses. Phenylalanine is an essential amino acid (one that you must get from food because it cannot be made in your body), a component of *tyrosine*, another amino acid.

Aspartame was approved by the Food and Drug Administration in 1981. It is approximately 160 to 200 times sweeter than sucrose (table sugar). It tastes like sugar and, unlike saccharin, it has no bitter aftertaste. Aspartame dissolves better in warm water than in cold, but it breaks down and loses its sweetening power when exposed to the high temperatures used in baking.

Aspartame is available under the brand name Nutrasweet. Nutrasweet is used commercially in many diet sodas, sugar-free beverages and low-calorie frozen desserts. For home use it is available as an ingredient in Equal, a low-calorie sweetening powder or liquid. Each packet of Equal powder contains dextrose with dried corn syrup, aspartame, silicon dioxide (to prevent caking), cellulose, tribasic calcium phosphate (an anticaking agent) and cellulose derivatives.

Nutritional profile. A one-serving packet of powdered aspartame sweetener (Equal) has 4 calories. It provides no protein, less than 1 g fat and less than 1 g carbohydrates.

How This Condiment Affects Your Body

Aspartame breaks down into methanol, phenylalanine and aspartic acid in the small intestine. All these substances are absorbed into your bloodstream.

Phenylalanine and tyrosine (which your body makes from phenylalanine) both appear to interfere with *neurotransmission* (the transmission of nerve impulses from one cell to another). Some scientists have suggested that this may cause changes in mood and behavior leading to depression or seizures. However, the Food and Drug Adminstration concluded in 1987 that although consuming aspartame does increase the amount of phenylalanine in your blood and brain, there is no conclusive evidence to show that it actually affects neurotransmission or changes behavior. (In fact, there is less phenylalanine in 500 mg [0.5 g] aspartame than in three ounces of beef or six ounces of milk.) The Food and Drug Administration has set the Acceptable Daily Intake of aspartame at 50 milligrams for each kilogram (2.2 pounds) of bodyweight. For a 150-pound adult man, this translates to 3.4 grams, the amount of aspartame in 20 cans of diet soda.

Benefits. Aspartame's chief benefit is its ability to sweeten with fewer calories than sugar, making it useful in a diet designed to control weight. Aspartame may also be useful for people with diabetes who must control their sugar intake. However, if you have diabetes, check with your doctor before changing your diet in any way.

Adverse effects. Because your body breaks aspartame down into phenylalanine, the sweetener may be hazardous for children born with phenylketonuria (PKU) and for pregnant women who were PKU infants. People with PKU are unable to metabolize phenylalanine. In newborns and infants the unmetabolized phenylalanine circulating in the blood may damage brain cells, thus causing mental retardation. As a protective measure, all newborns in the United States are given a simple blood or urine test to detect PKU, and PKU babies are put on a special diet low in phenylalanine.

In 1981 researchers at the Children's Medical Center in Boston suggested that women who were PKU babies should return to a protective diet (which would exclude foods sweetened with aspartame) when they become pregnant to avoid developing high blood levels of phenylalanine, which might damage fetal brain cells. To protect people with PKU, the 1981 FDA approval for aspartame included a requirement that the label on any product containing aspartame carry the warning: Contains phenylalanine.

Because the chemical structure of aspartic acid is similar to that of monosodium glutamate (MSG), people who are sensitive to MSG may also be sensitive to aspartame, which may cause hives and swelling of tissue in the throat. According to a 1986 study at Washington University in St. Louis, these symptoms may show up immediately after a person who is sensitive to aspartame drinks a diet soda, or they may not appear for several hours.

Although some people have complained of headaches after consuming foods that contain aspartame, a 1987 Duke University study of 40 patients with this complaint showed that when the patients were given either a placebo or an amount of aspartame equal to what they would get from 10 diet sodas, the patients who got aspartame were no more likely to develop a headache than the patients who got the placebo.

How to Use This Condiment

In cooking: One packet aspartame sweetener (Equal) has the sweetening power of 2 teaspoons sugar.

Because it breaks down and loses its sweetening power when exposed to high heat, aspartame cannot be used in cooking or baking. It can be added to foods after they have been cooked, used as a tabletop sweetener for coffee and tea or sprinkled over cold cereals.

Always store diet sodas made with aspartame in a cool, dark place to prevent the aspartame from breaking down.

BAKING POWDER

ABOUT THIS CONDIMENT

Chemical name: Sodium bicarbonate plus a variety of acids (see below)
Also known as: (—)
Native to: (—)
Parts used as condiment: (—)
Medicinal properties: (—)
Other Uses: (—)

ABOUT THIS CONDIMENT AS FOOD AND FLAVORING

Baking powder is a mixture of *sodium bicarbonate* (baking soda), a "slow-acting" leavening agent, and a "fast-acting" leavening agent such as *calcium acid phosphate* (monocalcium phosphate monohydrate), *calcium sulfate* or *cream of tartar*. The product is called "double-acting" baking powder.

When you mix flour with water and beat the batter, the long protein molecules in the flour relax and unfold. Internal bonds (bonds between atoms on the same molecule) are broken and new external bonds between atoms on different molecules are formed. The result is a network of elastic gluten (protein). When you add baking powder to the batter, its fast-acting ingredient releases carbon dioxide immediately (you can see the carbon dioxide as bubbles in the batter). The slow-acting sodium bicarbonate will release carbon dioxide later, when the batter is heated in the oven. Slow-acting leavening agents stabilize the batter's protein network and freeze it into its final ("risen") form.

The combination of a slow-acting and a fast-acting leavening agent, first used around 1835 in England and available commercially since about 1850, works best in thin batters such as pancakes and quick breads or muffins. These cook too quickly to be made with yeast, which releases carbon dioxide very slowly.

Nutritional profile. One teaspoon double-acting baking powder made with sodium bicarbonate plus sodium aluminum sulfate and calcium acid phosphate (monocalcium phosphate monohydrate) has 5 calories. It provides a trace of protein, no fat, 1 g carbohydrates, 58 mg calcium (7% of the RDA for an adult) and 329 mg sodium. There are no vitamins in baking powder.

One teaspoon double-acting baking powder made with sodium bicarbonate plus sodium aluminum sulfate, calcium acid phosphate (monocalcium phosphate monohydrate) and calcium sulfate has 5 calories and provides a trace of protein, no fat, 1 g carbohydrates, 183 mg calcium (22% of the RDA for an adult) and 290 mg sodium.

One teaspoon tartrate baking powder (sodium bicarbonate plus cream of tartar) has approximately 2.34 calories and provides a trace of protein, no fat, 0.5 mg carbohydrates, no calcium, 219 mg sodium and 114 mg potassium.

How This Condiment Affects Your Body

Sodium increases fluid retention. Cornstarch, used as a filler in some baking powders, is a potential allergen.

Benefits. (—)

Adverse effects. Sodium bicarbonate baking powders and baked goods made with them are ordinarily excluded from a sodium-restricted diet for people with heart disease and/or high blood pressure.

Baking powders contain cornstarch as a filler (approximately 1.2 tsp cornstarch for each 2 tsp baking powder). People who are sensitive to corn may be sensitive to the baking powders made with cornstarch filler, which can trigger such allergic side effects as hay fever, reddened eyes and stuffy nose.

How to Use This Condiment

In cooking: Tartrate baking powders have the quickest reaction time. They release their carbon dioxide as soon as they are added to the batter and should be used only in batters that will go straight into a heated oven. Never use a tartrate baking powder in a dough you plan to refrigerate.

The following combinations have the same leavening power as one teaspoon baking powder:

¼ tsp baking soda
plus
¾ tsp cream of tartar
or
½ cup buttermilk
or
½ cup yogurt
or
¼ cup to ½ cup molasses

To protect your baking powder, store it tightly closed in a cool place. Even under the best conditions baking powders become less potent with time. To test the powder, add 1 teaspoonful to a cup of water. If it bubbles, the powder is still working.

BAKING SODA

ABOUT THIS CONDIMENT

Chemical name:	Sodium bicarbonate
Also known as:	Bicarbonate of soda, sodium acid carbonate, sodium hydrogen carbonate
Native to:	(—)
Parts used as condiment:	(—)
Medicinal properties:	Antacid, antipruritic (relieves itching)
Other uses:	Household cleanser

ABOUT THIS CONDIMENT AS FOOD AND FLAVORING

Baking soda (*sodium bicarbonate*) is a white crystalline powder prepared from *sodium carbonate* (a naturally occurring crystal), water and *carbon dioxide* (gas). The most familiar use for baking soda is as an ingredient in baking powder (see BAKING POWDER). It is also used in carbonated beverages, effervescent bath salts, some cleaning compounds and some fire extinguishers.

Nutritional profile. One teaspoon baking soda contains 821 mg sodium.

HOW THIS CONDIMENT AFFECTS YOUR BODY

When it is moistened, baking soda decomposes into sodium carbonate and carbon dioxide. Sodium carbonate is a base (alkali). It neutralizes acids, is soothing to the skin and absorbs odors.

Benefits. Because sodium carbonate neutralizes acid, baking soda may be a useful antacid that temporarily relieves the pain and discomfort of an acid stomach. The Food and Drug Administration's Advisory Review Panel on OTC Miscellaneous Internal Drug Products has rated it safe for short-term use once in a while. The panel adds that even though people have been using it for years, there is no scientific research actually proving its effectiveness.

Baking soda is sometimes added to vaginal douches on the theory that it will make the vagina more basic (alkaline) and thus less hospitable to various microorganisms. The FDA's Advisory Review Panel on OTC Contraceptives and Other Vaginal Drug Products concluded that baking soda douches are safe, but that there is no scientific research to show that they have any effect on organisms in the vagina.

According to the FDA's Advisory Review Panel on OTC Oral Cavity Drug Products, a gargle solution of one teaspoon baking soda and ½ teaspoon salt in a glass of warm water is a safe and effective treatment for a sore throat. The solution appears to soften and dislodge mucus in your throat so that you can spit it out.

A paste of baking soda and water can sooth the itch of a mosquito bite; baking soda added to a warm bath can sooth itchiness due to hives, eczema or minor sunburn. To date, there has never been a report of a toxic reaction to these uses of baking soda on the skin, but **neither baking soda nor any other home remedy should ever be used for any severe burn, including acid burns. These are injuries that require immediate medical attention**.

Adverse effects.   Virtually all the problems caused by baking soda are associated with its use as an antacid. Over-the-counter antacids and laxatives that contain baking soda are high-sodium products. They may be hazardous for people with heart disease or hypertension who are sensitive to salt.

Some Common Antacids and Laxatives	Sodium Content
Alka Seltzer	276 mg/dose
Brioschi	710 mg/dose
Metamucil	Instant Mix 250 mg/dose
Sal Hepatica	1,000 mg/dose
Soda Mint	89 mg/dose

SOURCE: *The Sodium Content of Your Food.* Home and Garden Bulletin no. 233. (USDA, 1980).

It is important to use these products *only* in the recommended doses.

If you use a baking soda product as an antacid too often or if you use too much of it, you may experience belching and bloating or begin to retain fluid (which can be particularly hazardous for people with kidney disease). In some cases, particularly after a heavy meal, the carbon dioxide released from large amounts of baking soda may distend the stomach walls or, as one report has noted, actually rupture the stomach.

Baking soda interacts with some medications. It increases the effects of pseudoephedrine, a decongestant found in many allergy and cold products. In large doses it makes aspirin less effective. It decreases the effectiveness of the antidiabetic drug chlorpropamide (Diabinese); the mood-altering drug lithium (Cibalith-D, Eskalith, Lithobid, Lithonate, Lithotabs); and the tetracycline antibiotics. It may interfere with your body's absorption of iron supplements.

How to Use This Condiment

In cooking: See BAKING POWDER

As a home remedy: To soothe the itch of a mosquito bite, make a stiff paste of baking soda and water and apply the paste to the bite.

To relieve the pain of minor sunburn, add ¼ cup baking soda to a tepid bath and soak in it. Remember: Any serious sunburn requires your doctor's attention.

To ease the discomfort of weepy poison ivy, your doctor may suggest covering the rash with a sterile gauze pad dipped in a solution of 1½ teaspoons baking soda in 2 cups warm water. As with any home remedy, check with your doctor before prescribing for yourself.

To relieve the pain of a canker sore, rinse with a solution of ½ teaspoon baking soda in 1 cup warm water. **White spots in your mouth may be an early sign of oral cancer. Any "canker sore" that does not disappear within 10 days should be examined by your dentist.**

As a cosmetic: Baking soda is a cheap and handy substitute for pricey effervescent bath salts. Dissolve ¼ cup baking soda in a tubful of warm water and luxuriate for pennies. Carbonates, while soothing, are drying to the skin. If you have dry skin, this bath is not for you.

In a pinch, you can use plain baking soda as an underarm deodorant, but it's not an antiperspirant. If you perspire heavily, baking soda won't keep you—or your clothes—dry.

Baking soda is a gently abrasive cleanser that can be used as a substitute for toothpowder. **If you have extensive gum recession, baking soda may be too abrasive to be used on the exposed roots of your teeth. Ask your dentist's advice.**

Around the house: Baking soda is an effective scouring powder for your kitchen sink, pots and utensils. To make an all-purpose household cleanser, dissolve 2 tablespoons baking soda in 1 quart warm water. This will clean bathroom tile, plaster walls and any porcelain surfaces, such as the bathroom sink and tub.

Baking soda is an effective refrigerator deodorizer. It absorbs smelly particles floating in the refrigerator, trapping them until air and moisture in the refrigerator cause the baking soda to break down into sodium carbonate and carbon dioxide. Then some of the trapped odor particles remain in the carbonate crystals; the rest float away in the carbon dioxide gas. Throw out the box of used baking soda, and you throw out most of the smelly particles. For best results replace the box every three months.

BACON BITS

ABOUT THIS CONDIMENT

Chemical name: (—)
Also known as: (—)
Native to: (—)
Parts used as condiment: (—)
Medicinal properties: (—)
Other uses: (—)

ABOUT THIS CONDIMENT AS FOOD AND FLAVORING

Bacon bits are small pieces of imitation bacon made from soy products. A typical list of ingredients in bacon bits includes soy flour, soybean oil, salt, soya, natural and artificial flavors, hydrolyzed vegetable protein, caramel and artificial colors.

Nutritional profile. (—)

HOW THIS CONDIMENT AFFECTS YOUR BODY

Soy flour is very high (37%–47%) in protein, and products made from soy flour are also high in protein. But the amount of bacon bits used as a seasoning is generally too small to add any appreciable amounts of protein to your diet.

Benefits. Soy flour is very low (0.9%–20%) in fat, and soybean oil is composed chiefly (62%) of polyunsaturated fats. Neither the flour nor the oil has any cholesterol, so bacon bits are low in saturated fats, contain no cholesterol and may be permitted on a low-cholesterol, controlled-fat diet that prohibits bacon. They are also useful for vegetarian cooks.

Adverse effects. Soy products, artificial colors and artificial flavors may trigger allergic reactions in sensitive people.

HOW TO USE THIS CONDIMENT

In cooking: One tablespoon bacon bits equals one slice of bacon, cooked and crumbled.

Bacon bits must be added after a dish is cooked; otherwise they may dissolve.

BALM

About This Plant

Botanical name: *Melissa officinalis*
Also known as: Common balm, lemon balm, melissa, sweet balm
Native to: The Mediterranean, the Near East
Parts used as herb: Leaves
Medicinal properties: (—)
Other uses: Perfumery, insect repellent

About This Herb as Food and Flavoring

Balm is a member of the mint family. When you crush or tear its leaves, you rupture cell walls in the leaf, releasing the fragrant oils that give the herb its characteristic lemon scent. Balm's oil is a blend of *citral* and *citronellal*, which smell strongly of lemon; *geraniol*, which smells like roses and is the principal constituent of oil of roses; and *linalool*, which smells like French lavender.

Fresh balm leaves (which are usually available only from your own garden) can be used to add a lemony taste and aroma to salads. The tender young leaves are the most flavorful. You can dry balm leaves and store them for later use, but they lose their flavor and aroma quickly. To store, pack them in air-tight containers.

Balm, whose botanical name, *melissa*, is Greek for "bee," is sometimes used by beekeepers to attract bees to hives. Its oil is used in perfumes.
Nutritional profile. (—)

How This Herb Affects Your Body

Citronellal, geraniol and linalool are irritants.
Benefits. (—)
Adverse effects. Prolonged contact with balm plants or leaves may cause contact dermatitis (itching, stinging, burning, reddened or blistered skin) or it may sensitize you to other allergens.

How to Use This Herb

In cooking: For the most lemony flavor, crush balm leaves before you use them. Crushing tears cells, releasing the plant's flavorful scented oils.

For a lemony tea, pour a cup of boiling water over one or two tablespoons of crushed fresh or dried balm leaves. Let the tea steep 5 to 10 minutes. (Unlike many other herbs, balm does not get bitter with long steeping.) Balm leaves can also be used to garnish iced tea, carbonated sodas or fruit punches.

For a lemony tang in wine, add one or two balm leaves to an open bottle and let it steep until you are ready to serve the wine.

As a cosmetic: To make a lemon-scented bath, tie ¼ cup crushed balm leaves into a handkerchief or washcloth. Let the water run through the bag until the tub is filled.

In England, wine in which balm leaves have been steeped is sometimes used as a mouthwash. The alcohol in the wine draws out the flavor and aroma of the leaves. To make a mouthwash without alcohol, steep the leaves in boiling water. (Cold water doesn't draw out the oils.)

Around the house: Crushed dried balm leaves can be used in lemony scented pillows or potpourris. Or you can stash them in your dresser drawers to give your clothes a lemon scent.

In the garden: Balm and other lemon-scented herbs that contain citronella oil repel mosquitos and other insects in the garden. The active chemical appears to be *methyl heptanone*, a constituent of citronella oil. These plants make safe, natural insect repellents because they don't poison people, pets or wild animals that wander through to forage.

BASIL

ABOUT THIS PLANT

Botanical name:	*Ocimum basilicum*
Also known as:	Common basil, sweet basil
Native to:	India, Africa, southern Asia
Parts used as herb:	Leaves
Medicinal properties:	Carminative
Other uses:	Perfumery

ABOUT THIS HERB AS FOOD AND FLAVORING

Basil is a member of the mint family, a bushy annual with broad, light green, oval leaves that release a spicy scent when bruised. Their aroma and flavor come from their essential oil, which contains *anethole*, the major constituent of oil of anise; *estragole*, which tastes like tarragon; spicy *eucalyptol*; *eugenol*, the major constituent of oil of cloves; and *linalool*, which smells like French lavender.

Basil, which is particularly tasty with tomatoes, is characteristically identified with Italian tomato sauces, pizza and *pesto*, the oil-and-herb Italian condiment. Basil is widely available in grocery stores as either fresh leaves or crumbled or ground dried leaves. The fresh leaves are much more flavorful than the dried ones.

You can easily grow your own in the garden or in a pot as part of a window box herb garden. In addition to plain basil, you may want to try dark *opal basil*, which has purple leaves with a distinctly peppery flavor—some people find overtones of mint and cloves; *anise basil*, whose leaves have a licorice flavor; *lemon basil*, which tastes lemony; and *cinnamon basil*, which has a flavor reminiscent of cinnamon. These are not widely available; you may have to grow them in your own garden.

Nutritional profile. One ounce of fresh basil leaves has 12 calories. It provides 0.9 g protein, 0.3 g fat, 2 g carbohydrates, 91 mg calcium, 0.3 mg iron, approximately 12,380 IU vitamin A and 8 mg vitamin C.

One teaspoon (1.4 g) ground basil has 4 calories. It provides 0.2 g protein, a trace of fat, 0.9 g carbohydrates, 30 mg calcium, 0.6 mg iron, 131 IU vitamin A and 0.9 mg vitamin C.

How This Herb Affects Your Body

Some sweet basil oils contain estragole and *safrole*. Both are known carcinogens, that have caused tumors when fed or injected into laboratory rats and mice. However, basil contains such small amounts of these chemicals that it is not considered hazardous for human beings. Anethole, eucalyptol, eugenol and linalool are potential allergens that may cause contact dermatitis or sensitize you to other chemicals.

Benefits. Basil is a good source of *beta*-carotene, the vitamin A precursor in deep yellow fruits and vegetables. According to the American Cancer Society, a diet rich in these foods may lower the risk of some forms of cancer.

Vitamin A also protects your eyes. In your body the vitamin A from basil is converted to 11-cis retinol, the most important constituent of *rhodopsin*, a protein in the rods in your retina (the cells that enable you to see in dim light). One ounce of fresh basil leaves has about as much vitamin A as 1.75 ounces of boiled carrots, 309% of the vitamin A a healthy woman needs each day and 247% of the daily requirement for a healthy man.

Fresh basil leaves are also a good source of calcium. Once ounce of the leaves provides 11% of the calcium an adult needs each day. Basil is rich in vitamin C. One ounce provides 13% of the RDA for a healthy adult. Cooking reduces the amount of vitamin C you get from basil but doesn't affect the calcium or the vitamin A.

Adverse effects. Prolonged handling of the basil plant may cause contact dermatitis (itching, burning, stinging, and reddened or blistered skin).

How to Use This Herb

In cooking: Do not tear or cut basil leaves until you are actually ready to use them. When you cut into a food rich in vitamin C, its cells release an enzyme called ascorbic acid oxidase. This chemical destroys vitamin C and reduces the nutritional value of the food.

Chlorophyll, the green coloring in plants, is sensitive to acids. When you heat basil leaves, their chlorophyll reacts with natural acids in the leaves or in the cooking water, forming a brown compound called *pheophytin*. The pheophytin in turn reacts with the yellow carotene pigments in the leaves, turning the cooked basil dark brown. To prevent this color change, prevent the chlorophyll from reacting with the acids by cooking it for as short a time as possible. To protect its color, always add basil at the very last minute.

To protect the flavor and aroma of fresh basil leaves, pack them in a tightly sealed glass jar and store in the refrigerator.

To maintain basil's flavor and aroma during longer-term storage, blanch the leaves, then wrap them whole or minced in tightly sealed plastic bags and store in the freezer.

Basil is used most frequently with tomatoes, but it tastes good with fruit. As an experiment, sprinkle some on a baked apple.

In the garden: Like marigolds, rosemary, sage, tansy and a number of other plants with a strong aroma, basil is a safe, natural insect repellent for your garden. Oil of basil repels houseflies and mosquitos; one of its components, eucalyptol, also repels cockroaches. In addition, researchers have identified two compounds in basil oil, *juvocimene 1* and *juvocimene 2*, which appear to interfere with hormonal activity, stopping some insects from maturing.

Bay Leaf

About This Plant

Botanical name: *Laurus nobilis*
Also known as: Bay laurel,
Grecian laurel,
sweet laurel
Native to: The Mediterranean
Parts used as herb: Leaf
Medicinal properties: (—)
Other uses: Insect repellent

About This Herb as Food and Flavoring

Bay leaves come from an evergreen tree that can grow as tall as 40 feet in its native Mediterranean area. The leaves have a spicy fragrance; when you crush them, they smell like bay rum. The leaves get their flavor and aroma from laurel leaf oil. Its major constituent is spicy *eucalyptol*, which smells like camphor. Bay leaves are used in pickling spice and to flavor vinegars and toothpastes.

Leaves from the California laurel (*Umbellularia californica*), also known as bay laurel, Pacific myrtle or pepperwood, are often sold as "bay leaves," but they taste and smell bitter. Leaves from the West Indian bay tree (*Pomenta acris*) are not used in cooking, but they are distilled to produce oil of bay. The primary constituent of oil of bay (which is also known as oil of Myrcia) is *eugenol*, the most important component of oil of cloves. Oil of bay is used in making bay rum and as a fragrance in medicines.

Never use leaves from the mountain laurel (*Kalmia latifolia*) or the cherry laurel (*Prunus laurocerasus*) as substitutes for bay leaves. The leaves of the cherry laurel contain *prulaurasin*, a chemical that releases cyanide in your stomach. All parts of the mountain laurel contain *andromedotoxin*, a poison that may slow your pulse, lower your blood pressure, impair your coordination and cause convulsions, paralysis and death. Andromedotoxin is potent enough to poison honey made by bees that alight on the mountain laurel.

Nutritional profile. One ounce of bay leaves has 54 calories. It provides 1.2 g protein, a trace of fat, 13 g carbohydrates, 53 mg calcium, 1.5 mg iron, 3,000 IU vitamin A and 15 mg vitamin C. However, since bay leaves are usually removed from a cooked dish before it is served, they do not contribute any appreciable amount of nutrients to your diet.

How This Herb Affects Your Body

Laurel leaf oil contains several aromatic chemicals—*eucalyptol, geraniol, linalool, pinene,* and *phellandrene*—which are irritants and allergens.

Benefits. (—)

Adverse effects. Foods made with bay leaves and toothpastes made with bay oil have been reported to cause *cheilitis* (peeling and bleeding of the lips).

Whole bay leaves should *always* be removed before a dish is served. They are large enough to stick in the throat making them particularly dangerous for young children because they can obstruct a child's throat, cutting off the air supply and causing suffocation. Even if you succeed in swallowing a bay leaf, you may still not be out of the woods. Bay leaves are very hard to digest. They may actually remain intact long enough to obstruct the intestines, in which case they may have to be surgically removed.

How to Use This Herb

In cooking: Bay leaves are one of the few herbs that should be added early in cooking because they require a lot of simmering or marinating before their flavor permeates food. The leaves do not disintegrate in cooking; they can be boiled for hours and still hold their shape and texture.

For an unusual flavor, add a bay leaf to the water in which you boil potatoes, noodles or spaghetti.

Around the house: Bay leaves appear to repel roaches, moths and fleas. The active chemical in the leaf is eucalyptol (also known as *cineole*). Put a whole leaf in a canister of flour to keep the insects out, or put whole leaves on the floor of your closet, in drawers where woolen clothes are stored or around the drain under the sink in your kitchen. **Keep the leaves out of reach of children and pets.**

BLACK PEPPER

About This Plant

Botanical name: *Piper nigrum*
Also known as: Pepper

Native to:	India and the East Indies, Sumatra, Java, Sri Lanka
Parts used as spice:	Fruit (berry)
Medicinal properties:	Irritant, diaphoretic
Other uses:	Natural insecticide

About This Spice as a Food and Flavoring

Green, black and white peppercorns are the fruits of a tropical vine, *Piper nigrum*, a species entirely different from the capsicum peppers (bell peppers, cayenne pepper, chili pepper).

Black peppercorns are berries that are picked unripe and allowed to dry in the sun, which develops their color and flavor. They are sold whole or as a powder. Green peppercorns are also unripe berries, but unlike black peppercorns, they are sold whole and soft, never dried. White peppercorns, sold whole or as a powder, are berries that are allowed to mature before they are picked. After they are picked, they are soaked in water, stripped of their outer covering and allowed to dry in the sun, which bleaches them. Although white pepper is considered more attractive than black pepper in cream sauces and soups, it tastes just like black pepper. Green peppercorns have a different flavor, sometimes described as "fresh."

All three kinds of peppercorns get their flavor from the alkaloids *piperine, piperidine* and *chavicin.* Whole peppercorns hold their flavor better than ground pepper, which eventually begins to taste bitter.

Nutritional profile. One teaspoon (2.1 gram) black pepper has 5 calories. It provides 0.2 g protein, a trace of fat, 1.36 g carbohydrates, 9 mg calcium and 4 IU vitamin A.

How This Spice Affects Your Body

Piperine, piperidine and chavicin are diaphoretics (chemicals that make you perspire) and irritants. Black pepper also contains small amounts of *safrole,* a known carcinogen also found in sassafras. In experimental research, extracts of black pepper have caused tumors in labortaory mice when administered daily for three months. The doses were more than 80 times as high as the average amount of pepper consumed each day by human beings. Pepper is not considered a human carcinogen.

Benefits. Because pepper irritates mucous membranes, highly spiced foods may be beneficial when you have hay fever or a head cold. The spice irritates tissues inside your nose and throat, causing them to weep a watery secretion that makes it easier for you to cough up mucus or to blow your nose. Pepper also makes you perspire. Because perspiration acts as a natural air conditioner, cooling your body as the moisture evaporates from your skin, peppery foods are popular in warm climates.

Adverse effects. Eating peppered foods may upset your stomach, irritate your bladder so that you have to urinate more frequently or even make urination itself painful.

Some people confuse this urinary irritation with an aphrodisiac effect. Others mistakenly believe that because pepper makes you urinate more frequently, it will cure a hangover. But that's not really true. Your body does eliminate alcohol when you urinate (as well as when you breathe and perspire), but you can only get rid of the alcohol after it has been metabolized (digested) by enzyme action.

When you drink more alcohol than your body can metabolize in a given period, the unmetabolized alcohol is stored in your tissues, causing headache, muscle aches and upset stomach. As time passes, the excess alcohol is metabolized and eliminated, and your discomfort eases. There is no way to speed up the process because you can't speed up your body's production of the necessary enzymes.

How to Use This Spice

In cooking: Grind peppercorns right before you use them; the intact peppercorn holds its flavor better than ground pepper. Whole peppercorns can be stored in the freezer and ground while still frozen.

For maximum freshness, grind peppercorns in a metal or plastic peppermill rather than a wooden one. Wood, which absorbs oils from the peppercorns, is harder to keep clean and fresh.

Pepper has a natural affinity for dishes made with allspice, cinnamon or cloves, deepening the flavor and giving it a pleasant bite. Add a pinch of pepper to hot chocolate, eggnog, spiced wine punch, apple pie, baked apples or applesauce, baked pears and, of course, gingerbread.

Peppered Hot Chocolate

1 teaspoon plain cocoa powder
1 teaspoon sugar
Pinch cinnamon
Pinch ground black or white pepper
1 cup boiling water or 1 cup hot milk

Put the cocoa powder, sugar and cinnamon in a coffee cup, and add just enough hot water to make the powder into a smooth paste. Then stir in the rest of the boiling water.

As a home remedy: To relieve the congestion of a head cold or a cough, spice your chicken soup with some pepper (see above, How This Spice Affects Your Body).

In the garden: Piperine is a natural insecticide considered more toxic to houseflies than pyrethrins, the natural insecticide derived from chrysanthemums. To protect your plants, spray them with a solution of one-half teaspoon ground pepper in one quart of warm water.

BORAGE

ABOUT THIS PLANT

Botanical name:	*Borago officinalis*
Also known as:	Beebread, bee plant, burage
Native to:	Europe, the Mediterranean
Parts used as herb:	Leaves, flowers
Medicinal properties:	(—)
Other uses:	Honey plant

ABOUT THIS HERB AS FOOD AND FLAVORING

Borage is a decorative garden plant with coarse, hairy stems and leaves. The leaves, which can be eaten raw or cooked, are salty, and they taste and smell like cucumber. They are sometimes added to salads or used as a garnish for cold drinks. Borage is rarely available in grocery stores. If you like its flavor, you'll have to grow your own.

Borage's fresh flavor comes from *tannins,* the astringent chemicals that give a cup of tea its pleasant bite; *malic acid,* the chemical that makes immature apples sour; and *potassium nitrate,* which has a cooling, pungent taste.[*]

Nutritional profile. One-half cup (44 g) raw borage contains 9 calories. It provides 0.8 g protein, 0.3 g fat, 1.35 g carbohydrates, 41 mg calcium, 1.45 mg iron, 23 mg magnesium, 1,848 IU vitamin A and 15.4 mg vitamin C.

Three and a half ounces (100 g) cooked borage has 25 calories. It provides 2 g protein, 0.8 g fat, 3.6 g carbohydrates, 102 mg calcium, 3.64 mg iron, 4,385 IU vitamin A and 32.5 mg vitamin C.

---

[*] Potassium nitrate, which is used in matches, firecrackers and gunpowder, and as an additive in cigarettes to make the tobacco burn more evenly, makes borage pop and crackle when you burn it.

How This Herb Affects Your Body

Tannins are astringents. They coagulate the proteins on the surface of the mucous membrane lining of your mouth, making the tissues pucker. Malic acid and potassium nitrate are diuretics.*

Some recent research suggests borage may contain *lasiocarpine,* a liver carcinogen also found in comfrey, a poisonous herb (see appendix). Borage may also contain small amounts of two alkaloids, *lycopsamine* and *supinidine viridiflorate,* that may be poisonous. As a result, some experts suggest that it may be hazardous to consume large amounts of borage.

Benefits. Borage is a good source of *beta*-carotene, the pigment in deep yellow vegetables that is converted to vitamin A in your body. According to the American Cancer Society, a diet rich in these foods may lower the risk of some forms of cancer.

Vitamin A also protects your eyes. In your body the vitamin A from borage is converted to 11-cis retinol, the most important constituent of *rhodopsin,* a protein in the rods in your retina (the cells that enable you to see in dim light). One-half cup raw borage leaves gives a woman 46% of the vitamin A she needs each day and a man 37% of what he requires. Three and a half ounces of cooked borage has 109% of a woman's RDA for vitamin A, 88% of a man's.

Borage is also rich in vitamin C. One-half cup of fresh borage has 26% of the RDA for healthy adults; 3.5 ounces of cooked borage, 54%.

Like collard, dandelion, mustard and turnip greens, borage is high in calcium. Three and a half ounces cooked borage provides 13% of the calcium an adult needs each day. Borage rivals spinach as a source of *non-heme iron,* the kind of iron found in plants. (The form of iron found in meat, fish, poultry, milk and eggs is called *heme iron.*) One-half cup fresh borage leaves provides 10% of the iron a healthy woman needs each day and 15% of the RDA for a healthy man. You can increase the amount of iron you absorb from borage by eating the vegetable with meat. This increases the secretion of stomach acids, and iron is absorbed more easily in an acid environment. Or serve borage with a food rich in vitamin C. Vitamin C may change the non-heme iron from ferric iron to ferrous iron, a form of iron your body absorbs more easily.

Adverse effects. The bristles on borage stems are irritating. Handling the plant may cause contact dermatitis (itching, burning, stinging, reddened or blistered skin) in sensitive people.

Because it is high in calcium, borage may be prohibited for people who form calcium oxalate kidney stones.

---

* Large doses of potassium nitrate may cause violent gastric upset; repeated exposure to small amounts over a long period of time may cause anemia and kidney damage. Neither of these has been reported in people who eat borage.

How to Use This Herb

In cooking: Do not tear or cut borage leaves until you are actually ready to use them. When you cut into a food rich in vitamin C, its cells release an enzyme called *ascorbic acid oxidase*. This chemical destroys vitamin C and reduces the nutritional value of the food.

If you cook borage in an aluminum or iron pot, the tannins in the borage can react with ions from the metal to form dark pigments that discolor the pot and darken the borage. To prevent this chemical reaction, cook your borage in a glass or enameled pot.

Chlorophyll, the green coloring in plants, is sensitive to acids. When you heat borage leaves, their chlorophyll reacts with natural acids in the leaves or in the cooking water, forming a brown compound called *pheophytin.* The pheophytin in turn reacts with the yellow carotene pigments in the leaves, turning the cooked borage bronze. To prevent this color change, keep the chlorophyll from reacting with the acids in one of these ways: (1) cook the borage in lots of water to dilute the acids, (2) leave the lid off the pot so the acids can dissipate into the air or (3) steam the borage leaves very quickly so there is no time for the reaction to occur.

Dried borage leaves are less flavorful than fresh ones. They are also lower in vitamin C. **Use only unsprayed leaves.**

BURDOCK

About This Plant

Botanical name:	*Arctium lappa*
Also known as:	Great burdock
Native to:	Europe
Parts used as herb:	Leaves, roots, stems
Medicinal properties:	Skin protectant/antiseptic
Other uses:	(—)

About This Herb as Food and Flavoring

Burdock is a tall weed whose leaves are used in salads. Its stems can be peeled, boiled and eaten like asparagus or candied like angelica. Its long roots, which are grayish brown on the outside and white on the inside, can be sliced into soups and stews or Oriental stir-fried dishes. Or it can be boiled, buttered and served like turnips or potatoes. Dried burdock root is sometimes sold in health food stores as *lappa*, which is used to make burdock tea.

The starchy burdock root is composed chiefly (45%) of the complex carbohydrate *inulin*, the starch that gives Jerusalem artichokes their characteristic sweet flavor. The root also contains sucrose, bitter resin and some fats.

Nutritional profile. One cup (125 g) boiled and drained burdock root has 110 calories. It provides 2.6 g protein, 0.2 g fat, 26.4 g carbohydrates, 62 mg calcium and 0.9 mg iron.

How This Herb Affects Your Body

Inulin is sometimes used as a substitute for *sucrose* (table sugar) in baked goods for people with diabetes, an illness characterized by insufficient production of *insulin*, the pancreatic enzyme your body needs to metabolize (digest) sucrose.

Benefits. Like other starches, inulin appears to form a protective, soothing film when spread on the skin. Some studies suggest that there are antiseptic or antibacterial compounds in the fresh burdock root (they disappear when the root is dried), but there is currently no scientific proof that burdock root is effective either as a soothing dressing or as an external antiseptic.

Adverse effects. The burdock plant contains organic chemicals called *lactones* that can cause contact dermatitis (itching, burning and stinging, reddened or blistered skin) in sensitized people.

How to Use This Herb

In cooking: Burdock roots, which are brown on the outside but white on the inside, contain creamy anthoxanthin pigments that turn dark when they react with ions from an iron or aluminum pot. To keep cooked burdock roots white, prepare them in a glass or enameled pot. **Use only unsprayed plants.**

BURNET

ABOUT THIS PLANT

Botanical name:	*Sanguisorba minor* (garden burnet)
	Sangvisorba officinalis (greater burnet)
Also known as:	Salad burnet
Native to:	Eurasia (garden burnet)
	Europe (greater burnet)
Parts used as herb:	Leaves
Medicinal properties:	Astringent
Other uses:	(—)

ABOUT THIS HERB AS FOOD AND FLAVORING

The burnets are members of the rose family. You can tell them apart by their flowers. Garden burnet has light green to yellow green flowers; greater burnet has red ones. Like borage leaves, burnet leaves have a distinctly cucumber-like flavor that makes them a welcome addition to fresh salads and a useful garnish for cool summer drinks.

If you want to add burnet to your salads, you'll have to grow your own. This herb, which gets its fresh cool taste from a high concentration of *tannins*, is unlikely to be available at your grocery store.

Nutritional profile. (—)

HOW THIS HERB AFFECTS YOUR BODY

Tannins are astringents. They coagulate the proteins on the surface of your skin or the mucous membrane lining of your mouth and make the tissues pucker. When you eat or drink a food or beverage high in tannins, you experience a "cool" or "fresh" sensation. In folk medicine, high-tannin plants such as the burnets were used as a remedy for diarrhea or to stanch the flow of blood from open wounds (*Sanguisorba*, the burnets' family name, means "blood absorber"). Herbs rich in tannin have also been widely used as a folk remedy for minor burns, but none of these effects has been validated by the Food and Drug Adminstration.

Benefits. (—)

Adverse effects. (—)

How to Use This Herb

In cooking: When using burnet in salads, pick the tenderest leaves and use them as soon as possible: The flavor fades when the leaves dry out. **Use only unsprayed plants.**

CAPERS

About This Plant

Botanical name:	*Capparis spinosa*
Also known as:	(—)
Native to:	Southern Europe, the Mediterranean
Parts used as herb:	Flower buds
Medicinal properties:	(—)
Other uses:	(—)

About This Herb as Food and Flavoring

Capers are the unripened flower buds of a spiny shrub picked before they have a chance to open. The buds may be salted and pickled in vinegar or pickled in vinegar without having been salted. Capers are used to add a salty/sour piquancy to salad dressings or meat and chicken stews. They are particularly good in a sour cream sauce.

CAUTION: The caper spurge (*Euphorbia lathyris*) is an unrelated poisonous plant whose buds are sometimes mistaken for capers. People who pick and eat the buds of the caper spurge may experience a burning sensation in the mouth, nausea and gastric upset, paleness, irregular pulse, dizziness, delirium and collapse.

Nutritional profile. (—)

How This Herb Affects Your Body

Capers are high in sodium (defined as more than 125 mg sodium per serving). They may increase your body's retention of fluids and raise your blood pressure.

Benefits. (—)

Adverse effects. High-sodium foods are usually prohibited on salt-restricted diets for people with hypertension (high blood pressure) and heart disease who are sensitive to salt.

How to Use This Herb

In cooking: Capers can be used as a substitute for the Oriental condiment *fermented black beans* ("toushi").

In the garden: For salt-free capers, grow your own caper bushes. The plants, perennials which thrive in mild winter climates, can be started indoors from seed. Once there is no longer any possiblity of frost, move them outside. They will tolerate dryness, but they need full sun. To harvest the capers, pick off the flower buds before they show any color and steep them in vinegar to taste.

CARAWAY SEED

About This Plant

Botanical name:	*Carum carvi*
Also known as:	(—)
Native to:	Asia
Parts used as herb:	Fruit
Medicinal properties:	Carminative
Other uses:	Flavoring, perfume in drugs, cosmetics

About This Herb as Food and Flavoring

The caraway plant is a member of the carrot and parsley family. Its "seeds" (actually the dried ripe fruit) have a warm aroma and flavor that give rye bread and *kummel* their characteristic tastes. Young caraway leaves can be used to lend the flavor of caraway to salads.

Caraway gets its flavor and aroma from oil of caraway. The oil contains *carvone* (50%–60%), the flavor used in kummel, and *limonene* (40%–50%), a lemony smelling chemical also found in the oils of lemon, orange and dill.

Nutritional profile. One tablespoon (6.7 g) caraway seeds has 22 calories. It provides 1.32 g protein, 1 g fat, 3.3 g carbohydrates, 46 mg calcium, 1.09 mg iron and 24 IU vitamin A.

How This Herb Affects Your Body

Carvone and limonene are irritants. Limonene is also a photosensitizer, a chemical that makes your skin more sensitive to sunlight.

Benefits. (—)

Adverse effects. Handling the caraway plant can make your skin sensitive to sunlight.

How to Use This Herb

In cooking: Like whole peppercorns, whole caraway seeds hold their flavor and aroma for months at a time provided you store them in air-tight containers and protect them from light.

Add caraway seeds to a sauce after the dish is cooked; long cooking may turn their flavor bitter.

Caraway is sometimes known as "Roman cumin" because ground caraway has a flavor similar to (but slightly lighter than) ground cumin. You can grind or mash caraway seeds and use them as a substitute for cumin in homemade curry or chili powder.

CARDAMOM

About This Plant

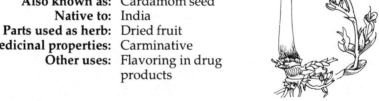

Botanical name:	*Elettaria cardamomum*
Also known as:	Cardamom seed
Native to:	India
Parts used as herb:	Dried fruit
Medicinal properties:	Carminative
Other uses:	Flavoring in drug products

About This Spice as Food and Flavoring

Cardamom is the world's third most expensive spice, right behind saffron and vanilla. The dried fruits ("seeds") are sold whole or ground. Some Indian grocery stores sell cardamom seedpods, either black (sun dried, deeply flavored) or green (milder flavored, dried indoors in large kilns).

Cardamom gets its flavor and aroma from oil of cardamon, a pale yellow liquid that contains spicy tasting, camphor-scented *eucalyptol*, lemony flavored *limonene* and *terpinene*, and peppery *borneol*. Cardamom is used in curry powders, baked goods and candies, and its oil is used to flavor liquors and pharmaceutical drug products.

Nutritional profile. One teaspoon (2 g) ground cardamom has 6 calories. It provides 0.2 g protein, 0.1 g fat, 1.37 g carbohydrates, 8 mg calcium and 0.3 mg iron.

How This Herb Affects Your Body

Borneol, eucalyptol and limonene are irritants. Limonene is also a photosensitizer, a chemical that makes your skin more sensitive to sunlight.

Benefits. Cardamom is reputed to be a carminative, a substance that breaks up intestinal gas.

Adverse effects. Prolonged handling of cardamom seeds may cause contact dermatitis (itching, burning, stinging, reddened or blistered skin) or make your skin more sensitive to sunlight.

How to Use This Herb

In cooking: A pinch of cardamom adds piquancy to after-dinner coffee.

Cardamom is most commonly used in spicy curries and chili dishes. You can also add a pinch to hamburger meat.

Around the house: Eucalyptol is a cockroach repellent found in bay leaves, as well as cardamom. A bay leaf in a canister of flour protects the flour from infestation; bay leaves under the sink keep the cockroaches away from there, too. Cardamom is too highly aromatic to toss into your flour canister unless you want your baked goods to smell of cardamom, but you could try scattering a few pods underneath the sink to see if they keep the cockroaches away. If you do, regard it as a useful scientific experiment. There are already laboratory studies showing that bay leaves repel cockroaches, but there aren't any showing the effects of cardamom.

CASSIA

ABOUT THIS PLANT

Botanical name:	*Cinnamomum cassia*
Also known as:	Chinese cassia
Native to:	Asia
Parts used as herb:	Bark
Medicinal properties:	Carminative
Other uses:	Perfumery

ABOUT THIS HERB AS FOOD AND FLAVORING

Cassia is the bark of an evergreen tree that belongs to the laurel family, a relative of *Cinnamomum zeylanicum*, the "true" cinnamon. Cassia is never sold under its own name. Instead, cassia bark may be ground and mixed with cinnamon to be marketed as "ground cinnamon" or rolled and sold as "cinnamon sticks." If you were to taste plan cassia and plain cinnamon, you would find cassia's flavor bitter, while cinnamon's is warm and sweet. Cassia also has a stronger scent and is darker in color (reddish brown versus tan). Cinnamon sticks made of true cinnamon look like quills (a single tube); cinnamon sticks made from cassia are rolled from both sides toward the center so that they end up looking like scrolls.

Both oil of cassia (known as "oil of cinnamon") and the oil of true cinnamon (known as "oil of cinnamon, Ceylon") get their flavor and aroma from *cinnamaldehyde*, a yellow, oily liquid with a strong cinnamon scent. The value of oil of cassia is determined by its cinnamaldehyde content. This runs as high as 80% or more. (Oil of cinnamon, Ceylon, is only 50%–65% cinnamaldehyde).

Cassia buds, the dried fruit of the cassia tree, are highly aromatic spices that look like cloves. In China they are used for adding a cinnamon flavor to candy and sweet pickles.

CAUTION: The cassia we use in food is not related to *Cassia marilandica* (wild senna) or *Cassia senna* (senna), plants that contain anthraquinone compounds, strong cathartics that may cause violent purging. Herbal teas made with plants from the *Cassia* genus may be hazardous.

Nutritional profile. One teaspoon (2.3 g) of a mixture of ground cassia and cinnamon labeled Cinnamon has 6 calories. It provides 0.09 g protein, 0.07 g fat, 1.84 g carbohydrates, 28 mg calcium, 6 IU vitamin A and 0.7 mg vitamin C.

How This Herb Affects Your Body

Oil of cinnamon, the yellow brown volatile oil in cassia, is a carminative, an agent that helps to break up intestinal gas. Both cinnamaldehyde and oil of cinnamon are irritants.

Benefits. (—)

Adverse effects. Some people find cassia and cinnamon irritating to the stomach.

How to Use This Herb

Around the house: To freshen the air in your kitchen, put one-half teaspoon cassia in two cups of water and boil on top of your stove.

To scent your drawers, put scrolls of cassia in the back.

Catnip

About This Plant

Botanical name:	*Nepeta cataria*
Also known as:	Catmint
Native to:	Europe, Asia
Parts used as herb:	Leaves
Medicinal properties:	Carminative, mild sedative
Other uses:	Attractant for cats

About This Herb as Food and Flavoring

Catnip is a member of the mint family. When you crush its flowers or its velvety gray green leaves, they release an oil that contains *nepatalactone*, a chemical whose aroma cats find irresistible. Catnip leaves can be used to add a minty flavor to salads or to brew a minty tea. Catnip is sometimes available as a tea in health food stores.

Nutritional profile. (—)

How This Herb Affects Your Body

Nepatalactone's chemical structure is similar to that of the *valepotriates*, chemicals used as sedatives in Europe. Some research with laboratory animals has suggested that nepatalactone has sedative effects and that it acts as a carminative, an agent that breaks up intestinal gas.

In 1969 an article in the Journal of the American Medical Association mistakenly suggested that smoking cigarettes made of catnip leaves produces euphoria in human beings. The error arose from the authors' confusing a drawing of the catnip plant with a drawing of the marijuana plant. (Catnip makes cats ecstatic only when they smell it; giving them catnip in their food has no such effect.)

The Food and Drug Administration presently classifies catnip as an herb of "undefined safety."

Benefits. (—)

Adverse effects. (—)

How to Use This Herb

In cooking: Moderate amounts of fresh catnip leaves add a pleasant minty flavor to a salad. To get the most flavor from the leaves, chop or rub them against the side of a colander or sieve. This releases the flavoring oils in the leaves.

Around the house: To give your cat a special treat, rub fresh catnip leaves against her scratching post.

In the garden: The odor of catnip is said to repel rats and insects. Planting catnip in a border around your garden may keep them both away, but keep a close watch on the catnip. You must clip off the flowers early, before the seeds are ready to fall. If you don't, catnip—which grows easily from seed—will start to take over your garden.

CATSUP

About This Condiment

Chemical name:	(—)
Also known as:	Ketchup, tomato catsup
Native to:	Malaysia
Parts used as condiment:	(—)
Medicinal properties:	(—)
Other uses:	(—)

ABOUT THIS CONDIMENT AS FOOD AND FLAVORING

Tomato catsup is a sweet tomato sauce made with tomatoes, onions, pepper, sugar and vinegar plus assorted spices such as allspice, cinnamon, mustard, garlic, cloves and nutmeg. It originated in Malaysia, where its name means "taste."

Nutritional profile. One tablespoon (15 g) catsup has 15 calories. It provides a trace of protein and fat, 4 g carbohydrates, 3 mg calcium, 0.1 mg iron, 2 mg vitamin C and 210 IU vitamin A.

One cup (273 g) catsup has 290 calories. It provides 5 g protein, 1 g fat, 69 g carbohydrates, 60 mg calcium, 2.2 mg iron, 41 mg vitamin C and 3,820 IU vitamin A.

HOW THIS CONDIMENT AFFECTS YOUR BODY

Benefits. Catsup is a respectable source of vitamin A. One tablespoon spread on a hot dog or hamburger provides 5% of the vitamin A a woman needs each day or 4% of the RDA for a man.

Adverse effects. Regular catsup is a high-sodium food (156 mg sodium per tbsp). It may cause an increase in blood pressure in people with hypertension who are sensitive to sodium. The alternative product—a low sodium dietary catsup—has, on average, only 3 milligrams sodium per tablespoon.

Catsup, a high-sugar food, is excluded from a sucrose-free diet. Each tablespoon of regular catsup has 3 grams sugar, accounting for 80% of the calories.

HOW TO USE THIS CONDIMENT

In cooking: When beef is cooked and stored in the refrigerator, the fats oxidize, giving the meat a characteristic "warmed over" flavor. You can slow the oxidation of fats and reduce the intensity of this flavor by cooking and storing the meat under a protective cover of antioxidant foods such as the high-acid, vitamin C–rich tomatoes in catsup.

CELERY SEED

ABOUT THIS PLANT

Botanical name: *Apium graveolens*
Also known as: (—)
Native to: Europe, Asia, Africa
Parts used as herb: Fruit
Medicinal properties: Carminative, diuretic
Other uses: Birdseed

ABOUT THIS HERB AS FOOD AND FLAVORING

Celery "seeds" are the dried fruit of a variety of wild celery popularly known as "smallage." They are the smallest of all the seeds used as flavorings. It takes about 760,000 celery seeds to make one pound.

Celery seeds are much more intensely aromatic than celery leaves or stalks because they contain proportionally more oil of celery. The oil is a pale yellow liquid scented and flavored with *apiin*, a glucoside (sugar/alcohol compound) also found in celery and parsley, plus lemony scented *limonene* and the bitter *furocoumarins bergapten* and *hydroxymethoxypsoralen*. Celery seeds are used in soups and stews, or ground and mixed with salt to make "celery salt." Oil of celery is used to flavor celery tonic and liqueurs and as a scent in perfumes and toilet soap.

Nutritional profile. One teaspoon celery seed (2 g) has 8 calories. It provides 0.4 g protein, 0.5 g fat, 35 mg calcium, 0.9 g iron, 1 IU vitamin A and 0.3 mg vitamin C.

HOW THIS HERB AFFECTS YOUR BODY

Limonene, bergapten and hydroxymethoxypsoralen are all photosensitizers, chemicals that can make your skin more sensitive to sunlight.

Benefits. Celery seeds act as a carminative, an agent that breaks up intestinal gas.

Adverse effects. Celery—which contains about 50 milligrams sodium in an average serving—is considered a high-sodium food, excluded from a sodium-restricted diet for people with high blood pressure or heart disease who are sensitive to salt. But a teaspoon of celery seeds sprinkled on a salad adds only 3 mg sodium, an amount considered low.

Prolonged handling of bruised or moldy celery may cause photosensitivity, which has been reported among food workers who handle this vegetable.

How to Use This Herb

In cooking: A commercial celery salt is approximately 10% to 25% ground celery seed. A simple way to make your own celery-flavored salt at home is to stir 2 teaspoons celery seeds into 6 teaspoons table salt, mixing thoroughly. Store the celery/salt mixture in a salt shaker, adding a few grains of rice to keep the salt from caking. Let the salt sit for a few days, and then use as needed. For a more intensely flavored celery salt, chop the seeds into small pieces before stirring them into the salt. When you cut the seeds, you tear the walls of cells inside the seed, releasing the oil of celery stored there.

CHAMOMILLE

About This Plant

Botanical name:	*Anthemis nobilis, Matricaria chamomilla*
Also known as:	Camomille, German chamomille manzanilla (*Matricaria*), Roman chamomille (*Anthemis*)
Native to:	Europe
Parts used as herb:	Flowers
Medicinal properties:	Anti-inflammatory (*Matricaria*), carminative, antispasmodic
Other uses:	Hair color rinse

About This Herb as Food and Flavoring

German chamomille ("sweet false chamomille") and Roman chamomille ("true chamomille") are members of the daisy family. Both smell and taste like apple and have pretty, pale green, feathery leaves and daisylike white flowers. Their golden centers are colored with *apigenin, luteolin, patuletin* and *quercitrin*, all bitter-tasting flavonoids (pigments). The flowers are the only edible parts of the plants.

You can add fresh or dried chamomille flowers from your garden to a salad or use them to make an apple-scented tea. Dried chamomille is also available in tea bags at the health food store.

Nutritional profile. (—)

How This Herb Affects Your Body

The oils of both German and Roman chamomille contain an anti-inflammatory and antipyretic (fever-reducing) chemical called *chamazulene.*

Apigenin, luteolin, patuletin and quercitrin, the flavonoids that make the centers of the chamomille flowers golden, are antispasmodics (substances that relax muscle spasms and are often used to soothe an upset stomach). However, a tea made from chamomille flowers contains such small amounts of these chemicals that it is hard to say whether the drink is effective.

In experiments with laboratory animals, chamomille teas show anti-inflammatory effects, relieving the symptoms of conditions such as arthritis that are ordinarily characterized by pain, redness and swelling. Although chamomille has long been used as a folk remedy for inflammations, there is at present no American scientific research showing that chamomille is effective for human beings.

Benefits. (—)

Adverse effects. The chamomilles are related to ragweed, asters and chrysanthemums. People who suffer respiratory allergy when exposed to these plants may also be sensitive to the chamomilles. They may develop hives, hay fever or asthma from eating chamomille flowers or drinking chamomille tea. Handling chamomille plants may cause contact dermatitis (itching, burning, stinging, reddened or blistered skin).

How to Use This Herb

In cooking: In cooking, use only chamomille flowers from your own garden, grown without any pesticides.

When you pick chamomille flowers, you may find the flowerheads full of seed-loving insects. To eliminate the pests, spread the flowers on a cookie sheet and dry them in the oven at 120 degrees F for half an hour. Then sift the flowers in a strainer or colander and discard the debris. Store the dried flowers in an air-tight container. Use as desired for teas.

The flowers of German chamomille are preferred for teas. Although they are not as strongly scented as leaves from Roman chamomille, they are sweeter.

As a cosmetic: For a golden rinse to highlight blonde or light brown hair, steep chamomille flowers in hot water, let the water cool and use as a rinse after shampooing.

For an apple-scented bath, add ½ pound chamomille flowers to 2½ quarts water. Bring the water to a boil to force the flowers to release their scented oil. Then let the water cool, and strain out the flowers. Add the water to your bath.

In the garden: Both chamomilles grow readily from seed and prefer full sun. Roman chamomille, an erect plant, is neater in the garden. German chamomille, which crawls along the ground, turns weedy if left untended.

CHERVIL

ABOUT THIS PLANT

Botanical name: *Anthriscus cerefolium*
Also known as: French parsley
Native to: Northern Europe
Parts used as herb: Leaves
Medicinal properties: (—)
Other uses: (—)

ABOUT THIS HERB AS FOOD AND FLAVORING

Chervil is a member of the carrot family. It looks like parsley, but its lacy leaves are lighter green, its flavor is sweeter and it is more aromatic, with a scent some say resembles tarragon's. Chervil is usually included in the French culinary herbal bouquet known as *fines herbes* (basil, chives, parsley, sage, savory and tarragon).

Like parsley, chervil comes with curly leaves ("true chervil") or flat leaves. Both curly leaved and flat-leaved chervil have the same pleasant flavor, but the curled leaf looks more decorative as a garnish. At well-stocked grocery stores, chervil is available fresh and dried.

Nutritional profile. One teaspoon dried chervil (0.6 g) has 1 calorie. It provides 0.1 g protein, a trace of fat, 0.3 g carbohydrates, 8 mg calcium and 0.2 mg iron.

How This Herb Affects Your Body

Chervil is almost never mentioned in herbal medicine, and to date there is no scientific evidence to support folk claims that it is useful as a diuretic and a digestive.

Benefits. (—)
Adverse effects. (—)

How to Use This Herb

In cooking: Chervil loses its delicate flavor quickly when dried. For the finest flavor, use fresh chervil whenever possible.

Chlorophyll, the green coloring in plants, is sensitive to acids and heat. Commercial herb packagers preserve the color in their chervil by drying the leaves at a very low heat. But when you use the leaves in cooking at home, their chlorophyll reacts with natural acids in the leaves or in the cooking liquid to form a brown compound called *pheophytin,* turning the leaves olive drab.

If your grocery store doesn't stock fresh chervil, you can approximate its flavor by combining one part fresh chopped tarragon with two parts fresh chopped parsley.

CHICORY

About This Plant

Botanical name:	*Cichorium intybus*
Also known as:	Coffeeweed
Native to:	Europe, India
Parts used as herb:	Leaves, roots
Medicinal properties:	(—)
Other uses:	Coffee substitute

About This Herb as Food and Flavoring

There are several varieties of *Cichorium,* including *Cichorium intybus,* the head of loosely wrapped leaves we call "chicory," and *Cichorium endiva,* which we call escarole. Another variety, Magdenburg, is grown specifically for its astringent-flavored roots.

Young chicory and escarole leaves, which have a slightly bitter tang, are used in salads. The older leaves can be cooked and served like spinach. Chicory root is composed primarily of *inulin*, the indigestible carbohydrate that gives Jerusalem artichoke its characteristic flavor. They also contain *fructose*; *pyrone* (a natural flavor enhancer that can make sucrose taste 10 to 300 times sweeter and has been approved by the Food and Drug Administration for use in baked goods); oils; bitter principles; and astringent *tannins*. When chicory root is roasted, its inulin is converted to oxymethylfurfurol, which smells like coffee but has no caffeine.

Nutritional profile. One-half cup (90 g) chopped chicory greens has 21 calories. It provides 1.5 g protein, 0.3 g fat, 4.2 g carbohydrates, 90 mg calcium, 0.8 mg iron, 3,600 IU vitamin A and 22 mg vitamin C.

One-half cup (45 g) raw chicory root has 33 calories. It provides 0.6 g protein, a trace of fat, 7.9 g carbohydrates, 18 mg calcium, 0.4 mg iron, 3 IU vitamin A and 2.3 mg vitamin C.

How This Herb Affects Your Body

Inulin is sometimes used as an ingredient in baked goods for people with diabetes, the illness characterized by an inability to use sucrose (table sugar).

Benefits. Fresh chicory leaves are a good source of vitamin C. One-half cup of fresh leaves in a salad provides 37% of the vitamin C an adult needs each day.

Chicory leaves are also rich in *beta*-carotene, the carotenoid pigment in deep yellow fruits and vegetables that is converted to vitamin A in your body. According to the American Cancer Society, a diet rich in these foods may lower the risk of some forms of cancer.

Vitamin A also protects your eyes, since your body can turn the vitamin A in chicory into 11-cis retinol, the most important constituent of *rhodopsin*, a protein in the rods in your retina (the cells that give you night vision, the ability to see in dim light). One-half cup fresh chicory leaves provides 90% of the vitamin A a woman needs each day; 72% of the RDA for an adult man.

People who are sensitive to caffeine's stimulant effects but don't like decaffeinated coffees may find coffee mixed with chicory a satisfactory alternative. It has less caffeine than plain coffee but is still pleasantly bitter.

Both the leaves and roots of the chicory plant have been used as a "bitter tonic" for treating digestive problems and as a diuretic or laxative.

Adverse effects. (—)

How to Use This Herb

In cooking: Do not tear or cut chicory leaves until you are actually ready to use them. When you cut into a food rich in vitamin C, its cells release an enzyme called ascorbic acid oxidase. This chemical destroys vitamin C and reduces the nutritional value of the food.

Chlorophyll, the green coloring in plants, is sensitive to acids. If you heat chicory leaves, their chlorophyll reacts with natural acids in the leaves or in the cooking water, forming a brown compound called *pheophytin*. The pheophytin then reacts with the yellow carotene pigments in the leaves, turning the cooked chicory bronze. To prevent this color change, you must keep the chlorophyll from reacting with the acids in one of these ways: (1) cook the greens in lots of water to dilute the acids, (2) leave the lid off the pot so the acids can dissipate into the air or (3) steam the leaves very quickly so there is no time for the reaction to occur.

CHILI POWDER

About This Condiment

Chemical name:	(—)
Also known as:	(—)
Native to:	The American Southwest
Parts used as condiment:	(—)
Medicinal properties:	Diaphoretic, irritant
Other uses:	(—)

About This Condiment as Food and Flavoring

Chili powder is a blend of spices created in the American Southwest during the 19th century. A representative chili powder is mostly red (cayenne) pepper, plus cumin, oregano, salt and garlic powder. It gets its bite chiefly from *capsaicin*, the most pungent chemical in cayenne peppers.

Nutritional profile. One tablespoon (7.5 g) chili powder containing red pepper (83%), cumin (9%), oregano (4%), salt (2.5%) and garlic powder (1.5%) has 24 calories. It provides 0.9 g protein, 1.26 g fat, 4.10 g carbohydrates, 1.07 mg iron, 21 mg calcium, 2,620 IU vitamin A and 4.8 mg vitamin C.

How This Condiment Affects Your Body

Virtually all of chili powder's effects on your body are due to the capsaicin in the red pepper, which is a *diaphoretic* (a substance that promotes perspiration) and an irritant. Capsaicin does not dissolve in cold water. That means it won't do any good to drink iced water when a hotly spiced chili-flavored stew makes your mouth burn. What you need instead is a glass of cold milk or a chilled beer: Both milk fat and alcohol dissolve capsaicin and relieve the stinging in your mouth.

Benefits. Chili powder is a good source of *beta*-carotene, the vitamin A precursor in deep yellow fruits and vegetables. According to the American Cancer Society, a diet rich in these foods may lower the risk of some forms of cancer.

Vitamin A also protects your eyes. In your body, the vitamin A from chili powder is converted to 11-cis retinol, the most important constituent of *rhodopsin*, a protein in the rods in your retina (the cells that enable you to see in dim light). One tablespoon provides 66% of the vitamin A a woman needs each day and 52% of the RDA for a man.

Eating food spiced with moderate amounts of chili powder may be helpful when you have hay fever or a head or chest cold. The capsaicin in the chili powder's red pepper irritates the mucous membranes lining your nose and throat. This irritation causes them to weep a watery secretion, making it easier for you to cough up mucus or clear your nose when you blow.

Foods spiced with chili powder may stimulate your appetite because they irritate the lining of your stomach and stimulate the flow of gastric juices, triggering the contractions we call hunger pangs.

Adverse effects. The cayenne pepper in chili powder may be irritating to the lining of your stomach and your bladder, causing gastric discomfort or a frequent urge to urinate.

How to Use This Condiment

In cooking: Store chili powder tightly closed in a cool place to protect its flavor and color.

You can enrich the flavor of any chili powder and make it more interesting by adding a pinch of one of the "sweet" spices: allspice, cinnamon, cloves and onion.

If you are making your own chili powder and don't have any cumin on hand, substitute ground caraway seeds, whose flavor is similar to cumin's, though more delicate.

CHIVES

About This Plant

Botanical name: *Allium schoenoprasum*
Also known as: (—)
Native to: Northern Europe, Asia
Parts used as herb: Leaves
Medicinal properties: (—)
Other uses: Insect repellent

About This Herb as Food and Flavoring

Chives are members of the onion family with mildly flavored bulbs and hollow, flat, green leaves used for their pleasant oniony flavor and aroma. The young pink, lavender, purple or white flower clusters of the chive plant are edible if used before seeds form. Once flowers appear, the leaves become much less flavorful.

Like onions, chives get their flavor and aroma from sulfur compounds. Garlic chives (*Allium tuberosum*), also known as Chinese or Oriental chives, have a mild garlicky flavor.

Nutritional profile. One tablespoon (3 g) chopped raw chives has one calorie. It provides 0.08 g protein, 0.02 g fat, 0.11 g carbohydrates, 2 mg calcium, 0.05 mg iron, 192 IU vitamin A and 2.4 mg vitamin C.

One tablespoon (0.2 g) freeze-dried chives has about one calorie. It provides 0.04 g protein, 0.01 g fat, 0.13 g carbohydrates, 2 mg calcium, 0.04 mg iron, 137 IU vitamin A and 1.3 mg vitamin C.

How This Herb Affects Your Body

The sulfur compounds in onions have antibiotic properties similar to those of *alliin* and *allicin*, the antibiotic chemicals in garlic. Eating onions and garlic seems to lower blood levels of low-density lipoproteins (LDLs), the "bad" cholesterol that clings to artery walls, an effect attributed to the oils in each plant.

Benefits. Because we use such small amounts of chives to season foods, we are unlikely to experience any of the medical benefits attributed to eating onions and garlic.

Adverse effects. See above, *Benefits.*

How to Use This Herb

In cooking: Freezing chives is the best way to preserve their flavor for long storage. Blanch the leaves and chop them, then store in airtight, freezer-proof containers. Use as needed right from the container; there's no need to defrost them first.

The chopped tops of green onions (scallions) can be used as a substitute for chives, but they are much more strongly flavored.

Chlorophyll, the green coloring in plants, is sensitive to acids. When you heat chives, their chlorophyll reacts with natural acids in the leaves or in the cooking water. A brown compound called *pheophytin* is formed, turning the chives olive drab instead of green and making them less decorative. Adding the chives as a garnish after the food is cooked prevents this color change.

In the garden: Many insects are repelled by the odors of garlic and onion plants, which appear to act as safe natural pest repellents. They keep the bugs away without poisoning people or pets.

CILANTRO

About This Plant

Botanical name:	*Coriandrum sativum*
Also known as:	Chinese parsley
Native to:	The Mediterranean
Parts used as herb:	Leaf
Medicinal properties:	(—)
Other uses:	(—)

About This Herb as Food and Flavoring

"Cilantro" is the Spanish name for the young, flat leaves of the plant whose fruits ("seeds") are sold as coriander. Cilantro leaves, which are also known as Chinese parsley, taste like a blend of lemon and parsley. They have a pungent odor some people find unpleasant. The flavor and aroma come from peppery *borneol*; lemon-scented *limonene,* lavender-scented *linalool*; sour *malic acid* (which gives immature apples their bite) and astringent *oxalic acid* and *tannic acid.*

Cilantro is used in Mexican and Oriental cuisine. It is widely available fresh, dried or freeze-dried, mostly in ethnic groceries. If you grow your own cilantro, pick the leaves while they are young, before the plant flowers and the cilantro turns bitter.

Nutritional profile. One tablespoon (1.86 g) dried cilantro has 5 calories. It provides 0.4 g protein, 0.09 g fat, 0.9 g carbohydrates, 22 mg calcium, 0.8 mg iron and 10 mg vitamin C.

How This Herb Affects Your Body

Linalool is an irritant.

Benefits. Cilantro is a good source of vitamin C. One tablespoon of dried cilantro leaves provides 17% of the RDA for a healthy adult. Because drying an herb reduces its vitamin C content, you can assume that fresh cilantro leaves are an even better source of this nutrient.

Adverse effects. Handling the coriander plant may cause contact dermatitis (itching, burning, or stinging, plus reddened or blistered skin).

How to Use This Herb

In cooking: Store fresh cilantro leaves standing upright in a jar of water. Cover the leaves with plastic wrap or a plastic food bag to keep them from drying out. Check the cilantro daily, discarding any wilted or damaged leaves.

Do not tear cilantro leaves until you are actually ready to use them. When you tear a vegetable rich in vitamin C, its cells release an enzyme called ascorbic acid oxidase. This chemical destroys vitamin C and reduces the nutritional value of the food.

CINNAMON

About This Plant

Botanical name: *Cinnamomum zeylanicum*
Also known as: Sweetwood, true cinnamon
Native to: Sri Lanka, Sumatra, Borneo
Parts used as herb: Bark
Medicinal properties: Carminative
Other uses: Flavoring for toothpaste, perfume

ABOUT THIS SPICE AS FOOD AND FLAVORING

Cinnamon comes from the dried inner bark of a tropical evergreen laurel tree, *Cinnamomum zeylanicum*. This spice is known as "true cinnamon" to distinguish it from cassia (*Cinnamomum cassia*), which looks and tastes like cinnamon.

After the bark is peeled off the tree it is left to dry and ferment for 24 hours. Then the outer layer of the bark is scraped off, leaving the inner, light-colored bark, which curls into quills as it dries. Removing the outer bark makes the cinnamon less biting and mellows its aroma.

Most of the "cinnamon" sold in the United States is actually a blend of cinnamon and cassia, but if you were to sample plain cassia and plain cinnamon, you would find cassia's flavor bitter, while cinnamon's is warm and "sweet." Cassia also has a stronger scent, and it is darker (reddish brown versus tan). "Cinnamon sticks" made of true cinnamon look like quills (a single tube); "cinnamon sticks" made from cassia are rolled from both sides toward the center so that they end up looking like scrolls.

Both oil of cassia (called "oil of cinnamon") and the oil of true cinnamon bark (known as "oil of cinnamon, Ceylon") get their flavor and aroma from *cinnamaldehyde*, a yellow, oily liquid with a pungent cinnamon scent. Oil of cassia many be as much as 80% cinnamaldehyde; oil of cinnamon, Ceylon, is approximately 55% to 70% cinnamaldehyde. The oil of true cinnamon bark also contains *eugenol*, the chemical that gives oil of cloves its flavor and scent, and several other aromatic oils, including *phellandrene*.

Nutritional profile. One teaspoon (2.3 g) of a mixture of ground cinnamon and cassia sold as "cinnamon" has 6 calories. It provides 0.09 g protein, 0.07 g fat, 1.84 g carbohydrates, 28 mg calcium, 0.9 mg iron, 6 IU vitamin A and 0.7 mg vitamin C.

HOW THIS SPICE AFFECTS YOUR BODY

Cinnamaldehyde, eugenol and phellandrene are all allergens and irritants that may cause contact dermatitis (burning, itching, stinging, and reddened or blistered skin) in sensitive individuals. Cinnamaldehyde and phellandrene may also be irritating to the gastrointestinal tract.

Benefits. Cinnamon is a carminative (an agent that helps break up intestinal gas).

Adverse effects. People who are sensitive to cinnamon may develop dermatitis after using perfume, soap, mouthwash or toothpaste scented or flavored with cinnamon.

How to Use This Spice

Around the house: To freshen your kitchen, boil 1 teaspoon of ground cinnamon or one cinnamon stick in 3 cups of water in an open saucepan on top of the stove.

To scent your bureau drawers, use cinnamon sticks as natural sachets. **Do not use the sticks if you are sensitive to cinnamon.**

CLOVES

About This Plant

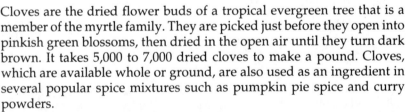

Botanical name:	*Syzygium aromaticum*
Also known as:	(—)
Native to:	The East Indies (Indonesia)
Parts used as spice:	Flower bud
Medicinal properties:	Dental analgesic
Other uses:	Pharmaceutical and cosmetic flavor, perfume

About This Spice as Food and Flavoring

Cloves are the dried flower buds of a tropical evergreen tree that is a member of the myrtle family. They are picked just before they open into pinkish green blossoms, then dried in the open air until they turn dark brown. It takes 5,000 to 7,000 dried cloves to make a pound. Cloves, which are available whole or ground, are also used as an ingredient in several popular spice mixtures such as pumpkin pie spice and curry powders.

The spicy sweet flavor and aroma of cloves comes from *eugenol*, the primary constituent (82%–87%) of oil of cloves, which also contains *caryophyllene*, an oily liquid that smells like a cross between cloves and turpentine; almond-scented *furfural*; *vanillin*; and fruity scented, peppery *methyl amyl ketone*. Oil of cloves is a popular perfume used in a wide variety of cosmetics including toothpastes, soaps and body lotions.

Nutritional profile. One teaspoon (2.1 g) ground cloves has 7 calories. It provides 0.1 g protein, 0.4 g fat, 1.29 g carbohydrates, 14 mg calcium, 0.2 mg iron, 11 IU vitamin A and 1.7 mg vitamin C.

How This Spice Affects Your Body

Eugenol is a local anesthetic used in dental fillings and cement; a rubifacient (an agent that irritates the skin and causes small blood vessels underneath to dilate so that more blood flows to the surface of the skin, making it warmer); and a carminative (an agent that breaks up intestinal gas). It is also an irritant and an allergic sensitizer. Eugenol is closely related to *safrole*, a known carcinogen that causes liver cancer in laboratory animals. At present, there is no evidence that eugenol is carcinogenic.

Benefits. (—)

Adverse effects. Contact with cloves may cause contact dermatitis (itching, burning, stinging, reddened or blistered skin). Because eugenol can be irritating to the intestinal tract, cloves are usually excluded from a bland diet.

How to Use This Spice

In cooking: Ground cloves, made without the clove heads, are milder in flavor and less irritating than whole cloves.

If you prefer cooking with whole cloves, be sure to remove them before you serve the dish. Put the cloves in a tea ball or stud them into an onion or carrot, them simply remove the tea ball or vegetable before serving the food.

Around the house: To make a nonchemical, perfumed air freshener for your closets, stick whole fresh cloves into the peel of a large firm orange until the entire orange is completely covered. Then roll the clove-studded orange in ground cinnamon. Wrap the cinnamon-dusted orange in tissue paper, and put it on your kitchen shelf until the orange dries and shrinks. When the orange is completely dried, unwrap it, dust off any loose cinnamon powder and hang the orange "pomander ball" in your closet. The scent will be lovely.

CORIANDER

About This Plant

Botanical name: *Coriandrum sativum*
Also known as: Coriander seed
Native to: The Mediterranean
Parts used as herb: Fruit
Medicinal properties: Carminative
Other uses: Cigarette flavoring

About This Herb as Food and Flavoring

Coriander "seeds" (the dried fruit) are gathered from the small white or purple-tinged flowers of the plant whose flat green leaves are known as cilantro ("Chinese parsley"). The leaves taste like a blend of lemon and parsley; the more intensely flavored seeds taste like a blend of lemon and sage. Unripe coriander seeds have an unpleasant odor that becomes warm and spicy when the seed matures. The fragrance comes from *linalool*, which smells like French lavender.

Most coriander seeds come from either Morocco or Romania. The Moroccan seeds are larger, but the more intensely flavored Romanian seeds are preferred by distillers and food manufacturers, who use them in gin, liqueurs and sausages (frankfurters). Coriander is also used to flavor chewing gum and to give cigarette tobacco a characteristically fragrant "American" flavor. Coriander seeds are widely available, whole or ground, or you can grow your own coriander plants and harvest either the leaves (cilantro) or the "seeds."

Nutritional profile. One teaspoon (1.8 g) coriander seed has 5 calories. It provides 0.2 g protein, 0.3 g fat, 1 g carbohydrates, 13 mg calcium and 0.3 g iron.

How This Herb Affects Your Body

Linalool is an irritant and an allergic sensitizer that may cause contact dermatitis (itching, burning or stinging, plus reddened or blistered skin).

Benefits. Coriander is a weak carminative, an agent that breaks up intestinal gas.

Adverse effects. Handling coriander plants may cause contact dermatitis (itching, burning, stinging, reddened or blistered skin).

How to Use This Herb

In cooking: To make your own coriander-flavored vodka, steep one tablespoon coriander seed in a bottle of vodka for 24 to 48 hours. Then strain the vodka to remove the seeds, and use as you like.

As a home remedy: To make a mildly carminative tea, add 2 teaspoons dried coriander seeds to a cup of boiling water and let steep for three to four minutes. Then strain and serve the tea.

In the garden: Coriander is a hardy plant that grows easily from seed in virtually any good garden soil and at temperatures as low as 10 degrees F. You can harvest the leaves (cilantro), or let the plant flower and then harvest the seeds. To harvest coriander seeds: Let the plants grow until the first fruits (seeds) are so dry they crack open when you squeeze them. Then either hang the plants upside down over cheesecloth and collect the seeds that fall, or wrap the plants in cheesecloth and hit them against a hard surface to separate the seeds from the plant. Once you have the seeds rub them in a strainer with openings about ⅛ inch wide. Catch the seeds, but let the chaff and bits of dirt fall through.

COSTMARY

About This Plant

Botanical name:	*Chrysanthemum balsamita*
Also known as:	Alecost, Bible leaf
Native to:	Asia
Parts used as herb:	Leaves
Medicinal properties:	(—)
Other uses:	Moth repellent

About This Herb as Food and Flavoring

Costmary is a member of the chrysanthemum family, a large plant with light green, mint-scented leaves and sparse, small flowers that look like daisies. The leaves can be used in soups, stews and sauces or to brew a minty tea.

Costmary is available only from your own garden.

Nutritional profile. (—)

How This Herb Affects Your Body

Benefits. (—)
Adverse effects: Like other members of the chrysanthemum family, costmary produces a pollen that may cause allergic reactions, including hives, asthma and stuffed or runny nose. Because costmary does not flower as profusely as its relatives—asters, chrysanthemums and ragweed—it produces less pollen and may be less likely to trigger allergic symptoms. But people who are sensitive to these plants may be better off avoiding related plants such as costmary or chamomille, either in the garden or as an herb in food and drink.

How to Use This Herb

In cooking: Costmary leaves can be used to brew a minty tea or to lend a minty accent to other teas. To protect the flavor, do not steep the leaves longer than three or four minutes—heat can turn the leaves bitter. **Use only unsprayed leaves.**

Around the house: Like other members of the chrysanthemum family, costmary contains natural insect repellents called *pyrethrins.* Dried costmary leaves scattered on the floor of your closet may be useful in protecting your clothes from moths.

CREAM OF TARTAR

About This Condiment

Chemical name:	Potassium bitartrate
Also known as:	(—)
Native to:	(—)
Parts used as condiment:	(—)
Medicinal properties:	Laxative
Other uses:	As mordant (color fixative in dying)

About This Condiment as Food and Flavoring

Cream of tartar is composed of white crystals formed naturally in the sediments ("lees") left when grapes ferment to produce wine. In food, cream of tartar is used to intensify the flavor of beverages and candy, and as a stabilizing agent to preserve colors and flavors.

The best known use for cream of tartar is as an acid ingredient in baking powder. It combines with baking soda, which is basic (alkaline), to release carbon dioxide.

When you mix flour with water and beat the batter, the long protein molecules in the flour relax and unfold. Internal bonds (bonds between atoms on the same molecule) are broken and new external bonds between atoms on different molecules are formed. The result is a network of elastic *gluten* (protein) that can stretch when filled with carbon dioxide released by leavening agents.

Cream of tartar is a "fast-acting" leavening agent that encourages the release of carbon dioxide at room temperature. It begins to stretch the gluten network as soon as you add it to the batter (you can see the gas as bubbles in the batter). Baking soda is a "slow-acting" leavening agent that decomposes at higher temperatures, releasing its carbon dioxide later, when the batter is heated in the oven. It stabilizes the batter's protein network into its final ("risen") form. Baking powders that contain baking soda and cream of tartar are called "double acting" baking powders.

Nutritional profile. (—)

How This Condiment Affects Your Body

Numerous studies on animals and humans have shown that cream of tartar is a safe and effective food additive.

Benefits. Tartrates, which attract and hold water in the digestive tract, are used in over-the-counter laxatives. The Food and Drug Administration's Advisory Review Panel on OTC (Over-the-Counter) Laxative, Antidiarrheal, Emetic and Antiemetic Drug Products rates tartrates as "conditionally approved active ingredients" in these products because neither their safety nor their effectiveness as laxatives has been scientifically unproven.

Adverse effects. Tartrates are used in over-the-counter antacid products. While the FDA Advisory Review Panel on OTC (Over-the-Counter) Drugs rates tartrates in antacids as safe and effective, it cautions that in high doses they may cause kidney problems.

How to Use This Condiment

In cooking: To make your own tartrate baking powder: ¼ teaspoon baking soda plus ½ teaspoon cream of tartar equals the leavening power of 1 teaspoon double acting baking powder.

If you add a pinch of cream of tartar to an egg white before you beat it, the acidic cream of tartar will stabilize the foam. It makes the egg white less basic (alkaline) and prevents its protein (albumen) molecules from bonding tightly to each other (coagulating), a phenomenon often described as "overbeating." Copper ions flaking off the sides of a copper mixing bowl do the same thing. That is why it is standard culinary practice to beat egg whites in a copper bowl.

Making candy or a sugar syrup? Add a pinch of cream of tartar to the sugar to slow down the clumping of sugar molecules, known as "crystallization." This gives you more time to either cool the candy into a clear syrup or beat it longer and make even more crystals.

CUMIN SEED

ABOUT THIS PLANT

Botanical name:	*Cuminum cyminum*
Also known as:	Comino
Native to:	The Mediterranean
Parts used as herb:	Seeds
Medicinal properties:	Carminative
Other uses:	(—)

ABOUT THIS HERB AS FOOD AND FLAVORING

Cumin seeds come from a plant related to parsley. The seeds look and smell like caraway seeds, but they are slightly longer, lighter in color and have a stronger flavor. Cumin is most widely used as an ingredient in curry and chili powders. In Germany it is used along with caraway in making *kummel*, the caraway-flavored liqueur; in Holland, cumin seeds are used to flavor cheese.

Cumin seeds contain oil of cumin, which is 30% to 40% *cuminaldehyde*, an oily liquid with a strong, persistent odor and stinging taste. Oil of cumin also contains *pinene* (which smells like turpentine) and lemony scented *dipentene*.

Cumin seeds are available whole or ground. If you shop in Indian grocery stores, you may come across black cumin (*Nigeria sativa*), an unrelated plant also known as nutmeg flower or Roman coriander. Black cumin, which is easier to grow than regular cumin, produces pods with small, dark seeds that smell like fennel and taste something like peppery nutmeg. You can pick the pods as they begin to yellow, dry them and then remove the seeds, grind and use like pepper. The flavor is distinctive, so try a little before you season a whole dish.

Nutritional profile. One teaspoon (2.1 g) cumin seed has 8 calories. It provides 0.4 g protein, 0.5 g fat, 0.9 g carbohydrates, 20 mg calcium, 1.4 mg iron, 27 IU vitamin A and 0.2 mg vitamin C.

How This Herb Affects Your Body

Like *capsaicin*, the flavoring agent in pepper, cuminaldehyde is practically insoluble in water. This is why drinking iced water doesn't cool the burning sensation caused by eating a hot curry or chili-flavored dish. What you need is either alcohol (beer) or milkfat (whole milk), both of which dissolve capsaicin and cuminaldehyde and ease the stinging in your mouth.
Benefits. (—)
Adverse effects. (—)

How to Use This Herb

In cooking: You can substitute ground caraway seeds for ground cumin. The flavor, though milder, is distinctly similar.

CURRY POWDER

About This Condiment

Chemical name:	(—)
Also known as:	(—)
Native to:	India
Parts used as condiment:	(—)
Medicinal properties:	Diaphoretic, irritant
Other uses:	(—)

About This Condiment as Food and Flavoring

Curry powder is a blend of as many as 16 to 20 different spices including cinnamon, cloves, cumin, fenugreek, ginger, pepper (red and black) and turmeric (which gives the curry powder its characteristic golden hue).

If you shop in Indian grocery stores, you may come across dried *curry leaves*. In India fresh curry leaves are used in cooking. The dried leaves, which look like small bay leaves, are the only ones available here.

Unfortunately, they have only a pale reflection of the fresh leaves' flavor and aroma.

Nutritional profile. One tablespoon (6.3 g) of a curry powder made with coriander seed (36%), turmeric (28%), cumin (10%), fenugreek (10%), white pepper (5%), allspice (4%), yellow mustard seed (3%), red pepper (2%) and ginger (2%) has 20 calories. It provides 0.3 g protein, 0.3 g fat, 3.7 g carbohydrates, 30 mg calcium, 1.86 mg iron, 62 IU vitamin A and 0.7 mg vitamin C.

How This Condiment Affects Your Body

Coriander, the main ingredient in most curry powders, is a carminative, an agent that relieves intestinal gas. Turmeric is a choleretic, an agent that increases the liver's output of bile. It also increases your body's ability to eliminate cholesterol. Black pepper and red pepper are diaphoretics, substances that increase perspiration. Pepper, allspice, mustard and ginger are all irritating to the skin and mucous membranes.

Benefits. Because it promotes perspiration, which acts as a natural air conditioner, cooling your body as the moisture evaporates on your skin, curry powder is a popular seasoning in warm climates.

Like other "hot" spices, curry powder may be useful when you have hay fever or a head or chest cold. The pepper in the mixture irritates the mucous membranes lining your nose and throat, causing them to "weep" a watery secretion. This makes it easier for you to cough up sticky mucus or clear your nose when you blow it.

Adverse effects. The peppers and mustard in curry powder can irritate the lining of your stomach and bladder, upsetting your stomach or causing you to urinate more frequently. It may even make urination painful for a while.

(Note: For more information on any of the spices in curry powder, see the individual listings.)

How to Use This Condiment

In cooking: For an unusual flavor, sprinkle a pinch of curry powder over an apple before you bake it, or add a pinch to a dish of applesauce, then warm it.

DANDELION

ABOUT THIS PLANT

Botanical name: *Taraxacum officinale*
Also known as: Lion's tooth
Native to: Europe
Parts used as herb: Leaf, root
Medicinal properties: Diuretic, laxative
Other uses: Winemaking, dye

ABOUT THIS HERB AS FOOD AND FLAVORING

The dandelion is a member of the daisy family whose pleasantly bitter leaves can be added fresh to salads or cooked and served as a vegetable. Ground, roasted dandelion roots and rhizomes (underground stems) can be used like ground, roasted chicory to deepen the bitter flavor of coffee without adding caffeine. Dandelion flowers are used to flavor and color dandelion wine.

Dandelion leaves get their bitter flavor from *taraxacin*. Dandelion roots and rhizomes contain bitter *taraxerol*; *levulin* and *inulin*, two complex carbohydrates; and the soluble fiber *pectin*.

Cultivated dandelions look just like the dandelions that grow wild on your lawn, but they are larger and produce more leaves. Because dandelions are so common, you may be tempted to simply pick them off your lawn, wash them and toss them into your salad. **But you should never eat dandelions growing wild on lawns unless you are certain the lawn has never been sprayed with pesticides or herbicides.**

Nutritional profile. One cup (55 g) chopped raw dandelion greens has 25 calories. It provides 1.5 g protein, 0.4 g fat, 5 g carbohydrates, 103 mg calcium, 1.7 mg iron, 7,700 IU vitamin A and 19 mg vitamin C.

One cup (105 g) boiled and drained chopped dandelion greens has 35 calories. It provides 2 g protein, 0.6 g fat, 6.7 g carbohydrates, 147 mg calcium, 1.9 mg iron, 12,285 IU vitamin A and 18.9 mg vitamin C.

HOW THIS HERB AFFECTS YOUR BODY

A tea made from dandelion leaves may be both mildly diuretic and mildly laxative; a tea made from dandelion roots is also mildly laxative. Exactly which components of the leaves or the root produce this effect is not known.

Benefits. Dandelion greens are a good source of *beta*-carotene, the vitamin A precursor in deep yellow fruits and vegetables. According to the American Cancer Society, a diet rich in these foods may lower the risk of some forms of cancer.

Vitamin A also protects your eyes. In your body, the vitamin A from dandelions is converted to 11-cis retinol, the most important constituent of *rhodopsin*, a protein in the rods in your retina (the cells that enable you to see in dim light). One cup fresh dandelion greens provides approximately twice the amount of vitamin A a woman needs each day and 150% of the RDA for a man.

Dandelion greens are also a good source of calcium (one cup cooked greens provides 13% of the calcium an adult needs each day); iron (one cup cooked greens provides 10% of the RDA for a woman); and vitamin C (one cup cooked greens provides 32% of the RDA for a healthy adult).

Adverse effects. People who are sensitive to other weeds may develop contact dermatitis (itching, burning, stinging, reddened or blistered skin) from handling dandelions. Dandelion flowers are also known to cause allergic rhinitis (a stuffy nose and/or reddened, weepy eyes).

How to Use This Herb

In cooking: You can make dandelion leaves less bitter by storing them in the refrigerator after they are picked or by waiting until the weather turns cold before you harvest the leaves. The dandelion root also becomes less bitter when exposed to cold.

Do not cut or tear dandelion leaves until you are actually ready to use them. When you cut the leaves, you tear the cells, which then release an enzyme called ascorbic acid oxidase. This chemical destroys vitamin C and reduces the dandelion's nutritional value.

Chlorophyll, the green coloring in plants, is sensitive to acids. When you heat dandelion leaves, their chlorophyll reacts with natural acids in the leaves or in the cooking water, forming a brown compound called *pheophytin*. The pheophytin then reacts with the yellow carotene pigments in the leaves, turning the cooked dandelion leaves bronze. To prevent this color change, you must keep the chlorophyll from reacting with the acids in one of these ways: (1) cook the dandelion leaves in lots of water to dilute the acids, (2) leave the lid off the pot so the acids can dissipate into the air or (3) steam the dandelion leaves very quickly so there is no time for the reaction to occur.

Non-heme iron, the kind of iron found in plants, is less available to the body than *heme iron*, the kind of iron found in meat. To increase your body's absorption of the iron in dandelion greens and other vegetables, serve the vegetable with meat. This increases the secretion of stomach acids, and iron is absorbed more easily in an acid enviroment. Or serve dandelions with a food rich in vitamin C. Vitamin C may change the iron from ferric iron to ferrous iron, which your body can absorb more easily.

Around the house: Dandelion flowers yield a golden yellow dye that colors wool and cotton; dandelion roots, a purple dye. To make the dyes, steep one quart crushed flowers or cut up roots overnight in a pot with just enough water to cover. The next day, boil flowers or roots in the water 15 minutes to two hours, adding more liquid as needed, until the water is the color desired. Now let the mixture cool. Strain it through a colander or sieve into a second large pot to remove all the plant material.

Wearing rubber gloves to protect your hands, immerse one clean, wet, cotton or woolen T-shirt, blouse or sweater in the bath, swishing it around so the dye comes in contact with every surface of the garment. Now boil the garment in the dye 30 minutes or less, until the color looks right. Turn off the heat, let the dye bath cool, remove the garment and hold it under cold running water until the water runs clear.

CAUTION: (1) Do not use this dye if you are sensitive to dandelions. (2) Always try *any* dye on an inconspicuous part of the garment first to see if you like the color. (3) Boiling will shrink some cotton or woolen fabrics. (4) Never dye any lined garment.

DILL

About This Plant

    Botanical name: *Anethum graveolens*
    Also known as: (—)
    Native to: Europe
    Parts used as herb: Leaves, fruit ("seeds")
    Medicinal properties: Carminative (seeds)
    Other uses: Insecticide

About This Herb as Food and Flavoring

Dill is a member of the parsley family with umbrella-like clusters of small, yellow flowers and feathery leaves. The plant yields two different herbs: dill seed (the fruit of the plant) and dill weed, the top eight inches

of the graceful leaves. The leaves and seeds get their slightly bitter, pungent flavor and aroma from *carvone*, which is also found in caraway and is used to flavor *kummel*.

Dill is most commonly used to give dill pickles their characteristic aromatic flavor and to add piquancy to fish and vegetable dishes, including baked or boiled potatoes, and cucumber and potato salads. Dried dill seeds are available whole; dill weed is sold fresh and as whole or chopped dried leaves.

Nutritional profile: One teaspoon (2.1 g) dill seed has 6 calories. It provides 0.3 g protein, 0.3 g fat, 1.2 g carbohydrates, 32 mg calcium, 0.3 mg iron and 1 IU vitamin A.

One teaspoon (1 g) dried dill weed has 3 calories. It provides 0.2 g protein, a trace of fat, 0.6 g carbohydrates, 18 mg calcium and 0.5 mg iron.

How This Herb Affects Your Body

Carvone is a carminative (an agent that breaks up intestinal gas). *Limonene* and *phellandrene*—an irritant found in oil of dill and many other essential oils—are photosensitizers (chemicals that make your skin more sensitive to sunlight).

Carvone is also an insecticide that increases the effectiveness of the garden insecticide parathion. Studies show that only 8% of fruit flies exposed to parathion alone die, but 99% die when exposed to the same amount of parathion plus carvone. Alas, no evidence exists right now to suggest that dill growing in your garden or scattered around the house has any such effect.

Benefits. (—)

Adverse effects. Handling dill plants may cause contact dermatitis (itching, burning, stinging, reddened or blistered skin) or make your skin more sensitive to sunlight. Both reactions are most likely to occur among food workers who handle dill.

How to Use This Herb

In cooking: The longer you cook dill leaves, the less flavor they have. To preserve the herb's pungency, add dill at the last minute, just before you serve the food.

Dill seeds taste like caraway seeds, only milder. In a pinch, you can use dill seeds instead of caraway seeds in rye bread. Both taste wonderful with cabbage.

As a home remedy: A tea brewed by steeping 1 teaspoon dill seeds in 1 cup boiling water is sometimes used to relieve intestinal gas.

FENNEL

ABOUT THIS PLANT

Botanical name: *Foeniculum vulgare*
Also known as: Garden fennel, sweet fennel
Native to: Europe, Asia Minor
Parts used as herb: Leaves, dried ripe fruit
Medicinal properties: Carminative, expectorant
Other uses: Cough syrup, fragrance in cosmetics

ABOUT THIS HERB AS FOOD AND FLAVORING

There are several varieties of fennel, including Florence fennel, which produces thick stalks that can be eaten like celery, and sweet fennel, whose fruit (seeds) is used as an herb. The sweet fennel plant has feathery leaves and small, yellow flowers, each of which produces two green or yellow brown seeds, about ⅛ to ⁵⁄₁₆ inches long. Some people say they look like tiny watermelons. Dried fennel seeds smell and taste like anise because oil of fennel contains *anethole* (50%–60%), *anisaldehyde* and *anisic acid*, the chemicals that give anise its characteristic licorice flavor and aroma. Oil of fennel also contains camphor- scented *fenchone;* *pinene*, which smells like turpentine; and lemony scented *limonene* and *dipentene*.

Sweet-fennel oil is used as a flavoring in pharmaceuticals, liqueurs, candy, pickles, condiments and sausages such as pepperoni, cappicola and the sausage used as pizza topping.

Nutritional profile. One teaspoon (2 g) fennel seed has 7 calories. It provides 0.3 g protein, 0.3 g fat, 1 g carbohydrates, 24 mg calcium, 0.4 mg iron and 3 IU vitamin A.

HOW THIS HERB AFFECTS YOUR BODY

Anethole and fenchone are irritants. Limonene is a photosensitizer, a chemical that makes your skin more sensitive to sunlight.

Benefits. Long use in folk medicine suggests that fennel tea can relax smooth muscles and that it is a carminative, an agent that can help break up and expel intestinal gas.

Adverse effects. Handling fennel plants may cause contact dermatitis (itching, burning, stinging, reddened or blistered skin) or make your skin extremely sensitive to sunlight.

How to Use This Herb

In cooking: In baking, you can substitute fennel seeds for aniseed.

Grilling fish over a fire built of fennel twigs scents the meat with a delicate licorice flavor and aroma. **Use only unsprayed plants.**

As a home remedy: For intestinal gas or spasms: Steep one tablespoon crushed fennel seeds in one cup boiling water for 5 minutes. Strain the tea and sweeten to your taste. **CAUTION: If your symptoms persist or worsen, don't rely on folk medicine—call your doctor.**

FENUGREEK

About This Plant

Botanical name:	*Trigonella foenum-graecum*
Also known as:	Greek hay seed, trigonella
Native to:	Southern Europe
Parts used as herb:	Seeds
Medicinal properties:	Emollient
Other uses:	Fabric dye

About This Herb as Food and Flavoring

Fenugreek is a member of the pea family. The plant produces pods, each of which contains 10 to 20 aromatic seeds. They are most commonly used as an ingredient in curry powders. Fenugreek seeds, which contain vanilla-scented *coumarin*, are also used in some chutneys and as the basic flavoring in imitation maple syrup.

Nutritional profile. One teaspoon (3.7 g) fenugreek seed has 12 calories. It provides 0.9 g protein, 0.2 g fat, 2.2 g carbohydrates, 6 mg calcium, 1.2 mg iron and 0.1 mg vitamin C.

How This Herb Affects Your Body

Fenugreek seeds are high (40%) in *mucilage*, an emollient soothing to the skin and used as an emulsifier in drugs and food. The seeds also contain *diosgenin*, a steroid that can be converted to *pregnenolone* (a steroid formed during the synthesis of hormones) and *progesterone*, the anti-estrogen hormone secreted by pregnant women. The major sources of diosgenin, which is used in the production of synthetic hormones, are Central and South American yams of the *Dioscorea* family.

Like lima beans, navy beans and peas, fenugreek seeds are reported to contain chemicals that inactivate *trypsin* and *chymotrypsin*, enzymes making it possible for your body to digest protein. But there is no evidence that fenugreek used to season food has any such effect. The same thing applies to coumarin and diosgenin; both can be toxic in very large doses, but neither appears to have produced any ill effects in people using fenugreek as an herb.

Benefits. Like beans and other legumes, fenugreek seeds are high in protein. The amount of protein you would get from using the seeds as a spice is negligible (about 1 g protein per teaspoon), but 3.5 ounces (100 g) of uncooked seeds supply 23 grams protein. This is exactly the same amount of protein as in a 3 to 3.5-ounce serving of meat, fish or poultry. In the Middle East, where a meatless diet is often the rule, fenugreek seeds are often boiled and served as a high protein main dish.

Fenugreek seeds contain *trigonelline*, a nitrogen compound found in many legumes. When trigonelline comes in contact with acids or is heated, it yields *nicotinic acid* (niacin), the B vitamin that prevents pellagra. (Three and a half ounces of fenugreek seeds provide 1.6 mg niacin, 12% of the RDA for a woman, 9% of the RDA for a man.)

Adverse effects. (—)

How to Use This Herb

In cooking: Fenugreek tea, available at the health food store, blends nicely with the flavor of mint.

FILÉ (SASSAFRAS)

About This Plant

Botanical name: *Sassafras albidum*

Also known as: Gumbo filé
Native to: East Coast (Maine to Florida),
Texas
Parts used as herb: Leaves
Medicinal properties: (—)
Other uses: (—)

About This Herb as Food and Flavoring

Filé, which is used to season Creole and Cajun dishes, is composed of dried sassafras leaves.

Sassafras root bark also contains *anethole,* found in anise and fennel; *eugenol,* the chief flavoring in oil of cloves; and gingery tasting *asarone.*

Nutritional profile. (—)

How This Herb Affects Your Body

Sassafras, the flavoring once used in root beer and the original chicle gum patented by Thomas Adams in 1871, is now considered unsafe. *Safrole,* its primary flavoring ingredient, is a naturally occurring precarcinogen that becomes an active carcinogen in body tissue and cells. Safrole has caused liver tumors in laboratory rats and mice.

Whether safrole causes cancer in human beings is unclear, but it is a known irritant that can trigger contact dermatitis, (itching, burning, stinging, reddened or blistered skin) and, in large doses, a hallucinogen. Only safrole-free extracts and sassafras leaves are approved for use in food in this country. (There are very small amounts of safrole in basil, black pepper, mace and nutmeg.)

Benefits: (—)

Adverse effects: (—)

How to Use This Herb

In cooking: Sassafras leaves contain mucilage for thickening a stew. Lacking file, use cornstarch or tapioca. You can approximate (but never quite match) filé's flavor with a mixture of equal parts ground aniseed, cloves and ginger. To avoid overseasoning, add the mixture carefully, a pinch at a time, tasting as you go.

GARLIC

ABOUT THIS PLANT

Botanical name: *Allium sativum*
Also known as: (—)
Native to: Central Asia,
Southern Europe
Parts used as herb: Bulbs
Medicinal properties: Antimicrobial,
carminative
Other uses: (—)

ABOUT THIS HERB AS FOOD AND FLAVORING

Garlic, a relative of the onion, is a member of the lily family with long, flat green leaves and white to pink flowers. To grow garlic, break the bulb apart and plant the cloves 2 to 8 inches apart in well-drained soil in full sun. Garlic grows best in a warm climate such as California, a center of garlic production in the United States.

Garlic is available fresh and as dried *garlic chips* (large pieces of dried garlic); *minced garlic* (small pieces of dried garlic); *garlic powder* (ground dried garlic plus an anticaking agent such as tricalcium phosphate, which keeps the garlic powder from absorbing moisture); and *garlic salt* (a blend of ground garlic and salt). The mildest garlic is "elephant garlic" (*Allium scorodoprasum*), a species with very large, very mild cloves.

All garlic gets its distinctive flavor and aroma from pale yellow oil of garlic, which contains the smelly sulfur compounds *allylpropyl disulfide, diallyl disulfide* and *allyl sulfide.*

Nutritional profile. One clove (3 g) raw garlic has 4 calories. It provides 0.2 g protein, a trace of fat, 1 g carbohydrates, 5 mg calcium, a trace of iron and 0.9 mg vitamin C.

One teaspoon (2.8 g) garlic powder has 9 calories. It provides 0.5 g protein, 0.02 g fat, 2 g carbohydrates, 2 mg calcium and 0.1 mg iron.

One teaspoon (6 g) garlic salt has 1,850 mg sodium.

HOW THIS HERB AFFECTS YOUR BODY

Garlic contains *alliin*, precursor of the antibiotic chemical *allicin*. When you crush or slice into a garlic clove, you tear its cell walls, releasing *allinase*, an enzyme that converts alliin to allicin. In laboratory experiments at the University of Oklahoma, garlic juice appeared to inhibit the growth of a wide variety of microorganisms, including bacteria, yeast and fungi. Garlic also contains *ajoene*, a chemical that may be as effective as aspirin in keeping blood platelets from clumping. Ajoene may account for the results of laboratory experiments suggesting that garlic oil offers some protection against heart attack and stroke.

Garlic's therapeutic value remains to be proven, but it is already clear that processed garlic is not as effective as fresh garlic. Heating or dehydrating the bulb destroys ajoene, and since all the biologically active chemicals in garlic are in its smelly garlic oil, "deodorized" garlic is almost certain to lack medical value.

Benefits. Oil of garlic is a carminative (an agent that helps break up and expel intestinal gas) and a rubefacient (a chemical that irritates skin and dilates the tiny blood vessels right under the surface, increasing the flow of blood and making the skin feel warmer).

Adverse effects. Diallyl disulfide is excreted in perspiration and in air exhaled from the lungs. That is why you smell garlicky after eating garlic.

How to Use This Herb

In cooking: To peel fresh garlic without having the skin stick to your fingers, drop the cloves in boiling water for 30 seconds, then drain, cool and peel.

To get the most flavor from fresh garlic, you must slice through the clove, releasing the odorous strongly flavored oil inside. Either mash the cloves, chop them or wring out the oil with a garlic press.

For a mild garlic flavor, cook the garlic. Heat destroys diallyl disulfide.

One-fourth teaspoon garlic powder equals two small, fresh garlic cloves.

Store dehydrated garlic products in tightly closed containers. This protects them from air and moisture that can make garlic powder cake or turn the fats in dried garlic rancid.

GENTIAN

About This Herb

Botanical name: *Gentiana lutea*
Also known as: Bitter root, yellow gentian
Native to: Central and Southern Europe

Parts used as herb: Rhizomes, roots
Medicinal properties: Appetite stimulant
Other uses: (—)

About This Herb as Food and Flavoring

Yellow gentian is an ornamental plant native to Europe. It is grown commercially for its root and rhizomes (underground stems), which produce a bitter extract used in digestive tonics and in "bitters," the spirits-based 45 to 90 proof (22%–45% alcohol) beverage. Gentian-flavored bitters, such as "angostura bitters," have a long-lived reputation as an appetite stimulant and folk remedy, partially because of the belief that the worse a medicine tastes, the more effective it is.

The bitter flavor of gentian roots and rhizomes comes from *amarogentian* and *gentiopicrin*. The rhizomes also contain yellow pigments (*gentisin, isogentisin* and *gentioside*), astringent *tannins*, the soluble food fiber pectin and *sugars*, including *sucrose*.

You may find powdered gentian for tea at your health food store. Sometimes—more often in Europe than in the United States—gentian is also sold as a dried root you can chop or crush to make your own tea powder.

Nutritional profile. (—)

How This Herb Affects Your Body

Gentian contains *gentisic acid*, an analgesic and antirheumatic chemical related to salicyclic acid. It also contains *gentianine*, a chemical that appears to act as an anti-inflammatory agent in laboratory animals.

Benefits. Like other bitter or spicy foods, gentian tonics seem to stimulate appetite by irritating the stomach and encouraging the secretion of gastric acid. This triggers the gastric contractions we call hunger pangs. Some other herbs and spices that do the same thing are American ginseng, caraway, hops and mustard.

Adverse effects. Gentian is a choleretic, an agent that stimulates the liver to increase its production of bile, the yellow brown or green fluid that helps emulsify fats in your duodenum and increases peristalsis, the rhythmic contractions that move food through your gastrointestinal tract. Choleretics are ordinarily beneficial for healthy people but may pose some problems for people with gallbladder or liver diseases. Some other choleretic herbs are onion, oregano and peppermint.

How to Use This Herb

In cooking: To make a tea with dried gentian root: Bring 1 teaspoon chopped root to a boil in 1 cup water, then simmer the liquid for about 15 minutes. Turn off the heat and let the root soak for another 5 minutes, then pour the liquid through a strainer into your teacup. Sweeten to taste with sugar or honey, or add a mint leaf.

GERANIUMS

About This Plant

Botanical name:	*Pelargonium graveolens*
Also known as:	Rose geranium, scented geranium
Native to:	South Africa
Parts used as herb:	Leaves
Medicinal properties:	(—)
Other uses:	Insect repellent

About This Herb as Food and Flavoring

Rose geraniums are annual plants grown for their small lavender flowers and wonderful rose aroma. There are also geraniums that smell like apple, cinnamon, coconut, lemon and mint. Collecitvely, these plants are known as "scented geraniums." Leaves from all the scented geraniums can be used to add an enticing aroma to fresh salads or to flavor desserts, baked goods, jellies and jams. All are grown commercially for their fragrant oils (particularly *geraniol*), which are used in perfumery. Scented geraniums also contain *citronella*, a lemony scented chemical once widely used as an insect repellent.

Nutritional profile. (—)

How This Herb Affects Your Body

Geraniol is an irritant.

Benefits. (—)

Adverse effects. Prolonged handling of the scented geraniums may cause contact dermatitis (itching, burning, stinging, reddened or blistered skin) in sensitive people.

How to Use This Herb

In cooking: Tear or bruise the scented geranium leaves to release their oils.

To bake a cake with the scent of one of the geraniums, line the pan with the leaves of the rose geranium, the apple geranium (*P. odoratissum*) or the mint geranium (*P. tomentosum*), and pour the batter on top.

To make a tea from geranium leaves, steep the fresh leaves in boiling water and flavor with fresh mint or lemon.

Around the house: Dried geranium leaves are perfect for sachets and potpourris.

To repel insects, sprinkle geranium leaves in drawers or closets.

In the garden: Like other plants which are lemon scented or contain citronella, geraniums planted in your garden may repel a number of pests without poisoning people or pets.

GINGER

About This Plant

Botanical name: *Zingiber officinale*
Also known as: Gingerroot
Native to: Southern Asia
Parts used as spice: Rhizones
Medicinal properties: Anti-motion sickness
Other uses: Preservative

About This Spice as Food and Flavoring

Ginger, a distant relative of the banana, gets its name from the Latin translation of the Sanskrit word *singabera*, which means "shaped like a horn." The ginger we use today comes from India, China, Jamaica and Sierra Leone.

Ginger's characteristic aroma and spicy flavor come from its pungent yellow oil, which contains spicy sweet *zingerone*, plus a number of sharpy flavored chemicals such as *borneol* (which smells like pepper and tastes like mint), *eucalyptol* (which smells like camphor and has a spicy, cooling taste); and lemony scented *citral*. Citral is most noticeable in

Indian ginger, a light yellow ginger with a hint of lemon flavor and aroma.

Ginger not only adds flavor to food, it may also act as an antioxidant, slowing the rate at which fats combine with oxygen and turn rancid. In 1986 researchers at the University of California at Davis added extract of freshly ground ginger root to salted pork patties, then cooked and refrigerated or froze the patties. The fats in the gingered pork patties turned rancid at a slower rate than the fats in patties that had been prepared without ginger. The more ginger there was in the patty the slower the rate of the rancidity reaction.

Ginger, which is widely used in soft drinks—including colas and ginger ale—is available ground or whole (whole pieces of gingerroot are called "hands").

Nutritional profile. One teaspoon (1.8 g) ground ginger has 6 calories. It provides 0.2 g protein, 0.1 g fat, 1.3 g carbohydrates, 2 mg calcium, 0.2 mg iron and 3 IU vitamin A.

How This Spice Affects Your Body

Zingerone is a pungent chemical that, like *piperine* in black pepper and *capsaicin* in red pepper, stimulates pain receptors in the skin and mucous membranes, producing the sensation we call "hot" in spicy foods.

Ginger may also relieve the misery of motion sickness. In 1982 researchers at Brigham Young University in Provo, Utah, gave 26 student volunteers either two capsules of Dramamine, two capsules of powdered ginger or two capsules of a placebo, then spun the students in a motorized chair for six minutes. (The researchers stopped the chair if the volunteers vomited or asked to stop.) None who had taken the placebo or the Dramamine made it through the whole six minutes, but half of the people who had taken the ginger capsules stayed the full time; it took twice as long for those who took the ginger to become sick as those who took Dramamine.

Why ginger works remains to be proved. Perhaps it interrupts messages between the brain and the stomach, or it may affect the inner ear. In any event, when the researchers released the report, they emphasized the fact that this is not a home remedy. To be safe and effective, the ginger root must be taken in medically prepared capsules *and* in moderation to avoid severe gastric irritation.

Benefits. Like piperine and capsaicin, zingerone irritates skin and mucous membranes. Applied to the skin, ginger makes the small blood vessels just under the surface dilate, increasing the flow of blood to the area and making the skin feel warm. Ginger also irritates the mucous membranes lining your nose and throat, causing them to "weep" watery secretions. This can make it easier for you to blow your nose or cough up mucus when you have a cold.

Ginger is a reputed carminative, an agent that helps break up and expel intestinal gas.

Adverse effects. Some people find gingered food irritating to the stomach.

How to Use This Spice

In cooking: Choose fresh ginger with smooth skin. If the skin is wrinkled, the root may be dried out.

Like garlic, ginger gets milder with cooking and turns bitter if burned.

One-half teaspoon ground ginger equals one to two teaspoons chopped fresh ginger.

Rinsed preserved ginger can be substituted in equal amounts for fresh ginger.

To make "pink ginger," the garnish commonly served in Japanese restaurants, buy very young ginger roots, peel or scrape away the skin, slice the ginger very thin, dip it in lemon juice and season with salt. The lemon juice turns the gingerroot pink.

As a home remedy: To relieve the congestion of a head cold, add a pinch of ginger to your tea (see above, How This Spice Affects Your Body).

In the garden: Ginger rhizomes can be potted, so you can grow your own ginger plants in your kitchen. When the roots are ready, simply reach in, pull them out and slice or grate to use in cooking.

Hops

About This Plant

Botanical name:	*Humulus lupulus*
Also known as:	Common hops
Native to:	Europe, North America
Parts used as herb:	Fruits
Medicinal properties:	Antimicrobial, sedative
Other uses:	(—)

ABOUT THIS HERB AS FOOD AND FLAVORING

Hops are dried strobiles (cone-shaped flowers) of the female plant. They are valued for their bitter resins (which give beer and ale their characteristic flavor) and their oils (which have a distinctive "beerlike" aroma). The most important flavoring chemicals in the hops resins are *lupulone* and *humulone*. These bitter acids have antibacterial properties that help keep bacteria from growing in the beer as it is being made. Hops also contain proteins, nitrogen compounds, sugars (fructose and glucose), pectins (soluble food fibers) and astringent tannins which give a brew its bite.

Nutritional profile. (—)

HOW THIS HERB AFFECTS YOUR BODY

Oil of hops contains a number of irritant chemicals including *myrcene, linalool, geraniol* and *citral.*

Lupulonic acid, a derivative of lupulone, is a chemical that produces effects in animals similar to those produced by estrogen. There is very little information about the effects of phytoestrogens on human beings.

Lupulone and humulone are antibiotics. In laboratory experiments, they have been shown to be active against *Staphylococcus aureus.*

Herbalists have long believed that teas brewed from dried hops have a sedative effect. It now appears that this effect may be due to an alcohol, 2-methyl-3-butene-2-ol, which reaches a concentration of 0.15% in dried hops. Given to laboratory rats, the alcohol made the animals quieter and less mobile. How it effects human beings remains to be shown.

Benefits. (—)

Adverse effects. The pollen of the hops plant can cause contact dermatitis (itching, burning, stinging, reddened or blistered skin) in people who handle the plant. Some reports suggest that as many as one in every 30 workers harvesting hops suffer some skin irritation.

HOW TO USE THIS HERB

Around the house: Throw-pillows stuffed with dried hops smell good. Some herbalists think the pillow's scent may help you fall asleep, but there is no scientific proof that it will work (see above, HOW THIS HERB AFFECTS YOUR BODY.)

HOREHOUND

ABOUT THIS PLANT

Botanical name: *Marrubium vulgare*
Also known as: Common hoarhound, white horehound
Native to: Europe, Asia
Parts used as herb: Leaves, stems, flowers
Medicinal properties: Expectorant
Other uses: Candy

ABOUT THIS HERB AS FOOD AND FLAVORING

Horehound, which is native to Europe and Asia but now grows wild in the United States, Canada and Mexico, is a member of the mint family, an erect perennial plant whose crinkled round or oval leaves and tall stems are covered with a whitish down. Horehound's musty, bittersweet flavor comes from *marrubiin*, a bitter reddish oil in the leaves and stems. The herb has traditionally been used to flavor candy, cough drops and cough syrups.

Nutritional profile. (—)

HOW THIS HERB AFFECTS YOUR BODY

Horehound leaves and stems are high in mucilage, which is a demulcent (an agent that soothes irritated mucous membranes). Marrubiin is an expectorant, an agent that increases the secretion of watery liquids from the mucous membranes lining the throat and bronchial tubes. Expectorants make it easier to cough up phlegm and mucus.

Horehound has a long history as a folk remedy for soothing an irritated throat or relieving a cough, but there is no scientific proof that it suppresses coughing or is effective as an expectorant. The Food and Drug Administration's Advisory Review Panel on Over-the-Counter Cold, Cough, Allergy, Bronchodilator and Anti-Asthmatic Products describes the herb as safe but not proven effective as a cold and cough remedy.

Benefits. (—)
Adverse effects. (—)

How to Use This Herb

As a home remedy: To make horehound tea, simmer leaves and/or stems in water to cover for 25 minutes, then strain and sweeten the thickish liquid with honey or sugar to taste. Drink this as a warm tea, or let it cool a bit then use as a gargle for a sore throat. **Use only unsprayed plants.**

HORSERADISH

About This Plant

Botanical name:	*Armoracia rusticana*
Also known as:	(—)
Native to:	Europe
Parts used as herb:	Roots
Medicinal properties:	Antiscorbutic, rubefacient
Other uses:	(—)

About This Herb as Food and Flavoring

Horseradish is a cruciferous vegetable, that is, a member of the cabbage family, which includes broccoli, Brussels sprouts and cauliflower. Like other crucifers, the edible horseradish root gets its flavor from sulfur compounds such as *allyl isothiocyanate* and its sharp smell from *sinigrin*, which releases an acrid odor when you slice into the radish and tear its cell walls. You produce the same reaction—but much stronger—when you slice into an onion, releasing sulfur compounds that make your eyes water.

Horseradish is widely available fresh or as a prepared condiment. Wasabi, the strong, green Japanese horseradish, is available in Japanese or Oriental grocery stores as a powder or paste. The "horseradish tree," *Moringa oleifera,* comes from a totally different plant family native to India and the Mediterranean. The tree has thick roots and pods sometimes used in curries and other dishes as a substitute for the stronger-flavored true horseradish.

Nutritional profile. One ounce (29 g) raw horseradish has 29 calories. It provides 0.9 g protein, a trace of fat, 5.6 g carbohydrates, 40 mg calcium, 0.4 mg iron and 23 mg vitamin C.

One ounce (29 g) prepared horseradish has 11 calories. It provides 0.4 g protein, a trace of fat, 2.7 g carbohydrates, 17 mg calcium and 0.3 mg iron.

How This Herb Affects Your Body

Like mustard, horseradish is a rubefacient. When applied as a poultice, it irritates the skin and causes the small blood vessels just under the surface to dilate, increasing the flow of blood and making the skin feel warm.

In laboratory tests, allyl isothiocyanate has produced chromosomal changes in hamster cells and cancer in rats; there is no evidence that it produces the same effects in human beings.

Benefits. Fresh horseradish is a good source of vitamin C. One ounce fresh grated horseradish supplies 38% of the vitamin C a healthy adult needs each day.

Adverse effects. Prepared horseradish, which is high in sodium (198 mg sodium/tbsp) is generally excluded from a sodium-restricted diet for people who have high blood pressure or heart disease and are sensitive to salt.

Like other cruciferous vegetables, horseradishes contain goitrin, *thiocyanate* and *isothiocyanate,* chemicals known as *goitrogens.* Goitrogens make it difficult for the thyroid gland to produce thyroid hormones. As a result the gland enlarges in an attempt to make more hormones. We call the swollen thyroid gland "goiter." Goitrogens are not dangerous for healthy people who eat moderate amounts of cruciferous vegetables, but they may create problems for people who have a thyroid disorder or who are taking thyroid medication.

Horseradish, again like other cruciferous vegetables, may interfere with the accuracy of the guaiac slide test for hidden blood in the stool. The active ingredient in this test is *alpha-guaiaconic* acid, which turns blue in the presence of blood. It also turns blue when it comes in contact with *peroxidase,* a chemical found naturally in crucifers. The result is a "false-positive" reading in people who really do not have any blood in their stool. So if you are to take this test, you may be advised to avoid eating these foods for three days prior to the test.

There have been at least two reports (one in New York and one in California) of a serious adverse reaction to wasabi: The diner became pale and confused, began to sweat profusely and collapsed after eating a large serving of the condiment. While there were no long-term effects, both reports suggested that this response may be serious in patients with weakened blood vessels in the heart or brain.

How to Use This Herb

In cooking: For the strongest flavor, use freshly grated horseradish.

The sulfur-containing mustard oil in prepared horseradish turns bitter when exposed to air. For the best flavor, use the horseradish within a few weeks after you open the jar.

To reconstitute dried wasabi powder, combine each teaspoon of powder with ¾ teaspoon water. For the best flavor, use immediately.

Hyssop

About This Plant

Botanical name: *Hyssopus officinalis*
Also known as: Garden hyssop
Native to: Eurasia
Parts used as herb: Leaves
Medicinal properties: Demulcent
Other uses: Perfumery

About This Herb as Food and Flavoring

Hyssop is a member of the mint family that produces small purple flowers and narrow, pungent leaves with a bitter, spicy mint flavor. Small quantities of fresh hyssop leaves may be used in salads or as a garnish for fruit soups, salads and desserts. Dried hyssop flowers are sometimes used to decorate soups or to brew a minty tea.

Hyssop's flavor and aroma come from oil of hyssop, a colorless or greenish yellow liquid whose most important constituent (50%) is *pinene*, which smells and tastes like turpentine. Oil of hyssop is sometimes used to flavor the French liqueurs Chartreuse and Bendictine, and as a base for perfumes. The herb may be available as a tea in your health food store; fresh leaves are available only from your own garden.

Nutritional profile. (—)

How This Herb Affects Your Body

Pinene is an expectorant, an agent that may increase the secretions of the mucous membranes lining the bronchial tubes, liquefying mucus so that you can cough it up more easily.

Benefits. (—)
Adverse effects. (—)

How to Use This Herb

In cooking: To obtain the most aromatic fresh hyssop leaves, pick them just before the plant flowers. **Use only unsprayed leaves.**

Use hyssop leaves with discretion; a little goes a long way toward flavoring any dish.

Hyssop leaves and flowers can be dried for use in herbal teas.

As a home remedy: As a folk remedy for the stuffed nasal passages that come with the common cold, steep fresh or dried hyssop leaves in hot water and inhale the vapors.

Around the house: Use hyssop to make a greenish dye for natural wool fabrics. Chop one pint hyssop leaves for each ounce of fabric, and soak the leaves overnight in water. Then discard the water used for soaking, add fresh water to cover and simmer the leaves up to an hour, until the water turns the color you want. Strain the liquid and add enough fresh water to make 4 gallons of dye for 1 pound of cloth; add the garment to be dyed and let it sit until the color is right, then rinse the fabric in cold water until the water runs clear. Theoretically this dye works on all natural fabrics, but it is much easier to get good results with wool than with silk and cotton. **CAUTION: In any case, it's a good idea to try the dye on a small inside spot to see how it looks—and how the material reacts—*before* you put the entire garment into the dye bath.**

In the garden: Pinene, the chief constituent of oil of hyssop, is used in making insecticides. Some gardeners maintain that its camphor/turpentine odor repels some varieties of butterflies and that planting hyssop in the garden provides a natural insect repellent.

JUNIPER

About This Plant

Botanical name:	*Juniperis communis*
Also known as:	Common juniper
Native to:	Europe, North America
Parts used as herb:	Berries
Medicinal properties:	Diuretic
Other uses:	(—)

ABOUT THIS HERB AS FOOD AND FLAVORING

Juniper is an evergreen shrub whose spicy blue-black or purplish berries contain juniper oil, the principal flavoring in gin. Oil of juniper (also known as juniperberry oil) is a colorless to pale green liquid used as a fragrance in perfumes, soaps, detergents, cosmetic lotions, and as a flavoring agent in cola drinks, root beer, ice cream, candy, chewing gum and sauerkraut. The amount of oil in juniper berries ranges from 0.2% to 3.4% depending on where the juniper is grown and how ripe the berries are.

Nutritional profile. (—)

HOW THIS HERB AFFECTS YOUR BODY

Benefits. (—)

Adverse effects. Because juniper and its extracts increase the natural contractions of the intestines and may trigger uterine contractions, they are not recommended for pregnant women.

Juniper oil contains 4-terpineol, a diuretic that irritates the kidneys and increases the elimination of liquids from the body. The amount of juniper oil in alcoholic beverages is so low (less than 1%) that it is unlikely to produce either of these effects in healthy people, but juniper and its extracts may be hazardous for people with kidney disease. Once used in medicine as a diuretic, juniper has been replaced by safer and more effective drugs.

HOW TO USE THIS HERB

In cooking: You can use juniper berries to give meat dishes, beans and soups a ginlike flavor. The flavor of 1 teaspoon of juniper berries in a marinade, soup or stew is equivalent to the flavor of ½ cup gin.

LAVENDER

ABOUT THIS PLANT

Botanical name:	*Lavandula officinalis*
Also known as:	Garden lavender, true lavender
Native to:	The Mediterranean
Parts used as herb:	Leaves, flowers

Medicinal properties: (—)
Other uses: Moth repellent, fragrance

ABOUT THIS HERB AS FOOD AND FLAVORING

Lavender is a perennial plant with narrow gray green leaves and long spikes with purple flowers. The fragrant leaves and flowers can be used fresh in salads and fruit dishes, or added to cooked sauces, candies and baked goods. When dried they are used in jellies. Lavender is grown primarily for the oil in its flowers, which is widely used as a fragrance in perfumes and cosmetic products and to flavor beverages and baked goods.

Oil of lavender contains small amounts of *coumarins,* which smell and taste like vanilla; astringent *tannins; linalyl acetate* and *linalool,* which smell like bergamot; turpentine-scented *pinene;* lemony scented *limonene;* and *geraniol,* which smells like roses and is used as an insect attractant.

Nutritional profile. (—)

HOW THIS HERB AFFECTS YOUR BODY

Linalool, limonene, geraniol and pinene are irritants. Limonene is also a photosensitizer, a chemical that makes your skin more sensitive to sunlight.

Coumarins are anticoagulants and known carcinogens that have been reported to cause cancers of the bile duct in laboratory rats. Their effects on human beings (especially in amounts as small as those you find in lavender) are uncertain.

Benefits. (—)

Adverse effects. Perfumes and cosmetic products scented with oil of lavender may make your skin more sensitive to sunlight.

HOW TO USE THIS HERB

Around the house: Lavender is reputed to repel moths. Sprinkle dried lavender flowers in your drawers or closets to protect your clothes.

To dry lavender flowers for sachets, pick the flowers just as they open and hang them upside down in an airy room until dry.

LEMON

ABOUT THIS PLANT

Botanical name: *Citrus limon*
Also known as: (—)
Native to: Northern India
Parts used as herb: Juice, rind
Medicinal properties: Antiscorbutic (juice)
Other uses: Pharmaceutical flavoring

ABOUT THIS HERB AS FOOD AND FLAVORING

Lemons give us two flavoring agents: lemon juice and lemon peel. The peel, known as "lemon zest" when grated, is more strongly flavored than the juice because it has a concentration of lemon oil. This oil is pale yellow or greenish and is also known as *cedro oil*. Lemon oil is about 90% lemony scented *limonene*. It also contains *citral* and *citronellal*, which also smell like lemon. The essential oils *phellandrene* and *pinene*, which smell like turpentine; and *hesperidin*, a flavonoid (pigment) with a bitter or astringent taste.

Dried lemon peel and bottled lemon juice are widely available.

Nutritional profile. One tsp (2 g) raw lemon peel provides a trace of protein, and fat, 0.3 g carbohydrates, 3 mg calcium, a trace of iron, and 2.6 mg vitamin C.

One ounce of fresh lemon juice has 7 calories. It provides 0.19 protein, a trace of fat, 2.4 g carbohydrates, 2 mg calcium, a trace of iron, 13 mg vitamin C and 5.7 IU vitamin A.

HOW THIS HERB AFFECTS YOUR BODY

Citral, citronellal, limonene, phellandrene and pinene are all irritating to the skin and mucous membranes.

In laboratory animals hesperidin appears to be used like vitamin C and to protect the strength of capillaries, the tiny blood vessels just under the skin. However, the effects of hesperidin and other flavonoids such as *rutin* (which are known collectively as vitamin P) have never been demonstrated in human beings.

Benefits. Lemon juice is a good source of vitamin C, which protects against scurvy, the disease caused by a deficiency of vitamin C. One ounce of juice provides 21% of the RDA for a healthy adult.

Adverse effects. Oil of lemon can cause contact dermatitis (itching, burning, stinging, reddened or blistered skin) including *cheilitis* (chapped, peeling or bleeding lips) in sensitive people who handle lemons or eat foods made with lemons, lemon juice or lemon peel.

How to Use This Herb

In cooking: Use only the lemon-colored part of the peel; the white membrane underneath is bitter.

Lemon rind is more intensely flavored than lemon juice because it is higher in lemon oil. One teaspoon grated lemon peel (zest) has flavor equal to 2 tablespoons fresh lemon juice.

To make lemon-flavored sugar, grate enough lemon peel to make 1 tablespoon zest. Stir the zest into 1 cup granulated sugar and store the sugar, tightly covered, in a cool, dry place. Use as needed. *Note:* Don't store the lemon-sugar in the refrigerator; the moist air causes it to cake.

One teaspoon freshly grated lemon peel (zest) has flavor equal to 2 teaspoons candied lemon peel.

As a cosmetic: Lemon juice is an effective conditioning rinse for blond hair. Shampoos are alkaline and may leave a sticky residue on your hair. The acid lemon juice dissolves the residue and makes your hair more manageable as well as shinier. To make the rinse, combine ¼ cup lemon juice with ¼ cup warm water and apply after rinsing; then rinse with water.

Lemon juice will gently lighten blond hair. It's not very strong, but if you paint lemon juice on your hair and sit in the sun, your hair will lighten slightly.

As a skin bleach. Rubbing "freckles" with the inside of a lemon rind is an old-fashioned bleach—mild, but not very effective. **CAUTION: If a "freckle" bleeds, darkens, crusts or enlarges—all possible warning signs of skin cancer—check with your doctor immediately.**

LEMONGRASS

ABOUT THIS PLANT

Botanical name: *Cymbopogon citratus*
Also known as: (—)
Native to: Southeast Asia
Parts used as herb: Leaf
Medicinal properties: (—)
Other uses: Perfume, insect repellent

ABOUT THIS HERB AS FOOD AND FLAVORING

Lemongrass is a perennial plant with tall, gray-green grasslike leaves that grows best in cooler tropical climates. The plant is used as a source of lemon flavor and aroma in Asian cooking. Lemongrass can be used fresh or dried. Fresh lemongrass is often available in Oriental grocery stores; dried lemongrass is easier to find.

Lemongrass oil is a light oily liquid with a strong lemon scent that comes from *citral*, also found in lemon and orange oil. Citral is used in the synthesis of vitamin A and as a lemony accent in perfumes, colognes and scented soaps. Lemongrass oil also contains *methyl heptanone*, an insect repellent, and lemony scented *limonene* and *citronellal* .

Nutritional profile. (—)

HOW THIS HERB AFFECTS YOUR BODY

Citral and citronellal are irritants. Limonene is a photosensitizer, a chemical that makes your skin more sensitive to sunlight.

Benefits. (—)

Adverse effects. Prolonged handling of lemongrass may cause contact dermatitis (itching, burning, stinging, reddened or blistered skin). People who handle the plant and then expose their skin to sunlight may end up with a severe sunburn on the exposed surfaces.

HOW TO USE THIS HERB

In cooking: When you slice or cut into a lemongrass leaf, you tear its cell walls, releasing the lemony scented and flavored oil inside. To use a fresh lemongrass leaf in stir frying, peel the leaf, slice or chop it into small pieces, then pound the pieces to let out the flavor and aroma.

For seasoning, one stalk of lemongrass is equivalent to about 2 to 3 tablespoons of dried lemongrass.

You can use the whole leaf in a soup or stew. Bruise or nick it before adding to the pot, and remove before serving the dish.

In the garden: Lemony or citronella-scented plants such as lemon verbena, lemon balm and lemongrass are useful because they appear to repel insects in the garden without being poisonous to people or pets.

LEMON VERBENA

ABOUT THIS PLANT

Botanical name:	*Aloysia triphylla*
Also known as:	(—)
Native to:	Latin America
Parts used as herb:	Leaves
Medicinal properties:	(—)
Other uses:	Insect repellent, perfumes

ABOUT THIS HERB AS FOOD AND FLAVORING

Lemon verbena is a woody shrub with narrow, shiny, pale green leaves that taste like lemon and smell like a combination of lemons and limes. Lemon verbena leaves are particularly useful herbs because they don't lose their flavor or aroma when you dry or cook them.

The oil that gives lemon verbena leaves their flavor and aroma is approximately 35% lemony scented *citral*; plus *borneol* (which smells like pepper and tastes like mint); *citronellal* and *limonene* (which both smell like lemon); camphor-scented *eucalyptol*; and rose-scented *geraniol*.

Nutritional value. (—)

HOW THIS HERB AFFECTS YOUR BODY

All the aroma chemicals in the oil of lemon verbena are potentially irritating to skin and mucous membranes.

Benefits. (—)

Adverse effects. Handling the lemon verbena plant or eating foods flavored with lemon verbena leaves may cause contact dermatitis (itching, burning, stinging, reddened or blistered skin) or cheilitis (chapped or bleeding lips) in sensitive people.

How to Use This Herb

Around the house: Use fresh or dried lemon verbena leaves to scent your closets and drawers and—perhaps—keep the insects away (see *In the garden*).

In the garden: Lemon- and citronella-scented plants such as lemon verbena appear to act as natural insect repellents in the garden, protecting the plants without being poisonous to pets or people.

LICORICE

About This Plant

Botanical name:	*Glycyrrhiza glabra*
Also known as:	Licorice root, sweet licorice, sweet wood
Native to:	Southern Europe, Asia
Parts used as herb:	Roots and woody stems
Medicinal properties:	Demulcent
Other uses:	Flavoring for drugs, tobacco and cosmetics

About This Herb as Food and Flavoring

Licorice, which grows wild in Europe and Asia, is cultivated mainly for its sweet-tasting rhizomes (underground stems) and roots, which are used as flavorings. From 1 to 21% of the weight of the licorice root is *glycyrrhizic acid*, the sweet compound extracted and used as a flavoring in food, drugs and cosmetics. Ammoniated licorice, an extract obtained by boiling licorice root in water and sulfuric acid and then neutralizing the solution with dilute ammonia, is the form of licorice used as a natural flavoring. This extract is 50 to 100 times as sweet as the sucrose (table sugar) obtained from sugarcane or sugar beets.

Ninety percent of all natural licorice employed as a flavoring agent is used in tobacco (cigarettes, cigars, pipe tobacco). Licorice candy, which rarely contains more than 2% natural licorice extract, is more likely to be flavored with anise (which is chemically unrelated to licorice) or with a synthetic licorice flavoring. Neither anise nor synthetic licorice flavoring produces the adverse effects associated with natural licorice.

Nutritional profile. (—)

How This Herb Affects Your Body

Glycyrrhizic acid increases your body's retention of sodium and water. Licorice root also contains mucilage, making it a natural demulcent, a substance that soothes skin and mucous membranes.

Benefits. Licorice root (known medically as glycyrrhizia) is used as a demulcent base, but it is not as widely used as the vegetable gums acacia and tragacanth. In experimental studies, *carbenoxolone sodium,* which is synthesized from a derivative of glycyrrhizic acid, appears to promote the healing of duodenal ulcers. At present, carbenoxolone sodium is considered an experimental drug; it is not available for general use in the United States.

Ammoniated licorice, which is soluble in water or alcohol, is used to flavor or disguise the taste of bitter medicines, and licorice extract is used as a flavoring agent in toothpastes and powders. Licorice root has also been used to sweeten cough syrups. Some modern research suggests that sweet foods trigger the production of endorphins (natural painkillers) in the brain, which may explain their nearly universal use to treat a sore throat.

Adverse effects. Because glycyrrhizic acid increases your body's retention of sodium and water, it may exacerbate existing hypertension and interfere with the effectiveness of antihyperactive drugs (including diuretics), as well as drugs used to treat heart disease. People who consume as little as an ounce of candy containing natural licorice flavoring or who drink alcoholic beverages flavored with natural licorice may develop elevated blood pressure, as well as edema (swelling due to water retention), muscle contractions and convulsions. All of those disappear when the licorice is withdrawn from the diet.

In human beings, doses of 280 mg/kg (an amount equal to 0.6 ounce for a 150-pound person) of licorice a day for four weeks produced hypertension, cardiac problems and gastrointestinal symptoms including diarrhea, ulceration and constipation.

How to Use This Herb

As a home remedy: Teas made by boiling a piece of peeled licorice root in water are said to relieve a cough or sore throat.

LOVAGE

ABOUT THIS PLANT

Botanical name: *Levisticum officinale*
Also known as: Love parsley, sea parsley
Native to: Europe, Asia Minor
Parts used as herb: Leaves, stems
Medicinal properties: Carminative, diuretic
Other uses: (—)

ABOUT THIS HERB AS FOOD AND FLAVORING

Lovage tastes and smells like celery. It is a tall plant with large dark green leaves, which can be used fresh in salads. Lovage leaves and stems are particularly useful in soups and stews because their strong celery flavor persists even after long cooking. Lovage stems can also be candied, and the stem bases blanched and served as a vegetable.

Nutritional profile. (—)

HOW THIS HERB AFFECTS YOUR BODY

When extracts of lovage root are injected into laboratory rats and mice, the animals urinate more frequently. While there is no proof that lovage root has the same effect on human beings, it is still used in European diuretic teas.

Benefits. Lovage root is a carminative, an agent that helps break up and expel intestinal gas.

Adverse effects. Prolonged contact with lovage plants has been known to cause photosensitivity (an increased sensitivity to sunlight), a common problem with plants in the carrot family, such as dill and fennel.

HOW TO USE THIS HERB

In cooking: *Chlorophyll,* the green coloring in plants, is sensitive to acids. When you heat lovage leaves, their chlorophyll reacts with natural acids in the leaves or in the cooking water, forming a brown compound called *pheophytin.* The pheophytin then reacts with the yellow carotene pigments in the leaves, thus turning the cooked lovage bronze. The color change doesn't affect the flavor. **Use only unsprayed leaves.**

MACE

About This Plant

Botanical name: *Myristica fragrans*
Also known as: (—)
Native to: Indonesia
Parts used as spice: Seed covering
Medicinal properties: Hallucinogen
Other uses: Flavoring for tobacco

About This Spice as Food and Flavoring

The nutmeg tree is an evergreen native to Indonesia but now cultivated in the West Indies as well. It produces two spices—nutmeg and mace. Nutmeg is the seed kernel inside the tree's fruit; mace is the lacy covering (the aril) on the fruit. When the nutmeg fruit is harvested, its outer husk is broken open and the aril is separated by hand from the seed shell inside. The seed kernel (nutmeg) is left to dry inside the shell. The broken pieces of the aril, known as *blades*, are dried to develop their strong aroma, then ground to make the powder we call mace. If the mace comes from Indonesia, it is orange-color; mace from the West Indies is yellowish brown.

Oil of nutmeg from the plant's leaves is also known as oil of mace. Oil of nutmeg from the kernel, which flavors the aril (mace), is also known as oil of myristica. Oil of nutmeg contains peppery scented, mint-flavored *borneol*; spicy, clove-scented *eugenol*, the chief constituent of oil of cloves; rose-scented *geraniol*; lavender-scented *linalool*; and two suspected hallucinogens, *myristicin* and *elemicin*. Oil from nutmegs grown in Indonesia contains *safrole*, the principal flavoring in sassafras.

Nutritional profile. One-fourth teaspoon (0.5 g) ground mace has 2 calories. It provides approximately 0.03 g protein, 0.1 g fat, 0.2 g carbohydrates, 1 mg calcium, 0.06 mg iron and 4 IU vitamin A.

How This Spice Affects Your Body

Oil of nutmeg is approximately 4% myristicin, a reputed hallucinogen. In high doses, very close to what is considered a toxic amount, oil of nutmeg may produce symptoms such as euphoria, detachment from reality or the sensation of floating; flushed skin; and visual and auditory hallucinations. These symptoms are unlikely to be caused by the small amounts of mace used to season food.

Safrole, which is found in black pepper as well as sassafras, is known to cause liver tumors in laboratory rats and mice, but its effects on human beings are not proven. Nevertheless, the Food and Drug Administration no longer permits it to be used as a food flavoring. The sassafras sold legally in this country must be "safrole free" (See FILÉ). Nutmeg contains only very small amounts of safrole.

Benefits. (—)
Adverse effects. (—)

How to Use This Spice

In cooking: Although its flavor is slightly stronger, mace can be used as a substitute for nutmeg.

MALLOW

About This Plant

Botanical name:	*Malva sylvestris, Malva rotundifolia*
Also known as:	Cheeseplant, common mallow (Malva sylvestris), dwarf mallow (Malva rotundifolia)
Native to:	Europe, Asia
Parts used as herb:	Flowers, leaves, seed pods, shoots
Medicinal properties:	Emollient, antiscorbutic
Other uses:	(—)

About This Herb as Food and Flavoring

Common mallow (*Malva sylvestris*) and dwarf mallow (*Malva rotundifolia*) are ancient herbs that have been cultivated since the era of the Romans. Both mallows now grow wild in North America. Mallow produces small, round leaves that can be boiled and eaten as a vegetable or brewed into a delicately flavored tea. Its shoots, green seed capsules (known as "cheeses") and pink flowers can be chopped and added to salads.

Mallow leaves are high in mucilage. Mallow seeds are 5% to 7% fatty oils. Mallow flowers contain tannins that give them a slight astringency.

Nutritional profile. One ounce (29 g) dwarf mallow leaves contains 36 mg vitamin C.

How This Herb Affects Your Body

Mucilage, a gelatinlike substance, is an emollient, an agent that softens skin and soothes and relieves irritated skin or mucous membranes.

Benefits. Mallow is a source of vitamin C. One ounce of dwarf mallow leaves provides 56% of the RDA for a healthy adult.

Adverse effects. (—)

How To Use This Herb

In cooking: Do not tear or cut mallow leaves until you are actually ready to use them. When you cut into a food rich in vitamin C, its cells release an enzyme called ascorbic acid oxidase, which destroys vitamin C. **Use only unsprayed leaves.**

Chlorophyll, the green coloring in plants, is sensitive to acids. When you heat mallow leaves as a pot herb, their chlorophyll reacts with natural acids in the leaves or in the cooking water, forming a brown compound called *pheophytin.* The pheophytin then reacts with the yellow carotene pigments in the leaves, turning the cooked mallow bronze. To prevent this color change, you must keep the chlorophyll from reacting with the acids in one of these ways: cook the mallow in lots of water to dilute the acids; (2) leave the lid off the pot so the acids can dissipate into the air; (3) steam the leaves very quickly so there is no time for the reaction to occur.

As a home remedy: Although there is no scientific study to prove it true, long use in folk medicine suggests that the mucilaginous tea brewed from mallow leaves may soothe the sore throat that comes with a cold, and that a poultice made of mashed mallow leaves may soothe the itch from a mosquito bite.

MARIGOLD

About This Plant

Botanical name:	*Calendula officinalis*
Also known as:	Calendula, pot marigolds
Native to:	Southern Europe
Parts used as herb:	Flowers, leaves
Medicinal properties:	(—)

Other uses: Coloring agent, natural pest
repellent

About This Herb as Food and Flavoring

Marigolds are ornamental plants that produce large orange, yellow or
creamy white edible flowers. Fresh young marigold leaves can be used
in salads or to add a touch of color and a mild flavor to soups and stews.
Powdered dried flowers are sometimes used in baked goods, and rice
and fish dishes as an inexpensive substitute for saffron, the world's most
expensive seasoning.

Marigolds owe their faintly bitter bite to astringent *tannins.*

The colors of marigold flowers come from a combination of natural
pigments including yellow *beta-* carotene (the carotenoid your body
converts to vitamin A), red *lycopene* (a carotenoid with no vitamin A
activity), red *rubixanthine* and red blue *violaxanthine.* There is so little
beta-carotene in marigolds that they are not considered a source of
vitamin A.

Nutritional profile. (—)

How This Herb Affects Your Body

The tannins in marigolds are astringents. They coagulate the proteins on
the mucous membrane lining of your mouth, making the tissues pucker
and creating a slightly unpleasant tingling effect when you eat marigold
flowers. The effect can be relieved by drinking milk.

Benefits. (—)

Adverse effects. Marigolds are related to asters, chamomille,
chrysanthemums and ragweed. People sensitive to these plants may also
be sensitive to marigolds and may develop respiratory symptoms
(asthma, runny nose, hay fever) or cheilitis (peeling, bleeding lips) from
eating marigolds. Contact with the plant may produce contact dermatitis
(itching, burning, stinging, reddened or blistered skin).

How to Use This Herb

In cooking: **Use only plants that have not been sprayed with pesticides.** Cut the flowers off while they are still in bloom, pull off the petals
and wash them thoroughly to remove dust and insects.

To make an inexpensive substitute for saffron, dry the marigold
flowers in a cool, dark place, then pulverize the centers. Store the powder
in a tightly sealed glass jar to protect it from air and moisture.

Around the house: Use marigolds to make an orange dye for wool.
Tear up 1 pint of marigold flowers for each ounce of wool you want to

dye. Put the flowers in a large pot, and add enough water to cover. Boil the flowers for 30 minutes; then strain out the flowers and add enough fresh water to make 1 quart of dye solution for each ounce of wool to be dyed. Wet the wool yarn, fabric or unlined garment in warm water; squeeze out excess water; add the yarn, fabric or garment to the dye bath; and let simmer (do not boil) for about 30 minutes. Now turn off the heat, let the solution cool, remove the yarn or garment and rinse it in cool water until the water runs clear. In theory, this natural marigold dye works on any natural color, 100% wool yarn or fabric, **but it is always possible the color may not be to your liking or it may be uneven if the yarn, fabric or garment is stained or faded. It is always a good idea to try any dye on a small inconspicuous spot to see how it looks before you dye the entire garment.**

In the garden: Like basil, garlic, peppermint and other strongly scented garden plants, some marigold plants appear to be natural pest repellents that keep insects away without being poisonous to people or pets.

MARJORAM

About This Plant

Botanical name: *Majorana hortensis*
Also known as: Sweet marjoram
Native to: Asia, the Mediterranean
Parts used as herb: Leaves
Medicinal properties: (—)
Other uses: Perfumery

About This Herb as Food and Flavoring

Sweet marjoram is a member of the mint family, closely related to the herb we call oregano. In fact, botanists sometimes use the same botanical name—either *Origanum majorana* or *Majorana hortensis*—to describe both plants. The U.S. Department of Agriculture, however, distinguishes between them by using the name *Majorana hortensis* for the sweet-scented marjoram and the name *Origanum vulgare* for the more acrid oregano.

Marjoram has small green leaves that taste like very mild oregano. The fresh leaves can be used in salads. Dried or ground leaves are used to flavor vegetables, meats (including sausages such as liverwurst and bologna), poultry stuffing and tomato sauces. Pot marjoram (*Origanum onites*), which has slightly larger leaves and a slightly more thymelike flavor than sweet marjoram, can be used in place of sweet marjoram.

Nutritional profile. One teaspoon (0.6 g) dried marjoram leaves has 2 calories. It provides 0.1 g protein, 0.04 g fat, 0.4 g carbohydrates, 12 mg calcium, 0.3 mg vitamin C and 48 IU vitamin A.

How This Herb Affects Your Body

Benefits. (—)
Adverse effects. (—)

How to Use This Herb

In cooking: You can substitute marjoram for oregano and vice versa, but not in equal quantities. Always use the same form of the herb (fresh leaves, dried whole leaves or ground dried leaves). When using oregano in place of marjoram, use a little less oregano; when using marjoram instead of oregano, use a little more marjoram or add some thyme.

One and one-half teaspoons marjoram leaves equals the flavor of 1 teaspoon oregano leaves.

One-half teaspoon oregano leaves equals the flavor of 1 teaspoon marjoram leaves.

MARSHMALLOW

About This Plant

Botanical name:	*Althaea officinalis*
Also known as:	Althea
Native to:	Europe, Asia
Parts used as herb:	Roots, leaves
Medicinal properties:	Emollient
Other uses:	Candy making (antiquated)

About This Herb as Food and Flavoring

Marshmallow is a tall plant with oval leaves and purple to pinkish white flowers that bloom from July through October. It is native to Europe and Asia and now grows wild on the edges of North American marshes.

The marshmallow was once a favorite with doctors and cooks. The plant's root and leaves contain a mucilaginous juice used as a folk remedy for soothing the skin. Cooks mixed the juice with eggs and sugar, whipping the liquid to a foam that hardened to form the original "marshmallow" candy. (Modern marshmallows are made by whipping a protein solution such as gelatin with sugar syrup and allowing the foam to harden.)

Marshmallow roots and young green tops were used as vegetables. Today, dried marshmallow root, sometimes called *althea* from the Greek word meaning "to heal," is occasionally available at health food stores.

Nutritional profile. (—)

How This Herb Affects Your Body

Benefits. The juice of the marshmallow root and leaves does soothe irritated skin and mucous membranes. But **check with your doctor before using to be sure your skin problem is nothing more than a slight irritation. Marshmallow root has no power to heal specific skin diseases.**

Adverse effects. (—)

How to Use This Herb

As a home remedy: Peeled marshmallow root, boiled with sugar or honey and orange or lemon juice, makes a soothing tea or gargle for a sore throat. Some people believe that it also soothes a cough.

MATÉ

About This Plant

Botanical name: *Ilex paraguariensis*
Also known as: St. Bartholomew's tea, yerba maté
Native to: South America
Parts used as herb: Leaves

Medicinal properties: Central nervous system stimulant
Other uses: (—)

About This Herb as Food and Flavoring

The maté tree, which thrives in Argentina, Brazil and Paraguay, is a member of the holly family. It has red berries like the northern holly, but its oval leaves are longer, lighter and less shiny. After maté leaves are harvested, they are dried, powdered and aged for up to a year to make maté tea, a bitter aromatic brew extremely popular in South America. Among the chemicals that give maté tea its characteristic flavor are astringent *tannins*, *citric acid* (one of the chemicals that makes lemons sour), *malic acid* (the chemical that gives immature apples their bite) and very small amounts of *vanillin*. Maté leaves also contain *caffeine* and *theophylline*, the central nervous system stimulants in coffee and tea, and *theobromine*, the muscle stimulant in cocoa.

Caffeine content in 5-oz cup coffee, maté & tea

Drip-brewed coffee	110–150 mg
Percolated coffee	64–124 mg
Decaffeinated coffee	2–5 mg
Maté tea	21–42 mg
Tea bag, 5-min brew	47 mg
Tea bag, 1-min brew	29 mg

Sources: The American Dietetic Association, *Handbook of Clinical Dietetics* (New Haven: Yale University Press, 1981); Briggs, George M., and Calloway, Doris Howes, *Nutrition and Physical Fitness*, 11th ed. (New York: Holt, Rinehart & Winston, 1984); Tyler, Varro E., *The New Honest Herbal* (Philadelphia: George F. Stickley Company, 1987)

Your health food store may carry maté, which is sometimes promoted as a "natural coffee substitute."

Nutritional profile. (—)

How This Herb Affects Your Body

Virtually all maté's benefits and adverse effects come from its caffeine. Some people are more susceptible than others to caffeine. People who drink caffeinated beverages every day are less likely to react strongly to caffeine than people who drink caffeinated beverages only once in a while.

Benefits. Caffeine is a stimulant. It makes you more alert, you can concentrate more easily, your muscles are more responsive, it speeds up your heartbeat and lifts your mood. Caffeine is a mild diuretic that increases urination. It constricts the blood vessels in your brain—that is why caffeinated beverages sometimes relieve headaches caused by engorged blood vessels. In contrast, it dilates the blood vessels in the rest of your body and increases the flow of blood to the heart. Some studies have shown that it may increase pain-free exercise time in people with angina. But because it also speeds up the heartbeat, or may make it irregular, doctors are divided on whether people with heart disease should use caffeinated beverages.

Adverse effects. Caffeinated beverages contain flavoring oils that can upset your stomach, but maté is probably less irritating than coffee or tea because it contains significantly less oils. A kilogram (2.2 lbs) of coffee has about 50 times more flavoring oil than a kilogram of mate (10 mg versus 410 mg), a kilogram of tea about 550 times as much (10 mg versus 6,000 to 7,900 mg).

Caffeine interacts with several drugs. It reduces the effectiveness of the anti-gout drug allopurinol; the antibiotics ampicillin, erythromycin, griseofulvin, penicillin and tetracyclines; anti-ulcer drugs, including cimetidine (Tagamet); and iron supplements. Drinking a caffeine beverage while you are taking any drugs that contain caffeine, such as the anti-asthma drug theophylline or nonprescription products such as cold remedies, diuretics, pain relievers and weight-control products, may increase the risk of caffeine side effects.

How to Use This Herb

In cooking: South Americans sometimes use maté to add a bitter note to baked goods, much as North Americans use coffee to intensify the flavor of chocolate in mocha desserts or Mexicans use bitter chocolate in a *mole* sauce. If you can find maté at your health food store, you may wish to experiment with maté tea in place of coffee in various recipes.

MAYONNAISE

About This Condiment

Chemical name: (—)
Also known as : (—)
Native to: (—)

Parts used as condiment: (—)
Medicinal properties: Emollient
Other uses: Food preservative, hair conditioner

ABOUT THIS CONDIMENT AS FOOD AND FLAVORING

Mayonnaise is a simple food with a sophisticated chemistry. It is made, basically, of oil and water. Since water is a *polar* molecule with a positive electrical charge at one end and a negative electrical charge at the other, and oil is a *nonpolar* molecule with its electrical charge evenly distributed all over the molecule, the two cannot attract each other.

To keep oil and water from separating, you need an *emulsifier*, a chemical that holds them together. The emulsifier in old-fashioned, homemade mayonnaise is lecithin, which is found in egg yolk. Lecithin is polar at one end, so it can hook onto water, and nonpolar at the other, so it can hook onto oil. When you add the egg yolk, the oil and water in the mayonnaise "mix."

Commercial mayonnaises and mayonnaise-type dressings also use flour to hold their oil and water together. The flour traps the oil and water molecules in a starch network so they cannot separate, so long as you do not beat the dressing, and break the network and free the liquids.

The Food and Drug Administration's "standard of identity" (representative recipe) for a typical commercial mayonnaise is:

Vegetable oil (not less than 65% of the total weight of the mayonnaise)

Vinegar or lemon or lime juice (not less than 2.5% of the weight of the mayonnaise)

Egg (whole eggs or frozen, liquid or dried yolks)

Salt

Sweetener (sugar, dextrose, honey, corn syrup, etc.)

MSG

Calcium disodium EDTA or disodium EDTA (these are *sequestrants,* chemicals that attract and hold metal atoms that would otherwise darken the dressing or make it turn rancid)

Nutritional profile. One tablespoon (14 g) mayonnaise has 100 calories. It provides a trace of protein, 11 g fat, 8 mg cholesterol, a trace of carbohydrates, 3 mg calcium, 0.1 mg iron and 40 IU vitamin A.

One tablespoon (15 g) imitation (low-fat) mayonnaise has 35 calories. It provides a trace of protein, 3 g fat, 4 mg cholesterol, 2 g carbohydrates, and a trace of calcium.

One tablespoon (15 g) mayonnaise-type salad dressing has 60 calories. It provides a trace of protein, 5 g fat, 4 mg cholesterol, 4 g carbohydrates, 2 mg calcium, a trace of iron, 30 IU vitamin A.

How This Condiment Affects Your Body

Benefits. (—)

Adverse effects. Commercial mayonnaise and mayonnaise-type dressings contain moderate amounts of sodium (50 to 125 mg per serving). They may be prohibited on some sodium-regulated diets.

How to Use This Condiment

In cooking: Contrary to popular belief, mayonnaise does not necessarily speed food spoilage. In fact, commercially prepared mayonnaise actually protects the food because it contains venegar or lemon juice, acids that retard the growth of the *Salmonella* and *Staphylococcus* organisms, the commonest causes of food poisoning. In 1982 researchers at the Food Research Institute of the University of Wisconsin confirmed that commercial mayonnaise helps retard spoilage but cautioned that this should *never* be interpreted to mean that any food, including food mixed with mayonnaise, does not need to be refrigerated. Keeping foods properly cold (or properly hot) is still the best way to slow bacterial growth and prevent food poisoning. **CAUTION: Freezing salads made with mayonnaise may be hazardous. Freezing slows bacterial growth but does not kill bacteria, which begin to multiply quickly again while the food is defrosting.**

When you peel or slice a fruit or vegetable, you tear cell walls, releasing polyphenoloxidase, an enzyme that converts phenols in the fruit or vegetable to brownish compounds that darken its flesh.

You can slow this reaction by coating the fruit or vegetable with an acid. That's why we dip sliced apples or potatoes in lemon juice, or mix guacamole (avocados), Waldorf salad (apples and walnuts) or potato salad with acidic, commercially prepared mayonnaise. The mayonnaise has two virtues. Not only is it an acid, it is also a protective coating that keeps out oxygen, which also turns the fruit and vegetables dark.

As a cosmetic: Mayonnaise is an efficient, handy hair conditioner. Scoop the mayonnaise out of the jar *with a clean spoon,* rub it on your hair, and wrap your head in aluminum foil or plastic wrap. Wait for about half an hour, and then wash your hair, rinsing thoroughly to remove excess oils.

Meat Tenderizer

About This Condiment

Chemical name:	(—)
Also known as:	(—)
Native to:	(—)
Parts used as condiment:	(—)
Medicinal properties:	Proteolytic
Other uses:	(—)

About This Condiment as Food and Flavoring

The active ingredient in commercial meat tenderizers is papain, a proteolytic (*proteo* = protein; *lyse* = disintegrate) enzyme from fresh papayas.[*]

Proteolytic enzymes tenderize meat by breaking its long protein molecules into smaller pieces. Papain, also known as vegetable pepsin, works so effectively that as little as one-fourth ounce (7 g) of papain will tenderize as much as 8.8 pounds of meat.

A representative commercial meat tenderizer contains salt, dextrose, proteolytic enzyme (papain), MSG, tricalcium phosphate to prevent caking and a partially hydrogenated vegetable oil such as cottonseed oil or soybean oil.

Nutritional profile. One teaspoon regular meat tenderizer contains 1,750 mg sodium. One teaspoon low-sodium meat tenderizer has 1 mg sodium.

---

[*] Other proteolytic enzymes are bromelain, from fresh pineapple, and ficin, from fresh figs. These enzymes are inactivated by heat; canned or dried papaya, pineapple and figs will not tenderize meat.

How This Condiment Affects Your Body

Benefits. Papain destroys the protein venom injected by many stinging insects, particularly mosquitos. A paste made of papain meat tenderizer and water is a time-honored folk remedy endorsed by many medical experts for relieving the itch caused by these insect stings. **CAUTION: If you are allergic to any insect venom NEVER rely on any home remedy. If stung, seek medical advice IMMEDIATELY.**

Adverse effects. Chemically tenderized meat may be prohibited if you are using an MAO-inhibitor, a class of drugs used to treat depression. When a meat tenderizer breaks down the proteins in meat, one of the chemical by-products is *tyramine*. Tyramine is a pressor amine, a chemical that constricts blood vessels and raises blood pressure. Ordinarily, tyramine is broken down and eliminated from the body by the enzyme monoamine oxidase (MAO), but MAO-inhibitors prevent this enzyme from degrading and eliminating tyramine. If you eat a food high in tyramine while you are taking an MAO-inhibitor, the result may be a hypertensive crisis (sustained high blood pressure).

Meat tenderizers high in sodium are usually prohibited on a controlled sodium diet. Low sodium meat tenderizers may be permitted.

Because papain destroys protein, a meat tenderizer paste (or even fresh papaya) may cause contact dermatitis (itching, stinging, burning, reddened or blistered skin) by destroying the proteins on the surface of your skin.

How to Use This Condiment

In cooking: Proteolytic meat tenderizers do not work at temperatures below 140 degrees F or above 170 degrees F.

As a home remedy: To relieve the itch of a mosquito bite, make a paste of meat tenderizers and water and dot it sparingly on the bite. **CAUTION: This paste is potentially irritating. Do not spread it over large areas of skin. Also, see caution above regarding allergies to insect venom.**

MSG

About This Condiment

Chemical name: Monosodium glutamate
Also known as: (—)

Parts used as condiment: (—)
Medicinal properties: (—)
Other uses: (—)

About This Condiment as Food and Flavoring

MSG (monosodium glutamate) is one of a number of compounds derived from *glutamic acid*, a nonessential amino acid found in meat, fish, cow's milk, cereals and grains. MSG occurs naturally in seaweed, or it can be manufactured by extraction from the proteins in wheat, corn or soybeans. Today, more than 90% of the MSG we use is made by bacterial fermentation of carbohydrates such as the sugar from sugar beets.

Exactly how MSG works is still a mystery. It may act on the taste buds, where taste cells come in contact with nerves that transmit the sensation of taste. Or it may increase electrical signals from the brain to the taste buds. Either way, MSG clearly intensifies the flavor of salty or bitter foods, particularly foods that are high in protein. It has no effect on sweets.

Nutritional profile. One teaspoon (5 g) MSG contains 492 mg sodium. One serving (⅛ teaspoon) of a commercial brand name MSG may contain 75 mg sodium.

How This Condiment Affects Your Body

MSG is a diuretic and a potential allergen. It may be prohibited on controlled sodium diets, but two other glutamates, *monoammonium glutamate* and *monopotassium glutamate*, are sometimes used as salt substitutes. They, too, enhance the flavor of foods.

Benefits. (—)

Adverse effects. MSG is the culprit in "Chinese restaurant syndrome," the collection of symptoms including nausea, headache, and a feeling of pressure in your forehead, chest and behind your eyes that may come along with a Chinese meal.

These symptoms may show up in anyone who gets a high enough dose of MSG on an empty stomach. This is why it often follows close on the heels of the soup course in Chinese restaurants. People who are especially sensitive to glutamic acid or corn, wheat or sugar beets (from which MSG may be made) may develop symptoms after eating only minute amounts of MSG, though.

MSG interacts with diuretics. Both increase urination, which eliminates water-soluble vitamins such as vitamin C and the B vitamins, sodium and potassium, along with liquids.

How to Use This Herb

In cooking: Because MSG dissolves in water but not in fat, it works best in cooking if you add it to the liquid in the dish—the sauce or a soup—rather than sprinkling it directly on the food.

MUSTARD SEED

About This Plant

Botanical name: *Brassica nigra* (black mustard), *Brassica juncea* (brown mustard)
Also known as: (—)
Native to: Europe
Parts used as herb: Flowers, leaves, seeds
Medicinal properties: Counterirritant, emetic
Other uses: (—)

About This Herb as Food and Flavoring

Mustard is a thoroughly economical plant. Its greens can be boiled and served as a vegetable; its flowers and seed pods can be used in salads; and its seeds are ground to make the condiment we call "mustard," the second most popular spice in the United States (pepper is number one).

The most important flavoring chemical in black or brown mustard seed is *sinigrin.* Whole mustard seeds have no particular flavor, but when you crack or grind the seeds to make the powder ("mustard flour") sold as *dry mustard,* you tear their cell walls. This releases enzymes that cause sinigrin to break down into *allyl isothiocyanate,* which gives the mustard its characteristic bitter taste.

To develop the sharp, stinging flavor of the mustard oils in the seeds, you must add a liquid. The liquid that most effectively triggers the enzyme action that develops the flavor of the mustard is tepid water, but dry mustard mixed with water loses flavor quickly. To preserve the flavor of a mustard flour paste, you need an acid liquid, such as vinegar or wine. The simplest *prepared mustard* is mustard flour plus an acid (wine or vinegar) and a coloring agent such as turmeric to make the mustard yellower. Some prepared mustards also contain sugar and artificial flavors plus wheat flour to make the mustard smoother.

Nutritional profile. One teaspoon (3.3 g) mustard seed has 15 calories. It provides 0.8 g protein, 1 g fat, 1.1 g carbohydrates, 17 mg calcium, 0.33 mg iron and 2 IU vitamin A.

One teaspoon or packet (5 g) prepared yellow mustard has 5 calories. It provides a trace of protein, fat and carbohydrates, 4 mg calcium, 0.1 mg iron, 63 mg sodium and a trace of vitamin C.

One-half cup (70 g) cooked, drained mustard greens has 11 calories. It provides 1.6 g protein, 0.2 g fat, 1.5 g carbohydrates, 52 mg calcium, 0.5 mg iron, 18 mg vitamin C and 2,122 IU vitamin A.

How This Herb Affects Your Body

Oil of mustard is a rubefacient (*rube* = red; *faciere* = to make). It irritates the skin and dilates the small blood vessels underneath. This increases the flow of blood to the skin, turns it red and makes it feel warm. **In strong concentrations or if left on too long, "mustard plasters" may burn the skin.**

In concentrated form, mustard is an emetic, a substance that causes vomiting. It is also a secretagogue and irritant, stimulating the secretion of stomach acid and triggering the contractions we call hunger pangs. That's why many people believe it may help stimulate a flagging appetite.

Benefits. Mustard greens are an excellent source of *beta*-carotene, the vitamin A precursor in deep yellow fruits and vegetables. According to the American Cancer Society, a diet rich in these foods may lower the risk of some forms of cancer.

Vitamin A also protects your eyes. In your body, the vitamin A from mustard greens is converted to 11-cis retinol, the most important constituent of *rhodopsin*, a protein in the rods in your retina (the cells that enable you to see in dim light). One-half cup cooked mustard greens provides 53% of the vitamin A required each day by a healthy adult woman and 42% of the vitamin A required by a healthy adult man.

Adverse effects. Because it stimulates the production of stomach acid, mustard is prohibited on a bland diet, which also rules out black pepper, chili powder, cloves and nutmeg, and restricts alcohol, cocoa, coffee, colas and tea.

How to Use This Herb

In cooking: One teaspoon dry mustard equals the flavor of 1 tablespoon prepared mustard.

As a substitute for "Chinese mustard," mix dry mustard with just enough water to make a paste. For the best flavor, wait 10 minutes, then use immediately.

You can use mustard powder to hold an oil and water salad dressing together. Ordinarily, water and oil do not mix. Water is a *polar* molecule with a positive electrical charge at one end and a negative electrical charge at the other. Oil is a *nonpolar* molecule with its electrical charge evenly distributed all over the molecule. So the two cannot attract each other. But if you add mustard flour, it will absorb both water and oil molecules, holding them in place and allowing the two to "mix." Mustard flour can hold up to 1.5 times its weight in salad oil and twice its weight in water.

In the garden: Black mustard (*Brassica nigra*) is a hardy plant with narrow leaves and yellow flowers. It resists frost. To harvest its seeds, slice the plants at the bottom after the pods have browned (but before they have split open). Hang the cut plants over cheesecloth or newspaper to dry. Then wrap them in a cheesecloth bag and bang them against a counter to dislodge the seeds. Finally, sift the seeds through a collander or strainer to get rid of the extraneous debris.

CAUTION: Always handle the mustard seeds carefully; if you break the seeds and liberate mustard oil, it can irritate—or even blister—your skin.

Nasturtium

About This Plant

Botanical name:	*Tropaeolum majus*
Also known as:	Indian cress
Native to:	South America
Parts used as herb:	Leaves, flowers, stems, seed pods
Medicinal properties:	(—)
Other uses:	Natural insect repellent

About This Herb as Food and Flavoring

Nasturtium is an annual plant that grows in any good soil. It has round, light green leaves with a spicy, peppery flavor similar to that of its botanical cousin, the watercress plant (*Nasturtium officinale*). Both nasturtium and watercress get their flavor from mustard oils.

Nasturtium is a versatile plant. You can use the stems, leaves and flowers in salads. You can cook the leaves and serve them as a vegetable.

Nutritional profile. (—)

How This Herb Affects Your Body

Benefits. (—)
Adverse effects. (—)

How to Use This Herb

In cooking: *Chlorophyll*, the green coloring in plants, is sensitive to heat. When you heat nasturtium leaves, their chlorophyll reacts with natural acids in the leaves or in the cooking water, forming a brown compound called *pheophytin*. The pheophytin then reacts with the yellow carotene pigments in the leaves, turning the cooked nasturtium bronze. To prevent this color change, you must keep the chlorophyll from reacting with the acids in one of these ways: cook the leaves in lots of water to dilute the acids, leave the lid off the pot so the acids can dissipate into the air, or steam the leaves so quickly that there is no time for the reaction to occur. **Use only unsprayed plants.**

In the garden: Like marigolds, onions, garlic and radish, nasturtiums have a strong aroma that repels many garden pests. In your garden, nasturtium plants act as a natural insect repellent that isn't poisonous to people or pets.

NETTLE

About This Plant

Botanical name:	*Urtica dioica*
Also known as:	Common nettle, stinging nettle
Native to:	Europe
Parts used as herb:	Young tops
Medicinal properties:	Diuretic, counterirritant
Other uses:	Source of chlorophyll for green dye

About This Herb as Food and Flavoring

Nettle is a tall, straight plant with hairy oval dark green leaves. Its botanical name, *Urtica*, comes from the Latin word for the verb "to burn," which describes exactly how your hands feel when you touch this plant without wearing protective gloves. Because boiling for a period of at least 15 minutes inactivates the irritating chemicals in the nettle, the plant's leaves and young shoots can be used as a cooked vegetable. Commercially, nettle is used as a source of chlorophyll for green dyes.

Nutritional profile.(—)

How This Herb Affects Your Body

Nettle tea is a diuretic.

Benefits. Like spinach and other greens, nettle shoots are rich in *beta*-carotene, the pigment in deep yellow fruits and vegetables that your body converts to vitamin A. According to the American Cancer Society, a diet rich in these foods may lower the risk of some forms of cancer.

Vitamin A also protects your eyes. In your body, the vitamin A from nettle is converted to 11-cis retinol, the most important constituent of *rhodopsin*, a protein in the rods in your retina (the cells that enable you to see in dim light).

Adverse effects. Touching the nettle plant may cause severe contact dermatitis (itching, burning, stinging, reddened or blistered skin), including hives (which are known medically as "nettle rash" or "uticaria"). The hairs on the nettle's leaves sting by transferring an irritating substance stored in tiny sacks inside the leaves. Some experts believe that this irritating substance contains *histamine* and *acetylcholine*, which are potent vasodilators, and *5-hydroxytryptamine*, a precursor of a neurotransmitter, *serotonin*. However, this is still speculation; the exact chemical makeup of the nettle's toxin is still unknown.

How to Use This Herb

In cooking: Always wear protective gloves and long sleeves to cover your arms when handling the nettle plant, either in the kitchen or in the garden. **Use only unsprayed plants.**

When cooking nettle, use only the young leaves and shoots at the very top of the plant. Boil the nettle in water *for at least 15 minutes* to destroy the chemicals that make nettle sting.[*] Then season the nettles with salt and pepper, and serve as a vegetable mixed with rice or other vegetables.

---

[*] Nettles made without boiling may cause gastric upset, make your lips and mouth burn, and interfere with urination.

Chlorophyll, the green coloring in plants, is sensitive to acids. When you heat nettle tops, their chlorophyll reacts with natural acids in the leaves or in the cooking water, forming a brown compound called *pheophytin*. The pheophytin then reacts with the yellow carotene pigments in the leaves, turning the cooked nettle bronze. To prevent this color change, you must keep the chlorophyll from reacting with the acids either by cooking the nettle in lots of water to dilute the acids or by leaving the lid off the pot so the acids can dissipate into the air.

NUTMEG

ABOUT THIS PLANT

Botanical name: *Myristica fragrans*
Also known as: Myristica
Native to: Indonesia
Parts used as spice: Seed kernel
Medicinal properties: Hallucinogen
Other uses: Flavoring for tobacco and toothpaste

ABOUT THIS SPICE AS FOOD AND FLAVORING

The nutmeg tree is an evergreen native to Indonesia and now cultivated in the West Indies. It produces two spices—mace and nutmeg. Mace is the lacy covering (*aril*) on the dried fruit of the nutmeg tree; nutmeg is the seed kernel inside the fruit. When the nutmeg fruits are harvested, the outer husk is broken open and the aril is separated by hand from the seed shell. The nutmeg (kernel) is left inside the seed to dry. The *blades*, the broken pieces of the aril, are dried to develop their flavor, then ground to make the powder we call mace.

The oily nutmeg seed kernel dries to a yellow brown; ground nutmeg is tan. Nutmeg, whole or ground, gets its pungent flavor and aroma from oil of nutmeg, which contains peppery scented, mint-flavored *borneol*; spicy, clove-scented *eugenol*, the chief constituent of oil of cloves; rose-scented *geraniol*; and lavender-scented *linalool*. Oil of nutmeg also contains two suspected hallucinogens, *myristicin* and *elemicin*. The oil from nutmegs grown in Indonesia contains *safrole*, the principal flavoring agent in sassafras.

Nutritional profile. One teaspoon (2.2 g) ground nutmeg has 12 calories. It provides 0.1 g protein, 0.8 g fat, 1 g carbohydrates, 4 mg calcium, a trace of iron and 2 IU vitamin A.

How This Spice Affects Your Body

Borneol, geraniol and linalool are irritants that can cause contact dermatitis (itching, burning, stinging, reddened or blistered skin).

Safrole, which is also found in black pepper and sassafras, is an animal carcinogen that causes liver tumors in laboratory rats and mice. Its effects on human beings are unknown.

Benefits. (—)

Adverse effects. Like black pepper, chili powder, cloves, and mustard seeds, nutmeg is a gastric irritant that increases the secretion of stomach acids. It is usually prohibited on a bland diet.

Because oil of nutmeg contains hallucinogens, nutmeg can produce serious toxic effects if the spice is abused. Nutmeg is considered safe in the amounts normally consumed as a food flavoring, **but high doses, defined as one to three whole seeds or 5 to 15 grams (one-half oz) grated nutmeg, can cause euphoria, a sensation of floating, flushed skin, vomiting, circulatory collapse and visual or auditory hallucinations within one to six hours after the nutmeg is consumed. Very large doses may be fatal.**

How to Use This Spice

In cooking: One whole nutmeg grated equals 2 to 3 teaspoons of ground nutmeg.

ONION SEASONINGS

About This Plant

    Botanical name: *Allium cepa*
    Also known as: (—)
    Native to: Asia, the Mediterranean
    Parts used as herb: Bulb
    Medicinal properties: (—)
    Other uses: (—)

ABOUT THIS HERB AS FOOD AND FLAVORING

Onions are members of the lily family whose flavor comes from sulfur compounds activated by the enzyme allinase, released when you peel or slice the onion's bulb. Heat converts these sulfur compounds to sugars, which is why cooked onions taste sweeter than raw onions. Dried onions are dehydrated without being heated so their flavor is preserved.

When onions are dehydrated (dried), they lose about 96% of their moisture, so it takes nearly 8 pounds of fresh onions to make 1 pound of dried onions. Dried onions are marketed as onion flakes (large pieces of dried onion); minced onion (small pieces of dried onion); onion powder (ground dehydrated onion); and onion salt (onion powder plus shredded scallions and salt). Onion powder and onion salt usually contain an anticaking agent such as *tricalcium phosphate* (also known as *calcium phosphate, tribasic;* or *tricalcium orthophosphate*) to keep the powder from absorbing moisture and clumping.

Nutritional profile. One teaspoon (2.1 g) onion powder has 7 calories. It provides 0.2 g protein, a trace of fat, 1.7 g carbohydrates, 8 mg calcium and 0.3 mg vitamin C.

One ounce (29 g) dehydrated onion flakes has 100 calories. It provides 2.5 g protein, 0.4 g fat, 23 g carbohydrates, 47 mg calcium, 0.8 mg iron, 10 mg vitamin C and 57 IU vitamin A.

One teaspoon (5 g) onion salt has 1,620 mg sodium.

HOW THIS HERB AFFECTS YOUR BODY

Benefits. (—)
Adverse effects. (—)

HOW TO USE THIS HERB

In cooking: Two tablespoons onion flakes equals the flavor of ½ cup chopped raw onion.

One tablespoon minced dried onion equals the flavor of ¼ cup raw minced onion.

One tablespoon onion powder moistened with water equals the flavor of one medium onion.

If you plan to add dehydrated onion products to an acid solution (such as a stew flavored with wine) or to a dish that does not have enough water to rehydrate the onions, soak the onion products in water first to bring out the flavor, then add them to the pot.

ORANGE PEEL

ABOUT THIS PLANT

Botanical name: *Citrus aurantium, Citrus sinensis*
Also known as: Bitter orange (Citrus aurantium), sweet orange (Citrus sinensis)
Parts used as herb: Rind
Medicinal properties: Antiscorbutic, pharmaceutical flavoring
Other uses: Perfume

ABOUT THIS HERB AS FOOD AND FLAVORING

Orange peel from ripe sweet oranges (*Citrus sinensis*) is called "sweet orange peel." The peel from unripe bitter oranges (*Citrus aurantium*) is called "bitter orange peel." Both sweet orange peel and bitter orange peel get their flavor and aroma primarily from oil of orange, the yellow to orange liquid that tastes like oranges. Oil of orange contains lemony scented *limonene*, plus *citral* and *terpineol*, which also smell like lemons; *methyl anthranilate* (also known as neroli oil), the flavoring oil in orange blossoms; and lavender-scented *linalool*. The peel from sweet oranges has a sweet, fragrant scent; the peel from unripe bitter oranges contains *naringen*, a chemical that tastes as bitter as quinine. Both sweet orange peel and bitter orange peel are colored with *hesperidin*, a flavonoid (pigment) some people call vitamin P.

Nutritional profile. One ounce (29 g) raw orange peel provides 0.4 g protein, a trace of fat, 7.1 g carbohydrates, 46 mg calcium, 0.2 mg iron, 120 IU vitamin A, 38.8 mg vitamin C.

One ounce (29 g) candied orange peel has 90 calories. It provides a trace of protein and fat, and 23 g carbohydrates.

HOW THIS HERB AFFECTS YOUR BODY

Citral and limonene are skin irritants and potential allergic sensitizers (chemicals that can make you sensitive to other allergens).

In studies on laboratory animals, the flavonoid hesperidin seems to act like vitamin C, protecting the strength of capillaries, the tiny blood vessels just under the skin. However, the effects of hesperidin and other flavonoids such as rutin have never been demonstrated in human beings.

Benefits. Orange peel is a good source of vitamin C. One ounce of fresh orange peel provides 65% of the vitamin C a healthy adult needs each day.

Adverse effects. Oil of orange can cause contact dermatitis (itching, burning, stinging, reddened or blistered skin) in sensitive people who handle oranges or eat food made with orange peel.

How to Use This Herb

In cooking: Before grating fresh orange peel, scrub the orange to remove any wax.

Never grate past the orange-colored part of the peel. The white tissue underneath is bitter, not orange flavored.

One teaspoon grated orange peel equals the flavor of 1 teaspoon dried orange peel or 1 tablespoon fresh orange juice or 2 teaspoons candied orange peel, washed to remove the sugar.

As a substitute for bitter orange peel, mix 2 parts grated fresh orange peel with 1 part grated lemon peel.

OREGANO

About This Plant

Botanical name: *Origanum vulgare*
Also known as: Common oregano
Native to: Southern Europe
Parts used as herb: Leaves
Medicinal properties: (—)
Other uses: Perfumery

About This Herb as Food and Flavoring

Oregano, popularly known as "the pizza herb," is a member of the mint family, a relative of basil and marjoram. Its leaves are small, less than an inch long. They are unusual because they dry quickly and hold their flavor well.

Oreganos vary in flavor. Greek oregano (*Origanum heraclites*) and Spanish oregano (*Origanum vivens*) are strongly flavored; Italian oregano (*Origanum onites*) and common oregano (*Origanum vulgare*) are mild. Mexican oregano (*Lippia*), also known as Mexican marjoram or Mexican wild sage, is the strongest of the oreganos, strong enough to be used in chili powders and dishes flavored with chili peppers.

Oregano's flavor comes from oil of origanum, a yellow green, pleasantly scented liquid also used to flavor some liqueurs and to perfume toilet soaps. The most important ingredient in oil of origanum is *carvacrol* (also known as 2- *p*-cymenol), a thyme-scented liquid also found in thyme, marjoram and summer savory. Oregano sold in the United States is a mixture of various species of dried oregano plus marjoram and thyme.

Nutritional profile. One teaspoon (1.5 g) ground oregano has 5 calories. It provides 0.2 g protein, 0.2 g fat, 1 g carbohydrates, 24 mg calcium and 104 IU vitamin A.

How This Herb Affects Your Body

Carvacrol is an antifungal and anthelmintic (an agent that kills intestinal worms). It is sometimes used as a disinfectant in the syntheses of organic chemicals, but its most important commercial use is as a perfume.

Benefits. (—)

Adverse effects. Oregano is a choleretic, an agent that stimulates the liver to increase its production of bile, a yellow brown or green fluid. Bile helps emulsify fats in your duodenum and increases persistalsis, the rhythmic contractions that move food through your gastrointestinal tract. Choleretics are ordinarly beneficial for healthy people, but may pose some problems for people with gallbladder or liver disease. Some other choleretic herbs are gentian, peppermint and onion.

How to Use This Herb

In cooking: For the best flavor, dry oregano leaves whole. Crumble them just before you use them.

You can substitute oregano for marjoram and vice versa, but not in equal quantities. Always use the same form of the herb (fresh leaves for fresh leaves, dried whole leaves for dried whole leaves and ground leaves for ground leaves).

One and one-half teaspoons marjoram leaves equals the flavor of 1 teaspoon oregano leaves.

One-half teaspoon oregano leaves equals the flavor of 1 teaspoon marjoram leaves.

Paprika

About This Plant

Botanical name:	*Capsicum annuum*
Native to:	(—)
Parts used as spice:	Dried pods (fruit)
Medicinal properties:	Antiscorbutic
Other uses:	Food coloring

About This Spice as Food and Flavoring

Paprika is the powder made by grinding dried ripe bell peppers, the mildest members of the Capsicum genus (see RED PEPPER). Depending on where they are grown, the peppers used to make paprika may be small and round (Spain and Morocco) or long and cone shaped (Hungary and California). The chemicals that make red peppers pungent are found primarily in the seeds and veins of the pod. Some paprikas are pungent rather than mild because they include the veins, but no paprika is made with the hot, spicy seeds. Most of the paprika sold in America is sweet, made without the veins.

Commercially, the oils and resins extracted from paprika are used as a spice and as a food coloring in cheeses and meat products, listed on the label as Natural Color. Paprika may also be used in salad dressing as an emulsifier (an agent that allows oil and water to mix), and it is sometimes included in other spice mixtures, such as chili powder.

Nutritional profile. One tablespoon (6.9 g) paprika has 20 calories. It provides 1 g protein, 0.9 g fat, 3.8 g carbohydrates, 12 mg calcium, 5 mg vitamin C and 4,182 IU vitamin A.

How This Spice Affects Your Body

Benefits. Ounce for ounce, fresh sweet red peppers have more than seven times as much vitamin C as fresh oranges (105 mg/oz versus 14 mg/oz), but drying the peppers destroys much of the vitamin C. One tablespoon of paprika has only 8% of the vitamin C a healthy adult needs each day.

Paprika is an excellent source of *beta*-carotene, the pigment in deep yellow fruits and vegetables that your body converts to vitamin A. According to the American Cancer Society, a diet rich in these foods may lower the risk of some forms of cancer.

Vitamin A also protects your eyes. In your body, the vitamin A from paprika is converted to 11-cis retinol, the most important constituent of *rhodopsin*, a protein in the rods in your retina (the cells that enable you to see in dim light). One tablespoon paprika provides 104% of the amount of vitamin A a healthy adult woman needs each day and 84% of the daily requirement for a healthy adult man.

Adverse effects. Some paprikas are very hot. For adverse effects, see RED PEPPER.

How to Use This Spice

In cooking: To protect paprika's vitamin A and its color, store the spice in a cool, dark place in a tightly covered container.

Paprika scorches easily. This can be a virtue if you are dusting paprika on meat to brown it, but if you are using paprika to flavor a stew such as Chicken Paprika, it will taste best if you add the paprika near the end of the cooking process.

You can use paprika to hold an oil and water salad dressing together. Ordinarily, water and oil will not mix. Water is a *polar* molecule with a positive electrical charge at one end and a negative electrical charge at the other, while oil is a *nonpolar* molecule with its electrical charge evenly distributed all over the molecule—the two cannot attract each other. But if you add paprika, the powder will absorb both water and oil molecules, holding them in place and allowing the two to "mix" for a while. The mix is not permanent, though. Each time you use the dressing, you must shake it to make it smooth once again.

Parsley

About This Plant

Botanical name:	*Petroselinum crispum*
Also known as:	Common parsley
Native to:	The Mediterranean
Parts used as herb:	Leaves, stems
Medicinal properties:	Diuretic
Other uses:	Breath freshener

About This Herb as Food and Flavoring

Parsley is a member of the carrot family. It comes in two basic versions: flat leaved and curly leaved. The curley leaf is prettier as a garnish, but the flat leaf has a stronger, more intense flavor. The leaves and stems of both kinds of parsley get their characteristic flavor and aroma from parsley leaf oil, which is less bitter than the oil in parsley seeds. Parsley leaf oil is mostly parsley-flavored *apiole*, plus *myristicin*, lavender-scented *bergapten*, alcohol and the yellow flavonoids (natural pigments) *apiin* and *apigenin*.

Nutritional profile. One-half cup (30 g) chopped fresh parsley has 10 calories. It provides 0.7 g protein, a trace of fat, 2.1 g carbohydrates, 39 mg calcium, 1.9 mg iron, 27 mg vitamin C and 1,560 IU vitamin A.

One teaspoon (0.3 g) dried parsley has 1 calorie. It provides a trace of protein and fat, 0.2 g carbohydrates, 4 mg calcium, 0.3 mg iron, 0.4 mg vitamin C and 70 IU vitamin A.

One tablespoon (0.4 g) freeze-dried parsley has 1 calorie. It provides 0.1 g protein, a trace of fat, 0.2 g carbohydrates, 1 mg calcium, 0.2 mg iron, 0.6 mg vitamin C and 253 IU vitamin A.

How This Herb Affects Your Body

Apiole and myristicin are mild diuretics, but there is so little in fresh parsley that they have no practical effect. Parsley seeds, however, have more parsley oil than the leaves and may actually be mildly diuretic.

Apiole and myristicin are uterine stimulants (agents that make the muscles of the uterus contract). Again, the amount of apiole and myristicin in fresh parsley is too small to affect the body, but the pure oil extracted from parsley is considered extremely hazardous for pregnant women.

Bergapten is a furocoumarin, a class of chemicals known to irritate the skin and make it extremely sensitive to sunlight.

Parsley has long been used as a folk remedy to sweeten the breath, but there is no scientific proof that it works.

Benefits. Fresh parsley is a good source of vitamin C. One-half cup of chopped fresh parsley provides 45% of the vitamin C a healthy adult needs each day.

Fresh parsley is also rich in *beta*-carotene, the pigment in deep yellow fruits and vegetables that your body can convert to vitamin A. According to the American Cancer Society, a diet rich in these foods may lower the risk of some forms of cancer.

Vitamin A also protects your eyes. In your body, the vitamin A from parsley is converted to 11-cis retinol, the most important constituent of *rhodopsin*, a protein in the rods in your retina (the cells that enable you to see in dim light). One-quarter cup fresh chopped parsley provides 780 IU vitamin A, 20% of the vitamin A a woman needs each day, 16% of the RDA for a man.

Adverse effects. Prolonged handling of the parsley plant may cause contact dermatitis (itching, burning, stinging, reddened or blistered skin) and make the skin very sensitive to sunlight. These reactions occur most commonly in food workers who handle large amounts of parsley without wearing protective gloves; they have not been shown to occur in people who eat parsley as a vegetable.

How to Use This Herb

In cooking: Do not tear or cut parsley until you are actually ready to use it. When you cut into a food rich in vitamin C, its cells release an enzyme called ascorbic acid oxidase. This enzyme destroys vitamin C and reduces the nutritional value of the food.

Chlorophyll, the green coloring in plants, is sensitive to acids. When you heat parsley leaves, their chlorophyll reacts with natural acids in the leaves or in the cooking water, forming a brown compound called *pheophytin.* The pheophytin then reacts with the yellow carotene pigments in the leaves, turning the cooked parsley bronze or dark brown. To keep parsley from changing color, add the herb as a garnish after the dish is cooked.

Parsley is useful as a cooking aid for reducing the cooking odors of strong vegetables such as onions.

PEPPERMINT

About This Plant

Botanical name:	*Mentha piperita*
Also known as:	Brandy mint, lamb mint
Native to:	Europe
Parts used as herb:	Leaves
Medicinal properties:	Carminative, counterirritant, mild topical anesthetic
Other uses:	Perfume

About This Herb as Food and Flavoring

Peppermint is among the most strongly flavored of the mint herbs. This group includes spearmint, as well as the fruit-flavored mints such as lemon mint, orange mint and pineapple mint.

The flavor and aroma of peppermint's 2-inch long oval leaves come from oil of peppermint, a colorless to pale yellow liquid whose most important constituent is *menthol* (not less than 50%). Menthol tastes and smells like peppermint. Oil of peppermint also contains pleasantly scented *cadinene*, lemony *limonene*, peppermint-scented menthone and turpentine-scented *pinene*.

Oil of peppermint is among the most popular of all the perfumed oils derived from herbs and spices. It is used not only in foods but in all kinds of cosmetics including shampoo, body oils, toilet soaps, toothpastes and powders, and face masks.

Most of the dried "mint" leaves sold in grocery stores are spearmint leaves. The best source of fresh peppermint leaves are plants in your own garden.

Nutritional profile. (—)

How This Herb Affects Your Body

Menthol is an allergic sensitizer that may cause hives. Like limonene and pinene, it is an irritant that may cause contact dermatitis (itching, stinging, burning, reddened or blistered skin).

The menthol in oil of peppermint is an effective local anesthetic. It increases the sensitivity of the receptors in the skin that perceive the sensation of coolness and reduces the sensitivity of the receptors that perceive pain and itching (a mild form of pain). Menthol is also a counterirritant, an agent that causes the small blood vessels under the skin to dilate, increasing the flow of blood to the area and making the skin feel warm. When you apply a skin lotion made with menthol, your skin feels cool for a minute, then warm. Menthol's anesthetic properties also make it useful in sprays and lozenges for sore throats.

Long use as a folk remedy suggests that inhaling the pungent fumes from a cup of tea brewed from peppermint leaves may help you cough up mucus or clear a stuffy nose when you have a cold, but there is no scientific proof that this is so. The Food and Drug Administration's Advisory Review Panel on OTC (Over-the Counter) Cold, Cough, Allergy, Bronchodilator and Anti-Asthmatic Products considers oil of peppermint and menthol safe but not proven effective for use in various cold and allergy remedies.

Benefits. (—)

Adverse effects. Like coffee, fatty foods and carbonated beverages, the menthol in oil of peppermint may irritate the sphincter (muscle ring) at the base of your esophagus, thus permitting food from your stomach to flow back into the esophagus, creating the discomfort we call heartburn.

Peppermint is a choleretic, an agent that stimulates the liver to increase its production of bile. This yellow-brown or green fluid helps emulsify fats in your duodenum and increases peristalsis, the rhythmic contractions that move food through your gastrointestinal tract. Choleretics are ordinarily beneficial for healthy people but may pose some problems for people with gallbladder or liver disease. Some other choleretic herbs are gentian, onion and oregano.

How to Use This Herb

In cooking: To protect the flavor of fresh-picked mint leaves, store them in the refrigerator or freeze them in airtight plastic bags or containers.

To protect the flavor of dried mint leaves, do not crumble them until you are ready to use them.

As a home remedy: Peppermint tea may be a triple threat for minor health problems, relieving a mildly upset stomach, a sore throat and helping to clear the stuffy nose that comes with a cold. **CAUTION: Peppermint tea may be hazardous for very young children, who can experience a choking sensation from the menthol.**

PINE NUTS

About This Plant

Botanical name:	*Pinus* species
Also known as:	Pignolia, pinon, pinyon
Native to:	Europe
Parts used as condiment:	Seeds
Medicinal properties:	(—)
Other uses:	(—)

ABOUT THIS CONDIMENT AS FOOD AND FLAVORING

Pine nuts are the seeds in the cones of various kinds of pine trees. The cream white nuts may be thin and tapered or wide and round, or they may look like small kernels of corn; the shape depends on the kind of tree they come from. All pine nuts are soft and oily, and their flavor varies from sweet to pungent, again depending on the tree. Because they must be gathered by hand, pine nuts are a relatively expensive seasoning.

In America pine nuts are known as Indian nuts.

Nutritional profile. One ounce (29 g) shelled pinon has 181 calories. It provides 3.9 g protein, 17.3 g fat, 5.9 g carbohydrates, 3.4 mg calcium, 1.5 mg iron, a trace of vitamin C and 8.6 IU vitamin A.

HOW THIS CONDIMENT AFFECTS YOUR BODY

Benefits. Pine nuts are high in protein, but their proteins are sometimes described as "limited" or "incomplete" because they are deficient in the essential amino acids *methionine* and *cystine*. Combining pine nuts with a cereal food such as pasta, which is limited in lysine but contains sufficient amounts of the essential amino acids methionine an cystine, creates "complete" proteins.

Adverse effects. (—)

HOW TO USE THIS CONDIMENT

In cooking: Rancidity is a natural chemical reaction that occurs when fats come in contact with oxygen. The oxygen combines with the fat to produce chemicals called *hydroperoxides*, which eventually break down into components that taste and smell bad. Cold slows—but does not stop— the rancidity reaction. To protect shelled pine nuts, put them in a tightly closed container and store in the refrigerator. For longer storage, freeze the pine nuts.

To make a less expensive substitute for pine nuts, shell pumpkin seeds or seeds from other winter squashes and toast them at low heat in an ungreased skillet on top of the stove or on a cookie sheet in the oven. Stir often to keep the seeds from burning. They are done as soon as they are nicely golden. Salt to taste and serve.

POPPY SEED

ABOUT THIS PLANT

Botanical name: *Papaver somniferum*
Also known as: (—)
Native to: Europe, Asia
Parts used as herb: Seeds
Medicinal properties: (—)
Other uses: (—)

ABOUT THIS SPICE AS FOOD AND FLAVORING

Poppy seeds, which are so small that it takes nearly 10 million of them to make one pound, come from the pods of the poppy plant. When you slice into them, the unripe pods ooze a thick latex, the source of opium and its constituents, morphine and codeine. The latex rarely touches the seeds inside the pod; ordinarily, when the pod ripens, there are no narcotics in the seeds or in poppy seed oil, a pale yellow liquid with a pleasant odor and flavor that is used as a food and in making soap, paint and varnishes. (An edible grade of poppy seed oil is sold in Europe and in Asia.)

Nutritional profile. One tablespoon (8.8 g) poppy seeds has 47 calories. It provides 1.6 g protein, 3.9 g fat, 2.1 g carbohydrates, 127 mg calcium and 0.8 mg iron.

HOW THIS SPICE AFFECTS YOUR BODY

Benefits. Poppy seeds are a good source of protein. One tablespoon of seeds has as much protein as one ounce (⅕ cup) cooked, drained lima beans. The proteins in poppy seeds are considered "limited" or "incomplete" because they are deficient in the essential amino acid *lysine*, even though they contain sufficient amounts of other amino acids, including *methionine* and *cystine*. Combining the seeds with grains (flour) as a cake filling or as a topping for bread provides "complete" proteins because grains, which are limited in cystine and methionine, have sufficient amounts of lysine.

Adverse effects. Poppy seeds that have been contaminated with even infinitesimal traces of the latex may produce a false-positive result on a urine test for drugs, suggesting that you have used morphine or heroin, a derivative of morphine, when in fact you have not.

How to Use This Spice

In cooking: The simplest way to crush poppy seeds for use as a cake filling is to wrap the seeds in a kitchen towel and hammer them with a wooden mallet or rolling pin. A more elegant way to do the job is to pulverize the seeds with a mortar and pestle or to put them through a special mill designed for grinding seeds.

RASPBERRY

About This Plant

Botanical name: *Rubus idaeus*
Also known as: Red raspberry, garden raspberry
Native to: Europe
Parts used as herb: Leaves, roots
Medicinal properties: Astringent
Other uses: (—)

About This Herb as Food and Flavoring

Raspberry is a member of the rose family, a shrub with prickly stems and pale green leaves that produces white flowers followed by small red, yellow, black or purple berries. Raspberry leaves, which are high in *tannins*, are used to make an astringent herbal tea. Teas made with dried raspberry leaves are available in health food stores, but be sure to check the label. Since raspberry leaves don't taste or smell like raspberries, some "raspberry" tea mixes may actually be ordinary tea made with raspberry flavoring.
Nutritional profile. (—)

How This Herb Affects Your Body

Tannins are astringents. They coagulate the proteins on the surface of the mucous membrane lining of your mouth, making it pucker. Because tannins have similar effects on your skin or on the membranes lining your gut, plants high in tannins are sometimes used as poultices to stop bleeding from minor cuts or to brew teas that relieve minor diarrhea. (In fact, the North American Indians once used wild raspberry leaves to treat dysentery.)

However, tannins can upset your stomach, and long-term heavy consumption of tannin-rich teas, including ordinary orange pekoe, may be linked to the development of cancers of the nose and throat. Adding milk to the tea binds the tannins so that your body cannot absorb them.

Benefits. Raspberry leaf tea may be used as a mouthwash or to relieve the pain of a minor sore throat. It has no effect on the organisms causing the infection, but it makes your mouth feel pleasantly tingly.

Adverse effects. (—)

How to Use This Herb

As a home remedy: To make raspberry leaf tea, steep 1 tablespoon clean, fresh leaves in 2 cups of boiling water. Steep the leaves for 15 minutes, then strain the tea and sweeten it to taste with orange juice, apple juice, honey or sugar. **Use only unsprayed leaves.**

As a cosmetic: Unsweetened raspberry leaf tea can be used as an astringent "freshening" mouthwash.

RED PEPPER

About This Plant

Botanical name:	*Capsicum annuum, Capsicum frutescens*
Also known as:	Cayenne pepper, chili pepper, hot pepper
Native to:	Central America, South America, the West Indies
Parts used as herb:	Dried ripe seeds and pods
Medicinal properties:	Diaphoretic, counterirritant
Other uses:	(—)

About This Herb as Food and Flavoring

Red pepper, also known as cayenne pepper, is made from the seeds and pods of *Capsicum* peppers, a species completely different from *Piper nigrum*, the plant whose fruit is used as black pepper.

The *Capsicum* peppers are native to Mexico, Central America, the West Indies and much of South America. They may be long and thin like the cayenne pepper, large and firm like the Anaheim, cone shaped like the jalapeno or small and cherry shaped. Tabasco peppers, used to make a popular hot sauce, are a variety of hot peppers known as *Capsicum frutescens*.

Ground red pepper labeled *cayenne pepper* or simply *red pepper* is made by grinding the smaller, more pungent *Capsicums*. The term "red pepper" may also be used to describe ground red pepper milder than cayenne. *Crushed red pepper*, the spice you find in pizza parlors, is made from the seeds of the hot varieties of *Capsicum annuum* and *Capsicum frutescens*. *Chili powder* is a blend of red pepper with other herbs and spices (see CHILI POWDER).

The chemicals that make hot peppers hot are the *capsaicinoids* concentrated in the peppers' seeds and membranes. Capsaicinoids are strong irritants that act directly on the pain receptors in your skin and mucous membranes. The strongest capsaicinoids are *capsaicin* and *dihydrocapsaicin*. Capsaicin is so strong that a single drop diluted in one million drops of water will still warm your tongue. Like dihydrocapsaicin, it delivers a sting all over your mouth. A third capsaicinoid, *nordihydrocapsaicin*, produces a warmer, mellower sensation in the front of your mouth and palate. A fourth, *homodihydrocapsaicin*, packs a delayed punch, delivering a stinging, numbing burn to the back of your throat.

Red pepper gets its color from red, yellow and orange carotenoid pigments. At least three of these pigments—*alpha*-carotene, *beta*-carotene and cryptoxanthin—can be converted to vitamin A in your body.

Nutritional profile. One teaspoon (1.8 g) red pepper has 6 calories. It provides 0.2 g protein, 0.3 g fat, 1 g carbohydrates, 3 mg calcium, 1.4 mg vitamin C and 749 IU vitamin A.

How This Herb Affects Your Body

Capsaicin is a strong irritant. Applied to the skin, it causes the small blood vessels under the skin to dilate, increasing the flow of blood to the area and making the skin feel warm. Though once used as a warming poultice, it is so irritating that it is no longer considerd a safe remedy.

Capsaicin is also a diaphoretic (an agent that increases perspiration). It stimulates nerve endings in your mouth normally stimulated by a rising body temperature, sending impulses to your brain that trigger facial perspiration.

Recent research on laboratory animals suggests that capsaicin may be a low-level carcinogen. Paradoxically, it also appears to be an antioxidant capable of binding and neutralizing enzymes that might otherwise activate carcinogens such as the nitrosamines. Neither of these effects has been demonstrated in human beings, and the low rate of stomach cancer in Central and South America, where red peppers are a significant part of the diet, seems to weigh against their being carcinogens.

Benefits. Foods spiced with pepper may be beneficial when you have hay fever or a cold. The pepper irritates the mucous membranes lining your nose and mouth, causing them to "weep" watery secretion. This may make it easier for you to blow your nose. Because peppery foods make you perspire, they are popular in warm climates. The perspiration they inspire acts as a natural air conditioner, cooling your body as the moisture evaporates on your skin.

Beverages and food spiced with red pepper also stimulate the flow of saliva and encourage the secretion of gastric fluids that set off the contractions we call hunger pangs. This explains red pepper's reputation as an appetite stimulant.

Red pepper is a good source of *beta*-carotene, the pigment in deep yellow fruits and vegetables converted to vitamin A in your body. According to the American Cancer Society, a diet rich in foods high in *beta*-carotene may lower the risk of some forms of cancer.

Vitamin A also protects your eyes. In your body, the vitamin A from red pepper is converted to 11-cis retinol, the most important constituent of *rhodopsin*, a protein in the rods in your retina (the cells that enable you to see in dim light). One teaspoon red pepper provides 19% of the vitamin A a healthy woman needs each day and 15% of the requirement for a healthy man.

Fresh red peppers are also rich in vitamin C. Ounce for ounce, they have more vitamin C than fresh oranges (105 mg/oz versus 50 mg/oz), but drying the vegetables to make ground red pepper destroys most of the vitamin C.

Adverse effects. Eating red peppers may upset your stomach, irritate the lining of your stomach (red peppers are among the very few foods prohibited on an ulcer diet), irritate your bladder so that you have to urinate more frequently or even make urination painful. Some people confuse this urinary irritation with an aphrodisiac effect.

Others mistakenly believe that because pepper makes you urinate more frequently, it will cure a hangover. That's not really true. Your body does eliminate alcohol when you urinate, as well as when you breathe and perspire, but you can only get rid of the alcohol after it has been metabolized (digested) by enzyme action. When you drink more alcohol than your body can metabolize in a given period of time, the unmetablized alcohol is stored in your body tissues, causing headache, muscle aches and upset stomach. As time passes, the excess alcohol is metabolized and eliminated, and your discomfort goes away. There is no way to speed up this process, because you can't speed up your body's production of the necessary enzyme.

How to Use This Herb

In cooking: **Never pick or handle fresh hot chili peppers without protective gloves.** The capsaicin in the white material surrounding the seeds and veins is a severe skin irritant that can continue to burn your skin hours after you have worked with the peppers. Washing with soapy water won't help: Capsaicin does not dissolve in cold water and dissolves only slightly in hot water. It does dissolve in milk fat, alcohol or vinegar. Bathing your hands with one of these may ease the pain. As a culinary corollary, keep in mind that beer (alcohol) or milk (milk fat) really are the beverages of choice to accompany a rousing chili or curry.

As a home remedy: Spicing your hot chicken soup with pepper may help relieve the congestion that comes with a cold.

Rose Hips

About This Plant

Botanical name:	*Rosa* species
Also known as:	Hipberries
Native to:	Europe
Parts used as herb:	Fruit
Medicinal properties:	Antiscorbutic, diuretic
Other uses:	(—)

About This Herb as Food and Flavoring

Rose hips are the bright red ovoid fruits of several different species of wild rose bushes, including *Rosa canina* (the "dog rose"), *Rosa gallica*, *Rosa condita* and *Rosa rugosa* (the Japanese rose). Rose hips can be used straight off the bush as a delicate, fruity garnish for fruit dishes and beverages or brewed into a tea. Or you can remove the seeds and make the rose hips into a jelly or syrup.

Commercially, rose hips are available in tea bags and as loose tea blends. Extracts of rose hips are used in "natural" vitamin C supplements. Rose hips also contain *hesperidin*, a yellow flavonoid (pigment) sometimes known as vitamin P.

Nutritional profile. One ounce (29 g) whole, fresh rose hips provides 156 mg vitamin C.

How This Herb Affects Your Body

Fresh rose hips are an antiscorbutic, a food high in vitamin C that prevents or cures scurvy, the disease caused by a vitamin C deficiency. Teas brewed from rose hips may also be mildly diuretic.

In laboratory animals, hesperidin appears to be used like vitamin C and to strengthen capillaries, the small blood vessels just under the skin. However, the effects of hesperidin and other flavonoids such as rutin have not been demonstrated in human beings.

Benefits. Fresh rose hips are an excellent source of vitamin C. One ounce fresh whole rose hips provides 260% of the vitamin C a healthy adult needs each day. Ounce for ounce, the rose hips have three times as much vitamin C as fresh citrus fruits (156 mg/oz versus 50 mg/oz).

Depending on where the rose hips were grown and how they were collected, dried and stored, dried rose hips may have only 10% to 55% as much vitamin C as fresh hips.

Steeping rose hips in boiling water to make a pleasantly flavored tea extracts about 40% of the vitamin C from fresh rose hips and slightly more than 50% of the vitamin C in dried rose hips; a cup of tea brewed from one ounce of fresh rose hips provides 62 mg vitamin C, 104% of the RDA for a healthy adult.

Adverse effects. Rose pollen is an allergen that can trigger sneezing and watery eyes in sensitive people, and the geraniol in oil of roses may cause contact dermatitis (itching, burning, stinging, reddened or blistered skin) in people who handle the rose bushes. Luckily, neither the pollen nor oil of roses occcurs in rose hips.

How to Use This Herb

In cooking: **CAUTION: When picking fresh rose hips, be sure that the rose bushes from which you are gathering the fruits have never been sprayed with pesticides or grown with fertilizer that contains pesticides.**

As a home remedy: To brew a mildly diuretic rose hip tea, add 2 tablespoons fresh or 1 tablespoon dried rose hips to 1½ cup fresh water. Bring the water to a boil, turn off the heat and let the rose hips steep for 15 minutes. Then strain the tea and use plain or sweeten to taste with orange juice, apple juice, sugar or honey.

Rosemary

About This Plant

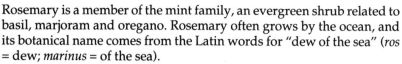

Botanical name:	*Rosmarinus officinalis*
Also known as:	Garden rosemary
Native to:	The Mediterranean
Parts used as herb:	Leaves
Medicinal properties:	(—)
Other uses:	Perfume, preservative, insect repellent

About This Herb as Food and Flavoring

Rosemary is a member of the mint family, an evergreen shrub related to basil, marjoram and oregano. Rosemary often grows by the ocean, and its botanical name comes from the Latin words for "dew of the sea" (*ros* = dew; *marinus* = of the sea).

Rosemary leaves, which look like tiny pine needles, are dark green with silver tips. Their bittersweet, slightly piney flavor comes from oil of rosemary, a colorless or pale yellow liquid that contains astringent *tannins*; peppery scented, sharply mint-flavored *borneol*; *camphor* and *eucalyptol*, which have a penetrating odor and a slightly bitter but cooling taste; and *pinene*, which smells like turpentine. Rosemary also contains the yellow flavonoids (pigments) *apigenin, diosmetin, diosmin,* and *luteolin*, sometimes known collectively as "vitamin P complex."

Rosemary leaves harvested for use as an herb are dried quickly to protect their oil and their dark green color. They are widely available, whole or ground. Oil of rosemary, extracted from the leaves and flowering tops of the plant, is used to flavor candies, baked goods and liqueurs and to perfume a variety of cosmetics, including soaps, creams, lotions, deodorants and hair tonics.

In 1987 researchers at Rutgers University in New Jersey patented a food preservative derived from rosemary. The preservative, a chemical known as *rosmaridiphenol*, is an extremely stable antioxidant that may be useful in cosmetics and in the plastic film used to make food packages.

Nutritional profile. One teaspoon (1.2 g) dried rosemary has 4 calories. It provides 0.1 g protein, 0.2 g fat, 0.8 g carbohydrates, 15 mg calcium, 0.4 mg iron, 0.8 mg vitamin C and 38 IU vitamin A.

How This Herb Affects Your Body

The borneol, camphor, eucalyptol and pinene in oil of rosemary are skin irritants.

In laboratory animals, flavonoids such as those in rosemary seem to work like vitamin C, protecting the strength of the capillaries, small blood vessels just under the skin. However, the effects of flavonoids have not been demonstrated in human beings.

Benefits. (—)

Adverse effects. Prolonged handling of fresh rosemary plants or using cosmetics scented with rosemary oil may cause contact dermatitis (itching, burning, stinging, reddened or blistered skin) in sensitive people.

How to Use This Herb

In cooking: Rosemary is a very pungent herb. As little as ⅛ to ¼ teaspoon of fresh or dried rosemary leaves will season a dish for four people.

To make rosemary vinegar, immerse a sprig of fresh rosemary in a bottle of vinegar and let it marinate for two weeks. Shake every other day to distribute the flavor. Then remove the rosemary. Use the vinegar in salad dressings or as a marinade.

Adding a sprig of fresh rosemary to a jar of honey or orange marmalade gives the sweet a pleasantly bitter undertone.

To dry fresh rosemary, hang the sprigs in a cool, dry place, and dry them quickly. An extra benefit: a lovely fragrance in the air. Store the dried rosemary in airtight containers (glass jars are usually most protective), and use as needed. If you prefer, simply freeze whole sprigs of rosemary; use them as needed in cooking, directly from the freezer.

In the garden: Like basil, peppermint, sage and tansy, rosemary plants have a strong, distinctive odor and appear to act as natural insect repellents in the garden.

SACCHARIN

About This Condiment

Chemical name:	1,2-Benzisothiazol-3(2H)-one 1,1-dioxide
Also known as:	(—)
Native to:	United States
Parts used as condiment:	(—)
Medicinal properties:	Noncaloric sweetener
Other uses:	Flavoring in medication

About This Condiment as Food and Flavoring

Saccharin is a crystalline by-product of petroleum discovered in 1879 by researchers at Johns Hopkins University in Baltimore. It was used originally as an antiseptic and food preservative; not until World War II, when sugar was in short supply, did saccharin become popular as a food sweetener. It is also used to sweeten oral medicines.

Although some people complain that it leaves a bitter aftertaste, saccharin is 300 to 500 times as sweet as ordinary granulated table sugar, so sweet that you can taste it even when diluted to a concentration of one part saccharin in one million parts water.

The saccharin powder sold as a sweetener is made with *saccharin soluble,* a form of saccharin specially treated to make it 150 to 225 times more soluble than ordinary saccharin. It takes 290 ml (9 oz) cold water or 25 ml (0.8 oz) boiling water to dissolve 1 gram regular saccharin. One gram saccharin soluble dissolves in 1.2 ml (0.04 oz) cold water. The packets of saccharin powder sold in grocery stores may contain dextrose (sugar), soluble saccharin, cream of tartar to keep the powder from darkening and calcium silicate or silicon dioxide, anticaking agents that keep the powder from absorbing moisture.

Nutritional profile. One packet saccharin has 2 to 4 calories. It provides no protein, up to 0.5 g carbohydrates, no fat and so little sodium (3.3 mg) per serving that it is considered "sodium free." **However, persons on low salt diets should check with their doctors before using saccharin.**

How This Condiment Affects Your Body

Benefits. Theoretically, saccharin's benefit lies in its ability to reduce the calories in your diet. But most people who save calories by drinking diet sodas or using saccharin instead of sugar in their coffee or tea add calories in other ways. The true value of artificial sweeteners such as saccharin and aspartame lies in their use by people who have diabetes or other medical conditions that require them to avoid sugar.

Adverse effects. Saccharin is excreted rapidly through the kidneys. Several studies with laboratory animals have shown that in large concentrations causes bladder tumors in rats. In 1977, for example, the Canadian government released a three-year study by the Health Protection Branch (the Canadian equivalent of our Food and Drug Administration) showing that large doses of saccharin (5% of the daily diet, equivalent to 800 cans of diet soda a day for a human being) were linked to bladder cancers in laboratory rats.

The FDA then proposed banning saccharin from foods and beverages while still allowing its sale as a nonprescription drug for use as a sugar substitute. Congress, responding to the objections of several major health organizations, including the American Medical Association, the National Academy of Sciences, and the American Diabetes Association, passed the Saccharin Study and Labeling Law, which prohibited the FDA from banning saccharin for 18 months. The prohibition, renewed several times since, is still in effect. However, Congress did pass a law requiring products containing saccharin to carry a warning label and requiring stores selling these products to display a warning poster.

Today, the generally accepted medical view is that saccharin is a weak carcinogen but that the doses required to produce tumors are unusually large. According to the American Dietetic Association, people who use artificial sweeteners have little or no greater risk of cancers of the urinary tract than people who do not use those products. At least three major studies since 1980 have shown no link between bladder cancer and the consumption of artificial sweeteners (although they did show a link between smoking and bladder cancers). Nevertheless, most experts agree that pregnant women should not use saccharin because it may accumulate in fetal tissues.

How to Use This Condiment

In cooking: One packet saccharin powder equals the sweetening power of 2 teaspoons table sugar (25 to 30 calories).

One-fourth teaspoon liquid saccharin solution equals the sweetening power of one packet powdered saccharin or 2 teaspoons granulated table sugar.

SAFFRON

ABOUT THIS PLANT

Botanical name: *Crocus sativus*
Also known as: (—)
Native to: Western Asia, Southern Europe
Parts used as herb: Stigma
Medicinal properties: (—)
Other uses: Natural coloring agent

ABOUT THIS HERB AS FOOD AND FLAVORING

Saffron is a seasoning composed of the dried red brown stigmas of the flower of a plant belonging to the crocus family. Each saffron flower has only three stigmas, which must be handpicked as soon as the flowers open. It takes nearly 60,000 flowers to yield the 225,000 flat, tubular, threadlike stigmas needed to make one pound of saffron. That is why saffron is the world's most expensive seasoning.

Saffron's color comes from carotenoid pigments, chiefly red *crocetin* and *crocin*, which is so powerful a coloring agent (reddish yellow) that one part pure crocin dissolved in 150,000 parts water turns the water distinctively yellow. Saffron also contains *lycopene*, the red pigment in tomatoes; *xanthophyll*, the yellow pigment in egg yolks; *zeaxanthin*, the yellow pigment in yellow corn; and yellow *alpha-*, *beta-* and *gamma*-carotene. Of all these carotenoids, only *alpha-* and *beta*-carotene can be converted by your body to vitamin A. Saffron contains such small amounts of pigments that it is not considered a source of vitamin A.

Saffron's bitter flavor comes from *picrocrocin* (also known as "saffron bitter"), which holds its flavor best in acid dishes. Oil of saffron contains *safranal*, a chemical produced when picrocrocin separates into its constituent parts as the flower stigmas are dried; *pinene*, which smells like turpentine; and *eualyptol*, which smells like camphor and has a spicy flavor.

Saffron is sold as whole or powdered stigmas. Powdered saffron, more concentrated than whole saffron threads, is usually sold in small opaque plastic packets containing about ¹⁄₁₆ of a teaspoon. Thread saffron is usually available in small packets containing about ¼ gram saffron, equal to about ½ teaspoon.

There are a number of other plants whose name includes the word "saffron." *American saffron* is safflower, the plant from which we get safflower oil. *Indian saffron* is a common name for turmeric, which may be used as an honest substitute for saffron or, unscrupulously, to stretch saffron powder. **CAUTION: Meadow saffron** *(Colchicum autumnale),* **which is neither a crocus nor related to saffron, is a poisonous plant, the source of colchicine, a drug used to treat gout. Amateur herbalists should be especially careful not to confuse these two plants, both of which flower in the autumn.**

Nutritional profile. One teaspoon (0.7 g) saffron has 2 calories. It provides 0.1 g protein, a trace of fat, 0.5 g carbohydrates, 1 mg calcium and 0.08 mg iron.

How This Herb Affects Your Body

Benefits. (—)

Adverse effects. Crocin is a choleretic, an agent that stimulates the liver to increase its production of bile. This yellow brown or green fluid helps emulsify fats in your duodenum and increases peristalsis, the rhythmic contractions that move food through your gastrointestinal tract. Choleretics are ordinarily beneficial for healthy people but may pose some problems for people with gallbladder or liver disease. According to the Food and Drug Administration, so little saffron is used in food that it is unlikely to cause harm.

How to Use This Herb

In cooking: Saffron's color, flavor and aroma are extremely sensitive to light. Protect your investment in this expensive seasoning by storing it in tightly closed containers in a cool, dark place.

To bring out the flavor of saffron, stir it into 1 tablespoon hot water before adding it to your dish. For saffron rice, add the saffron to the boiling water *before* you add the rice. For saffron rolls and biscuits, add ¼ teaspoon saffron steeped in 2 tablespoons hot water for each 6 cups of flour.

A little bit of saffron's strong, medicine-like flavor goes a very long way. If you are using saffron mainly for color, use no more than ¼ teaspoon saffron in 2 tablespoons hot water or white wine to season a dish meant for up to eight people.

Turmeric can be used as an inexpensive substitute for saffron. Use very little turmeric: Its acrid flavor can easily overwhelm the food.

SAGE

About This Plant

Botanical name: *Salvia officinale*
Also known as: Salvia
Native to: Southern Europe
Parts used as herb: Leaves, blossoms
Medicinal properties: Astringent
Other uses: Insect repellent

About This Herb as Food and Flavoring

Sage is a woody evergreen shrub that grows in Albania, Italy, Turkey and Yugoslavia. The plant is a member of the mint family, a relative of basil, marjoram and oregano, with violet blue flowers and wooly, gray green leaves.

Fresh, rinsed purple or white sage blossoms may be used to add a mildly spicy flavor to salads, cheese or fruit dishes. The more intensely flavored leaves contain oil of sage, whose penetrating odor comes from *camphor* (26%), plus lemon-scented *limonene*, pleasantly scented *ocimene* and *pinene*, which smells like turpentine. Sage's flavor comes from bitter tasting *thujone*; spicy, camphor-scented *eucalyptol* and astringent *tannins*.

Sage is available either "rubbed" or ground. Rubbed sage, which has gone through a minimum grinding, is a fluffy, velvety powder. Ground sage is a more finely grained powder.

Nutritional profile. One teaspoon (0.7 g) ground sage has 2 calories. It provides 0.1 g protein, 0.1 g fat, 0.4 g carbohydrates, 12 mg calcium, 0.2 mg vitamin C and 41 IU vitamin A.

How This Herb Affects Your Body

Camphor, eucalyptol, limonene, linalool, pinene and thujone are irritants that can cause contact dermatitis (itching, burning, stinging, reddened or blistered skin). Tannins are *astringents*. They coagulate the proteins on the surface of the mucous membrane lining of your mouth, making the tissues pucker.

Alpha-thujone, an important constituent of oil of sage, is also a major component of oil of wormwood, the principal flavoring in absinthe. Thujone is a colorless liquid that can cause gastric upset, irritability, stupor, convulsions resembling epileptic seizures and death. Although plants such as sage, tansy and wormwood that contain thujone cannot

be considered completely harmless, using dried sage leaves as a seasoning is unlikely to be hazardous because much of the thujone, a volatile
oil, appears to evaporate during drying and when the food is heated.

Benefits. Astringent sage tea, used as a gargle, may relieve the pain
of a sore mouth or throat.

Adverse effects. Drinking sage tea may cause cheilitis (peeling
cracked or bleeding lips) or stomatitis (an inflammation of the mucous
membranes lining the mouth) in sensitive people.

How to Use This Herb

As a cosmetic: If you are not sensitive to sage, you can use the herb
to make a scented aftershave. Buy two bottles of plain witch hazel. Pour
½ cup liquid out of one of the bottles, and add ¼ cup crumbled sage
leaves. Cap the bottle and shake it thoroughly. Let it stand for a week,
shaking vigorously each morning and night. At the end of the week,
pour out all the witch hazel in the second bottle, and strain the scented
liquid from the first bottle into the second through a coffee filter or a
clean linen handkerchief. Discard the wet sage leaves. The witch hazel
now has a distinct herbal aroma. If you prefer a stronger scent, repeat
the process, adding another 1/4 cup crumbled dried sage leaves to the
liquid. At the end of the second week, strain the liquid back into the
empty witch hazel bottle, discard the sage leaves and the empty bottle,
and use the liquid as an astringent aftershave.

Sage tea can be used as an after-shampoo rinse to make brunette hair
shiny and smooth. To make the rinse, pour 1 cup boiling water over 1
tablespoon rubbed or ground sage. Let the mix steep for 15 minutes.
Then strain the liquid through a coffee filter or a clean linen handkerchief; use after shampooing.

In the garden: Like basil, peppermint, rosemary, sage and tansy,
the strongly scented sage plant appears to act as a safe, natural pest
control that repels insects without being poisonous for people and pets.

Salt

About This Condiment

Chemical name: Sodium chloride
Also known as: Common salt, NaCl, table salt
Native to: (—)

Parts used as condiment: (—)
Medicinal properties: Essential nutrient
Other uses: Fire extinguisher

About This Condiment as Food and Flavoring

Table salt is a compound composed of two reactive chemicals: sodium (60.7%), a silvery metal that is the sixth most common element on earth, and chlorine (39.3%), a greenish yellow, suffocating gas that is found in the earth's crust and in seawater. When you put these two together, you get sodium chloride ($NaCl$), a white, crystalline substance that occurs in nature as the mineral *halite*.

We get the salt we use on food either by mining rock salt or evaporating seawater. No matter where it comes from, all salt is composed of exactly the same chemical elements. The principal difference between table salt and "sea salt" is that sea salt is naturally iodized, while table salt may or may not contain iodine as an additive.

Nutritional profile. One teaspoon (5 g) table salt has 1,938 mg sodium. The adequate dietary consumption of sodium for a healthy adult is estimated to be 1,100 to 3,300 mg a day depending on age, sex and physical activity.

How This Condiment Affects Your Body

Sodium and chlorine are essential to life. Like potassium, which regulates the balance fo fluids inside our body cells, sodium and chlorine regulate the balance of fluids outside the cells. Together, potassium, sodium and chlorine (known collectively as *electrolytes*), also regulate the acid/base balance of the body.

Sodium is absorbed from your intestines and excreted through your kidneys, under the control of adrenal hormones. It is also excreted in perspiration. If you do not take in enough sodium, or if you excrete too much, you may experience severe muscle weakness and cramps, as well as vomiting and circulatory problems that may culminate in coma and death. On the other hand, if you consume or retain too much sodium, your body may begin to retain water, and you may develop the characteristic swelling of the tissues known as *edema*.

Benefits. Iodized table salt is a valuable source of iodine. Iodine is vital to the thyroid gland, which needs the mineral to make thyroid hormones. If you don't get enough iodine, your thyroid gland swells in an attempt to make more thyroid hormone. This swelling is called goiter.[*]

Adverse effects. Excessive salt consumption has been linked to hypertension (high blood pressure), but how salt triggers high blood pressure is not clear. Some people appear to be more sensitive than others to the effects of salt in the diet. Because there is currently no simple test to tell exactly who will benefit from a low salt regime, the safest course for people with hypertension or a tendency to hypertension is to follow their physician's advice on diet.

How to Use This Condiment

In cooking: Sodium chloride crystals cake when they absorb moisture from the air. To prevent this, some manufacturers add anticaking ingredients such as calcium or magnesium chloride. At home, you can add a few grains of raw rice to the salt cellar to serve the same purpose.

To cook without fat in a pan that does not have a nonstick surface, pour 1 tablespoon salt into the pan, rub the salt into the pan with a paper towel or a dish towel, then pour out the salt. You should now be able to cook pancakes, waffles, potatoes or meat without having it stick.

As a home remedy: To hasten the healing of a cold sore, the American Academy of Otolaryngology–Head and Neck Surgery suggests making a paste of salt and water and putting it on the cold sore as soon as the blisters form. Theoretically, the salt solution will draw water out of the cells of the viruses causing the cold sore. The viruses will be unable to multiply and spread the infection, and the sore should heal.

To relieve a sore throat, gargle with warm saltwater solution. The warm salt gargle appears to loosen and wash away sticky material in your inflamed throat, momentarily easing discomfort. In fact, some studies suggest the warm saltwater gargle is as effective as gargles containing cetylpyridinium or phenol.

As a cosmetic: A slushy paste of salt and water is a cheap, effective dentifrice; a salt/water solution is a cheap and effective mouthwash.

---

[*] People who consume too much iodine may also suffer from goiter because an oversupply of inorganic iodine (the form found in food) keeps the thyroid gland from making organic iodine (the form used to make thyroid hormones). This kind of goiter is likely to occur when iodine consumption exceeds 2,000 micrograms (2 mg) a day. Iodine goiter has been reported in Japan, where seaweed, which is high in iodine, is important in the diet and iodine intake may be as high as 50 to 80,000 micrograms (50–60 mg) a day. According to the FDA, safe consumption of iodine ranges between 50 micrograms and 1,000 micrograms a day; the recommended consumption is 150 mcg a day for everyone older than 11.

SALT SUBSTITUTES

ABOUT THIS CONDIMENT

Chemical name: *Potassium chloride*
Also known as: Sylvite, sylvine
Native to: (—)
Parts used as condiment: (—)
Medicinal properties: Electrolyte replenisher
Other uses: Photography

ABOUT THIS CONDIMENT AS FOOD AND FLAVORING

Salt substitutes are products made with *potassium chloride* instead of *sodium chloride* (table salt). They are designed for people who must limit the amount of sodium in their diet. Potassium chloride is an odorless, salty, white crystalline powder that occurs in nature as deposits of the mineral *sylvine* or *sylvite*. Potassium chloride also occurs naturally in dairy foods, meat, fish, poultry, cereals and potatoes.

Commercial salt substitutes may also contain the antioxidants *potassium bitartrate* (cream of tartar) and *fumaric acid* to keep the seasoning from darkening, and *adipic acid* to give it a tart flavor. A seasoned salt substitute may contain garlic, sugar, onion, paprika and other spices. Some contain salt (sodium chloride), but so little—less than 5 mg—that the product is considered salt free.

Nutritional profile. One-half teaspoon salt substitute made with potassium chloride provides 664 mg potassium. Depending on age and sex, a healthy adult requires 1,875 to 5,625 mg potassium a day.

HOW THIS CONDIMENT AFFECTS YOUR BODY

Potassium is vital to life. It helps regulate the body's acid/base (pH) balance; aids in metabolizing carbohydrates in our liver and muscles; and protects us against the hypertensive effect of sodium. Medicinally, potassium chloride is given intravenously for the potassium depletion that may accompany kidney, liver or heart failure.

Benefits. Salt substitutes allow some people on a sodium-restricted diet to season their food with a salty condiment.

Adverse effects. Consuming excessive amounts of potassium chloride may cause pallor, numbness and tingling in your hands and feet, muscle weakness, gastrointestinal irritation, violent diarrhea, mental confusion and irregular heartbeat. While the amount of potassium chloride we get from salt substitutes is generally considered too small to pose problems for healthy people, the substitutes may be hazardous for people with heart disease, kidney disease, diabetes, too much potassium in the blood (*hyperkalemia*) or insufficient urination (*oliguria*).

Potassium chloride salt substitutes may cause hyperkalemia if taken along with certain diuretics such as spironolactone (Aldactizide, Aldactone) or triamterene (Dyazide, Maxzide). For these reasons, **the safest course is to use these products only on the advice of a physician.**

How to Use This Condiment

In cooking: Salt substitutes may be substituted in equal amounts for sodium chloride at the table and in cooking.

Savory

About This Plant

Botanical name: *Satureja hortensis*
Also known as: Garden savory, summer savory
Native to: The Mediterranean
Parts used as herb: Leaves
Medicinal properties: Antiseptic, astringent
Other uses: Perfumery

About This Herb as Food and Flavoring

Savory is a member of the mint family, related to basil, marjoram and oregano. It is a small, compact plant with pink or white flowers. The small, green or bronze green leaves add a peppery flavor and pungent aroma to meats and vegetables, particularly beans. Savory's spicy flavor and aroma come from oil of savory, which contains *carvacrol*, the chief constituent of oil of thyme; *cymene*, which is used in lemon- and spice-flavored candy and chewing gum; lemon-scented *limonene*; and astringent tannins.

A related plant, winter savory (*Satureja montana*), has stiff, dark green, pointed leaves. Winter savory, also known as Spanish savory, tastes like summer savory, but stronger. Its flavor and aroma come from an oil whose main ingredient is either carvacrol, cymeme or lavender-scented linalool, depending on where the plant is grown. The ground savory sold in grocery stores is summer savory. Winter savory, traditionally used in salamis, is available only from your own garden.

Nutritional profile. One teaspoon (1.4 g) ground summer savory has 4 calories. It provides 0.1 g protein, 0.1 g fat, 1 g carbohydrates, 30 mg calcium, 0.5 mg iron and 72 IU vitamin A.

How This Herb Affects Your Body

Carvacrol and cymene are antiseptics. Tannins are astringents, chemicals that coagulate the proteins on the surface of your skin or the mucous membranes lining your mouth, making the tissues pucker.

Benefits. The astringent tea brewed from summer savory may relieve the sore throat that comes with a cold or help control mild diarrhea.

Adverse effects. (—)

How to Use This Herb

In the garden: To harvest summer savory, cut the green tops while the plants are budding. Hang the stems in a cool, shaded place to dry. Store the dried leaves in a tightly closed container.

Winter savory is an evergreen plant. It can be harvested at any time, but its leaves are less flavorful in winter. Dry and store like summer savory. **Us only unsprayed leaves.**

SCALLIONS

About This Plant

Botanical name:	*Allium cepa* or *Allium fistulosum*
Also known as:	Green onions, spring onions
Native to:	The Mediterranean
Parts used as herb:	Bulb, leaves
Medicinal properties:	(—)
Other use:	Insect repellent

About This Herb as Food and Flavoring

Scallions are immature onions with a small bulb and lots of long green leaves. Like all onions, scallions get their flavor and aroma from sulfur compounds. These chemicals remain innocuous until you cut or peel the onion, tearing its cells and thus releasing an enzyme called *alliinase*, which activates the sulfur chemicals.

Scallions are available fresh or chopped and dried. Because heat converts the sulfur chemicals in onions to sugars (which is why cooked scallions taste sweet), dried scallions are dehydrated without being heated so their flavor is preserved.

Nutritional profile. One-half cup (50 g) chopped scallions (including the bulb and green tops) has 13 calories. It provides 0.9 g protein, a trace of fat, 2.8 g carbohydrates, 30 mg calcium, 0.9 mg iron, 22.5 mg vitamin C and 2,500 IU vitamin A.

How This Herb Affects Your Body

Benefits. If you include the green tops, scallions are a good source of *beta*-carotene, the vitamin A precursor in deep yellow fruits and vegetables. According to the American Cancer Society, a diet rich in these foods may lower the risk of some forms of cancer.

Vitamin A also protects your eyes. In your body, the vitamin A from scallion tops is converted to 11-cis retinol, the most important constituent of *rhodopsin*, a protein in the rods in your retina (the cells that enable you to see in dim light). One-half cup chopped scallion bulbs and tops has 63% of the vitamin A a healthy woman needs each day and 50% of the requirement for a healthy man.

Scallions are also a good source of vitamin C. One-half cup chopped bulbs and tops provides 38% of the RDA for a healthy adult.

Adverse effects. The most common side effect of eating onions (including scallions) is bad breath caused by the sulfur compounds in the onions. Cooking breaks down these compounds; cooked onions are less smelly than raw ones.

How to Use This Herb

In cooking: Do not tear or cut scallion tops until you are ready to use them. When you cut into a food rich in vitamin C, the cells release an enzyme called *ascorbic acid oxidase*. This enzyme destroys vitamin C and reduces the nutritional value of the food.

Chlorophyll, the green coloring in plants, is sensitive to acids. When you heat scallion tops, their chlorophyll reacts with natural acids in the leaves or in the cooking water, forming a brown compound called *pheophytin.* The pheophytin then reacts with the yellow carotene pigments in the leaves, turning the cooked scallion tops bronze. If you add the scallion tops at the end of the cooking process and cook them quickly enough to keep the chlorophyll from reacting with the acids, you can keep them green.

Use chopped fresh scallion tops as a substitute for chives.

In the garden: In the garden, onions (including scallions) appear to act as natural insect repellents, keeping the pests away without being poisonous for people or pets. Some other odorous herbs that act this way are basil, marigold, nasturtium, peppermint, rosemary, sage and tansy.

SEAWEED

About This Plant

Botanical name:	*Gelidium, Chondrus crispus, Laminaria, Undaria*
Also known as:	Agar, agar-agar, Chinese or Japanese isinglass, red algae (*Gelidium*), Irish moss, carrageen (*Chondrus crispus*), kelp, brown algae, kombu tangleweed (*Laminaria*)
Native to:	Pacific and Indian oceans, North Atlantic
Parts used as herb:	Whole plants or their extracts, leaves and extracted gums
Medicinal properties:	Iodine source
Other uses:	Laxatives, stabilizers

About This Herb as Food and Flavoring

Seaweed is used as a vegetable in Japan. In America it is used as a garnish or as a source of *alginates*, the indigestible gums used as thickeners and gelling agents.

Agar, also known as Chinese or Japanese isinglass, is dried to make an odorless, tasteless, colorless powder used as a gelling agent. It is also used in ice creams, salad dressings, icings and glazes, cosmetics, gelatin capsules for medications, impressions for dentures, fabric and paper sizing, adhesives and bacterial cultures. Agar forms a strong gel at about

96 degrees F (36 degrees C) and it stays firm even at temperatures as high as 202 degrees F (95 degrees C).

Carrageen, the alginate from Irish moss, became popular as a substitute for agar during World War II. It is used like agar, but it turns thin in acid foods.

Powdered kelp (sometimes labeled Brown Algae) is often sold as a "natural" alternative to table salt. In fact, all salt—whether extracted from seawater (sea salt), seaweed or mineral deposits in the earth—is the same chemical combination of sodium and chloride ions. Some table salts contain added iodine; all sea salts and powdered kelp salts are naturally iodized. Kelp also yields alginates used as thickeners in cosmetics and foods.

Wakame is a species of kelp.

Nutritional profile. One ounce (29 g) dried agar has 87 calories. It provides 1.8 g protein, 0.1 g fat, 23.1 g carbohydrates, 178.6 mg calcium and 7 mg iron.

Three and one-half ounces (100 g) raw Irish moss has 49 calories. It provides 1.5 g protein, 0.2 g fat, 12.3 g carbohydrates, 72 mg calcium and 8.9 mg iron.

Three and one-half ounces (100 g) raw kelp has 43 calories. It provides 1.68 g protein, 0.6 g fat, 9.6 g carbohydrates, 168 mg calcium, 2.9 mg iron and 116 IU vitamin A.

Three and one-half ounces (100 g) raw laver has 35 calories. It provides 5.8 g protein, 0.3 g fat, 5 g carbohydrates, 70 mg calcium, 1.8 mg iron, 39 mg vitamin C and 5,202 IU vitamin A.

Three and one-half ounces (110 g) raw wakame has 45 calories. It provides 3 g protein, 0.6 g fat, 9 g carbohydrates, 150 mg calcium, 2.2 mg iron, 3 mg vitamin C and 360 IU vitamin A.

How This Herb Affects Your Body

Because they absorb moisture, all the alginates extracted from seaweed are effective, bulk-forming laxatives. Carrageen is a demulcent (an agent that soothes skin and mucous membranes). It is also a suspected carcinogen, causing tumors when injected into laboratory animals.

Benefits. Seaweed is rich in calcium. One ounce dried agar provides 22% of the 800 milligrams calcium recommended each day for a healthy adult. Three and one-half ounces raw kelp provides 21% of the RDA for calcium; 3½ ounces raw wakame provides 18% of the RDA.

Seaweed is a good source of nonheme iron, the form of iron found in plants. Nonheme iron is five times harder for your body to absorb than heme iron, the organic iron found in meat, fish, poultry, milk and eggs. Eating seaweed with meat or a food rich in vitamin C increases the amount of iron you get from the seaweed. Meat increases the secretion of stomach acids, and iron is absorbed more easily in an acid environment. Vitamin C changes the iron in seaweed from the ferric form to the ferrous, which is more easily absorbed. One ounce dried agar has 46% of the 15 milligrams iron a healthy woman needs each day. Three and one-half ounces raw kelp has 19% of the RDA; 3½ ounces raw wakame provides 15%.

Laver is a good source of beta-carotene, the vitamin A precursor in deep yellow fruits and vegetables. According to the American Cancer Society, a diet rich in these foods may lower the risk of some forms of cancer.

Vitamin A also protects your eyes. In your body, the vitamin A from laver is converted to 11-cis retinol, the most important constituent of *rhodopsin*, a protein in the rods in your retina (the cells that enable you to see in dim light). One ounce laver provides 37% of the vitamin A a healthy woman needs each day and 30% of the requirement for a healthy man.

Finally, seaweed is a good source of vitamin C. Three and one-half ounces raw laver provides 69% of the 60 mg a healthy adult needs each day.

Adverse effects. Because it is high in sodium, seaweed is likely to be prohibited on a sodium-restricted diet. Powdered seaweed is **not** a low sodium substitute for table salt.

All seaweed is high in iodine. Exactly how much iodine there is in a serving of seaweed varies from species to species, but it is not uncommon for dried seaweed to have concentrations as high as 0.4–0.6%. This works out to 116–174 mg iodine per ounce, nearly 800 times the recommended daily allowance (150 micrograms).[*] Iodine is vital to the thyroid gland, which needs the mineral to make thyroid hormones. If you don't get enough iodine, your thyroid gland will swell in an attempt to make more thyroid hormone. This swelling is called goiter. People who consume too much iodine may also suffer from goiter because an oversupply of inorganic iodine (the form found in food) keeps the thyroid gland from making organic iodine (the form used to make thyroid hormones). This kind of goiter is likely to occur when iodine consumption exceeds 2,000 micrograms (2 mg) a day. Iodine goiter has been reported in Japan, where seaweed is important in the diet and iodine intake may be as high as 50,000 to 80,000 micrograms (50 to 80 mg) a day.

---

[*] One gram = 1,000 milligrams = 1,000,000 micrograms. A microgram is one-thousandth of a milligram or one-millionth of a gram.

How to Use This Herb

In cooking: Before using seaweed as a garnish or vegetable, you must soak it in cool water for at least 2 hours, changing the water several times to get rid of the "weedy" iodine taste.

SESAME SEEDS

About This Plant

Botanical name:	*Sesamum indicum*
Also known as:	Benne seed
Native to:	Africa, India, Afghanistan, Indonesia
Parts used as herb:	Seed
Medicinal properties:	Emollient, laxative
Other uses:	Medical solvent

About This Herb as Food and Flavoring

Sesame seeds come from a tall herb whose single hairy stalk can grow as high as seven feet, although a two to four foot stalk is much more common. The seeds are tiny flat ovals, less than ⅛ inch long and ¹⁄₂₀ inch thick. Whole sesame seeds can be dark (with their hulls), white (hulled) or tan (hulled and roasted). Crushed sesame seeds are known as "tahini," an oily paste that looks and tastes something like peanut butter.

Sesame oil, also known as benne oil ("benne" is the African word for sesame), is clear and golden when pressed from unroasted sesame seeds and dark amber when pressed from roasted seeds. The golden oil is used in cooking, in margarines, in cosmetics and as a solvent in medicines. The dark oil is used mainly in Oriental cooking. Sesame seed oil is exceptionally stable and much less likely to become rancid than other salad and cooking oils so long as you keep it in a cool, dark place.

Nutritional profile. One tablespoon (8 g) sesame seeds with the hull removed has 47 calories. It provides 2.1 g protein, 4.4 g fat, 0.8 g carbohydrates, 10 mg calcium, 0.6 mg iron and 5 IU vitamin A.

One tablespoon (15 g) tahini (ground sesame seeds) has 90 calories. It provides 3 grams protein, 8 grams fat, 3 g carbohydrates, 21 mg calcium, 0.7 mg iron, 1 mg vitamin C and 10 IU vitamin A.

One ounce (29 g) sesame oil has 253 calories. It provides 29 g fat.

How This Herb Affects Your Body

Sesame seed oil, like other vegetable oils, is a source of *tocopherol* (vitamin E), an antioxidant that appears to block the formation of *nitrosamines*, chemicals that cause cancer in laboratory animals. Laboratory studies also suggest that vitamin E may protect the lining of the lungs against the effects of air pollutants, and some laboratory studies suggest that it may retard the deterioration of body cells. As yet these effects have not been demonstrated in human beings.

Nor is there any proof that vitamin E relieves menopausal hot flashes and vaginal dryness or that it improves male sexual performance. This mistaken belief is based on a misinterpretation of an early study showing that male laboratory animals deficient in vitamin E were infertile. Vitamin E has no known effect on human infertility.

Benefits. Sesame seeds are a good source of protein. One ounce sesame seeds has as much protein as 8 ounces of milk, 1 ounce of cheddar cheese or ¼ cup cottage cheese. The proteins in sesame seeds are considered "limited" or "incomplete" because they are deficient in the essential animo acid lysine. But the seeds contain sufficient amounts of other amino acids, including methionine and tryptophan. Combining sesame seeds with grains or beans, which are limited in methionine and cystine, provides "complete" proteins.

To see how this works, consider the Protein Efficiency Ratio (PER) of a seed/bean combination versus the PER for the seeds alone. The PER is a number derived by calculating the grams of weight a laboratory rat gains for each gram of protein he consumes. The PER for casein (milk protein), a complete protein well absorbed by the human body, is arbitrarily set at 2.35. The PER for sesame flour is only 1.19, well below casein's. But a flour composed of 50% navy bean flour and 50% sesame flour has a PER of 2.30, just about equal to casein's.

Sesame seed, which has no cholesterol, is high in unsaturated fats. The oil is approximately 16% saturated fatty acids, 41% monosaturated fatty acids and 43% polyunsaturated fatty acids.

Adverse effects. (—)

How to Use This Herb

In cooking: To preserve the flavor of sesame seeds and sesame oils, store them in a cool, dark place. In warm weather, refrigerate the oil.

To make ½ cup tahini, put 2 tablespoons sesame seeds in a blender and grind until smooth. Then add ½ teaspoon sesame oil, ¼ teaspoon salt, and slowly pour in ¼ cup tepid water. Blend until smooth.

Tahini may be used as a substitute for peanut butter.

Sesame seeds can be used as a substitute for finely chopped almonds.

SHALLOTS

ABOUT THIS PLANT

Botanical name:	*Allium ascalonicum*
Also known as:	(—)
Native to:	Western Asia
Parts used as herb:	Bulbs, tops
Medicinal properties:	(—)
Other uses:	Insect repellent

ABOUT THIS HERB AS FOOD AND FLAVORING

Shallots smell and taste like onions, but they look like dark garlic, with clusters of brown-skinned bulbs at the bottom of the plant. Some shallots are gray skinned. The gray shallots have a sharper, stronger flavor than the brown-skinned ones.

Like all onions, shallots get their flavor from sulfur compounds that are activated by the enzyme alliinase when you cut or peel the bulb. When you cook shallots, the heat converts the sulfur compounds to sugars, which is why cooked shallots taste sweet, not sharp.

Shallots are available fresh or freeze-dried.

Nutritional profile. One tablespoon (10 g) chopped raw shallots has 7 calories. It provides 0.3 g protein, a trace of fat, 1.7 g carbohydrates, 4 mg calcium, 0.1 mg iron and 0.8 mg vitamin C.

One tablespoon (0.9 g) freeze-dried shallots has 3 calories. It provides 0.1 g proteins, no fat, 0.7 g carbohydrates, 2 mg calcium, a trace of iron and 0.4 mg vitamin C.

HOW THIS HERB AFFECTS YOUR BODY

Benefits. (—)

Adverse effects. The most common side effect of eating onions (including shallots) is bad breath caused by the sulfur compounds in the onions. Cooking breaks down these compounds, so cooked onions are less smelly than raw ones.

How to Use This Herb

In cooking: If you store shallots in a cool, dark cabinet, they can stay fresh for as long as four weeks.

To peel shallots, first immerse them in boiling water. Then lift them out with a slotted spoon, and plunge them into cold water. The papery skin should now slip off easily.

Three to four medium shallot bulbs equals the flavor of one medium yellow onion.

If you grow your own shallots, you can pull the green tops and use them as a substitute for scallions or chives.

In the garden: In the garden, strong-scented herbs such as onions and garlic appear to act as natural insect repellents, keeping the pests away without being poisonous to people or pets. Some other herbs that act this way are basil, marigold, nasturtium, peppermint, rosemary, sage and tansy.

SMOKE FLAVORING

About This Condiment

Chemical name:	(—)
Also known as:	Liquid smoke
Native to:	(—)
Parts used as condiment:	(—)
Medicinal properties:	(—)
Other uses:	(—)

About This Condiment as Food and Flavoring

Liquid smoke is a solution of water plus flavor compounds extracted from wood smoke. The smoke comes from wood burned with very little air and treated to remove some of the resinous materials ("tars") that contain cancer-causing *benzopyrenes*. The most popular woods used to make liquid wood smoke are the flavorful ones such as hickory, maple and mesquite. Liquid smoke is used chiefly in processed foods. At home it is used to lend a barbequed flavor to food prepared in the oven or broiler.

Nutritional profile. (—)

How This Condiment Affects Your Body

Benefits. (—)

Adverse effects. In 1981 the Food and Drug Administration published the results of three major toxicity studies showing that liquid smoke appeared safe even in amounts 4,000 times greater than those normally in food. When tested on bacteria, smoke flavorings did not appear to be mutagens, agents that cause mutations in genetic material. However, in 1988 researchers at the Massachusetts Institute of Technology (MIT) announced the results of another study. When liquid smoke was applied to human white blood cells in test tubes it was mutagenic at concentrations of about 20 parts per million (ppm), making it about five times more active than the solids from diesel smoke.

SORREL

About This Plant

Botanical name:	*Rumex acetosa*
Also known as:	Garden sorrel
Native to:	Europe
Parts used as herb:	Leaves
Medicinal properties:	Antiscorbutic
Other uses:	(—)

About This Herb as Food and Flavoring

Sorrel is a member of the *Rumex* family, a group of plants that includes yellow dock (*Rumex crispus*). Sorrel's dark green, arrow-shaped leaves get their distinctive bitter flavor from a combination of sharp tasting chemicals including oxalic acid (also found in spinach); *malic acid* (the chemical that gives immature apples and some mature sour apples their bite); astringent *tannic acid; tartaric acid*; and vitamin C (ascorbic acid).

As a vegetable, sorrel is usually combined with spinach or Swiss chard. As a garnish, it is used in small amounts to season eggs and meat, as an ingredient in sauces or as one of the herbs on which fish is steamed.

Nutritional profile. One-half cup (67 g) chopped fresh leaves of *Rumex* plants has 15 calories. It provides 1.3 g protein, 2.1 g carbohydrates, 29 mg calcium, 1.6 mg iron, 32.2 mg vitamin C and 2,680 IU vitamin A.

How This Herb Affects Your Body

Like spinach, sorrel is high in *oxalates*, which may be hazardous in large quantities. Oxalic acid is a caustic chemical that may irritate your skin and the lining of your stomach. It is also mildly laxative.

Benefits. Sorrel leaves are so high in vitamin C that they were once used as an antiscorbutic (a food that prevents or cures the vitamin C–deficiency disease, scurvy). One-half cup chopped fresh sorrel leaves provides 54% of the daily requirement for a healthy adult.

The dark green leaves of *Rumex* are a good source of the yellow carotenoid pigment, *beta*-carotene, the vitamin A precursor in deep yellow fruits and vegetables. According to the American Cancer Society, a diet rich in these foods may lower the risk of some forms of cancer.

Vitamin A also protects your eyes. In your body, the vitamin A precursors from plants are converted to 11-cis retinol, the most important constituent of *rhodopsin*, a protein in the rods in your retina (the cells that enable you to see in dim light). One-half cup chopped fresh *Rumex* leaves provides 67% of the vitamin A a healthy woman needs each day and 54% of the requirement for a healthy man.

Adverse effects. Sorrel's pollen is a potential respiratory allergen that may trigger allergic rhinitis (hay fever) and bronchial asthma in sensitive people.

Foods such as spinach and sorrel, which are high in calcium and oxalates, are prohibited on a low-calcium, low-oxalate diet for people who form calcium-oxalate kidney stones. They may also be prohibited for people with arthritis or gout. **Large quantities of sorrel tea may be poisonous.**

How to Use This Herb

In cooking: Do not tear or cut sorrel leaves until you are ready to use them. When you cut into a food rich in vitamin C, the cells release an enzyme called *ascorbic acid oxidase*. This enzyme destroys vitamin C and reduces the nutritional value of the food.

To reduce the oxalic acid content of sorrel leaves, blanch the leaves and discard the cooking water three times before using the sorrel for a vegetable dish or green sauce. **Use only unsprayed leaves.**

Chlorophyll, the green coloring in plants, is sensitive to acids. When you heat sorrel leaves, their chlorophyll reacts with natural acids in the leaves or in the cooking water, forming a brown compound called *pheophytin*. The pheophytin then reacts with the yellow carotene pigments in the leaves, turning the cooked sorrel bronze.

Sorrel, like spinach, is high in *tannins*, which react with metals to form dark pigments. If you cook sorrel or spinach in an aluminum or iron pot, these pigments discolor the pot and the leaves as well. To keep sorrel and spinach from darkening, cook them in a glass pot or a pot with an enameled surface.

SOY SAUCE

ABOUT THIS CONDIMENT

Chemical name: (—)
Also known as:—Shoyu, Tamari
Native to: Far East
Parts used as condiment: Fermented beans
Medicinal properties: (—)
Other uses: (—)

ABOUT THIS CONDIMENT AS FOOD AND FLAVORING

Soy sauce is a condiment made by adding salt to cooked soybeans and then setting the mixture aside to ferment. The result is a liquid containing amino acids, proteins, carbohydrates and other organic compounds in a solution of sodium chloride (salt).

The smoothest, most flavorful soy sauces are the "Oriental type" made from fermented soybeans, roasted wheat salt, yeast or malt and sugar. They are sometimes allowed to ferment for as long as a year and a half. "Light" soy sauces are paler and less intensely flavored, but saltier than "dark" soy sauces. The light soy sauces work well with fish and chicken, when you don't want the color or the flavor of the sauce to overwhelm the dish. Dark soy sauces work best in stews or with beef.

During fermentation up to 70% of the vitamins in soybeans are destroyed. Among the constituents of soy sauce are *adenine* (a B vitamin); *arginine* (an essential amino acid also found in gelatin); *choline* (a vitamin-like substance in plant and animal cells important in the transmission of impulses between nerves); *lysine* (an essential amino acid); *betaine* (closely related to choline); and *glutaminc acid* (a nonessential amino acid whose sodium salt, monosodium glutamate, is used as a flavor enhancer).

Nutritional profile. One tablespoon (18 g) soy sauce has 10 calories. It provides 2 g protein, no fat, 2 g carbohydrates, 3 mg calcium, 0.5 mg iron and 1,029 mg sodium.

How This Condiment Affects Your Body

Benefits. Adding soy sauce to vegetables appears to increase the amount of iron you absorb from them. *Non-heme iron*, the kind of iron found in plant foods, is much less easily absorbed than *heme iron*, the form of iron found in meat, fish, poultry and eggs. In 1988 scientists from the United States, China and Great Britain released the results of a five-year study showing that people in China have no widespread iron deficiencies even though they get their iron primarily from vegetables. The scientists concluded that soy sauce and other fermented condiments used by the Chinese make nonheme iron more available to the body. Exactly how this happens remains to be shown.

Adverse effects. Soy sauce, which is high in sodium, is usually prohibited on a sodium-restricted diet.

Soy sauce is high in *tyramine*, a natural by-product formed when proteins are fermented. Tyramine is a pressor amine, a chemical that constricts blood vessels and triggers an increase in blood pressure. Monoamine oxidase (MAO) inhibitors—drugs used as antidepressants—interfere with the action of enzymes that break down tyramine. If you eat a food such as soy sauce (which is high in tyramine) while taking an MAO inhibitor, the tyramine cannot be eliminated from your body. The result may be a hypertensive crisis (sustained elevated blood pressure).

How to Use This Condiment

In cooking: You can "tenderize" and season a tough cut of beef by marinating it in an acid such as wine, vinegar or soy sauce, which breaks down the muscle fibers in the beef. But these marinades may also destroy the thiamine (vitamin B_1) in the meat. A 1986 study from the Hawkesbury Agricultural College in Richmond, Australia, suggests that marinating beef in soy sauce may reduce the thiamine (vitamin B_1) content of the beef by as much as 44%. (According to the study, red wine is the marinade least likely to destroy thamine.)

SPEARMINT

ABOUT THIS PLANT

Botanical name: *Mentha spicata*
Also known as: Mint
Native to: The Mediterranean
Parts used as herb: Leaves; oil
Medicinal properties: Carminative, choleretics, expectorant
Other uses: Pest repellent

ABOUT THIS HERB AS FOOD AND FLAVORING

Spearmint is a member of the mint family with pointed, slightly crinkly, pale green leaves. Their flavor and aroma are sweeter and less pungent than those of peppermint leaves.

Spearmint's flavor and aroma come from oil of spearmint, a colorless, yellow or yellow green liquid that is at least 50% *l*-Carvone, a chemical that smells like spearmint. (*d*-Carvone, which smells like caraway, is the primary [more than 50%] ingredient in oil of caraway.) Oil of spearmint also contains lemon-scented *limonene; pinene*, which smells like turpentine; and a little bit of *menthol*.

Spearmint leaves taste best when they are freshly picked, but they are sold dried in grocery stores.

Nutritional profile. (—)

HOW THIS HERB AFFECTS YOUR BODY

Carvone, limonene, menthol and pinene are irritants that may cause contact dermatitis (itching, burning, stinging, reddened or blistered skin). Limonene and menthol are also allergic sensitizers; exposure to them may make you sensitive to other allergens. Carvone and menthol are *carminatives*; they help break up and expel intestinal gas.

Benefits. Long use as a folk remedy suggests that inhaling the pungent fumes from a cup of tea brewed from spearmint leaves may help clear a stuffy nose when you have a cold or the tea may act as an expectorant (an agent that causes the mucous membranes in your bronchial tubes to "weep" watery secretions that may help you cough up mucus), but there is no scientific proof that this is so.

Adverse effects. Like coffee, fatty foods and carbonated beverages, mint oils may irritate the sphincter (muscle ring) at the base of your esophagus, permitting food from your stomach to flow back into the esophagus and create the discomfort we call heartburn.

How to Use This Herb

In cooking: To protect the flavor of fresh-picked mint leaves, store them in the refrigerator or freeze them in airtight plastic bags or containers.

To protect the flavor of dried mint leaves, do not crumble them until you are ready to use them.

Adding two or three spearmint leaves per pint of your favorite recipe for tomato sauce will add a surprising, zesty note to the sauce.

As a home remedy: Spearmint tea may be a triple threat for minor health problems by relieving a mildly upset stomach, soothing a sore throat and helping clear the stuffy nose that comes with a cold.

Around the house: Mice are reputed to dislike the odor of mint, avoiding any area where mint grows or mint leaves are scattered.

In the garden: To make a natural pest repellent not poisonous to people or pets, pour 3 cups boiling water over 1 cup spearmint leaves, let steep for 30 minutes and then strain the liquid. Spray your garden plants to protect them from many common pests. For the best results, spray once a week.

STAR ANISE

About This Plant

Botanical name:	*Illicium verum*
Also known as:	Chinese anise
Native to:	The Far East
Parts used as spice:	Dried fruit
Medicinal properties:	Carminative, expectorant
Other uses:	Fragrance

About This Spice as Food and Flavoring

Star anise is a small evergreen tree that grows wild in southern China. The tree produces fruits that open out into the shape of a star as they ripen. This accounts for the "star" in star anise's name. The "anise" comes from the fact that, even though they are not botanically related, star anise tastes and smells like anise.

Despite the fact that they come from different plants, oil of anise and oil of star anise are considered to be interchangeable. Both are widely used as flavorings in commercial baked goods, cough syrups, cough drops, dentifrices, chewing gum, tobacco and the licorice-flavored liqueurs ouzo and anisette. Anisette is a nonpoisonous substitute for absinthe, the original licorice-flavored liqueur made with oil of wormwood (*Absinthum*). Oil of wormwood contains *thujone*, a central nervous system poison related to THC (*tetrahydrocannabinol*), the active ingredient in marijuana. Because thujone may cause gastrointestinal upset, nervousness, stupor, convulsions and death, absinthe has been banned in France since 1915 and is illegal in this country.

Neither oil of anise nor oil of star anise contains thujone. Their flavor comes from *anethole*, which tastes like licorice; *methylchavicol*, which is related to *chavicol*, one of the chemicals that gives black pepper its bite; and vanilla- flavored *anisaldehyde*. Oil of star anise also contains *estragole*, the main constituent of oil of tarragon; *eucalyptol*, a spicy cool chemical that smells like camphor; lemony scented *limonene*; *acrid quinic acid*; penetrating *terpineol*; and salty *trigonelline* (nicotinic acid). **CAUTION: Do not confuse Chinese star anise with Japanese star anise (*Illicium lanceolatum*), a poisonous plant used as an agricultural pesticide in the Far East.**

Nutritional profile. (—)

How This Spice Affects Your Body

Anethole ("anise camphor"), limonene and phellandrene are irritants. They may cause contact dermatitis (itching, burning, stinging, reddened or blistered skin). In laboratory animals anethole is poisonous when absorbed through the skin.

Eucalyptol and terpineol are expectorants, agents that increase the secretion of liquid from the mucous membranes lining the respiratory tract, thus making it easier for you to cough up mucus.

Oil of anise is a carminative, an agent that helps break up and expel intestinal gas.

Benefits. (—)

Adverse effects. Dentrifices flavored with oil of anise have been reported to cause cheilitis (dry, peeling and bleeding lips), sometimes mistaken for the simple chapping that occurs in cold weather.

How to Use This Spice

In cooking: Star anise is the main ingredient in Chinese five spice powder, which also contains fennel, cinnamon or cassia, cloves and Szechwan peppercorns.

To brew star anise tea, pour 1 cup boiling water over 1 teaspoon crushed star anise seeds. Let the tea steep for 5 minutes. Then strain into a warmed cup and, if desired, sweeten to taste with honey or sugar.

As a cosmetic: The Chinese chew whole star anise seeds as a breath sweetener.

Around the house: The scent of anise is attractive to rodents. Dusting star anise seeds on your mousetraps may make them more effective.

SUGAR

About This Plant

Chemical name:	Sucrose
Also known as:	Cane sugar, beet sugar, table sugar
Native to:	Tropical areas
Parts used as condiment:	(—)
Medicinal properties:	Demulcent, antiseptic
Other uses:	Preservative

About This Condiment as Food and Flavoring

Sugar, a sweetening agent made from sugarcane and sugar beets, is a crystalline powder that can absorb up to 1% of its weight in water from the air. In its simplest form, it is known as white sugar or table sugar. Brown sugar is essentially white sugar with molasses added.

Nutritional profile. One packet (6 g) table sugar has 25 calories. It provides 6 g carbohydrates and a trace of calcium and iron.

One tablespoon (12 g) table sugar has 45 calories. It provides 12 g carbohydrates and a trace of calcium and iron.

One cup (200 g) table sugar has 770 calories. It provides 199 g carbohydrates, 3 mg calcium and 0.1 mg iron.

One level cup (220 g) brown sugar has 820 calories. It provides 212 g carbohydrates, 187 mg calcium, 4.8 mg iron.

How This Condiment Affects Your Body

Benefits. Sucrose is a concentrated source of energy, but it provides no nutrients other than carbohydrates. Brown sugar provides only insignificant amounts of minerals and B vitamins from molasses.

Adverse effects. Sugars stick to your teeth, providing food for the bacteria that cause cavities.

Some people develop higher levels of triglycerides (fatty acids) in their blood when they eat a diet high in sugar, but there is no evidence that eating sugar causes heart disease.

Nor does eating sugar cause diabetes. However, people who have diabetes cannot use sucrose efficiently because they lack sufficient amounts of the pancreatic enzyme that enables the body to metabolize (digest) sucrose.

How to Use This Condiment

In cooking: One cup of white sugar has the sweetening power of 1 cup packed brown sugar *or* ¾ cups confectioner's sugar *or* 2 cups corn syrup *or* ⅓ cups molasses. Because these sweeteners contain different amounts of moisture, you cannot substitute them in cooking or baking without adjusting the liquid content of the recipe.

SWEET CICELY

About This Plant

Botanical name:	*Myrrhis odorata*
Also known as:	British myrrh, sweet chervil
Native to:	Europe
Parts used as herb:	Flowers, leaves, seeds
Medicinal properties:	(—)
Other uses:	(—)

About This Herb as Food and Flavoring

Sweet cicely is a decorative plant with lacy, fernlike leaves and small white flowers. The leaves, flowers and stem tips smell like anise and have a sugary sweet flavor with licorice overtones. All can be used fresh in salads or boiled to make a licorice-flavored liquid used in fruit pies and compotes. Sweet cicely's licorice-flavored small green seeds can be used in salads and fruit dishes or steeped in vodka to make a licorice-flavored drink.

Sweet cicely is available only from your own garden.

Nutritional profile. (—)

How This Herb Affects Your Body

Benefits. (—)
Adverse effects. (—)

How to Use This Herb

In cooking: When stewing fruit, substitute 2 to 4 teaspoons chopped fresh cicely leaves for 1 teaspoon sugar. Or boil ¼ cup cicely leaves and stem tips in 1 cup water and drain. Use in place of 1 cup water plus 2 teaspoons sugar when poaching fruit. **Use only unsprayed leaves.**

In baking, sprinkle dried cicely seeds on cookies for a sweet licorice flavor.

Around the house: Dried sweet cicely leaves and seeds add a licorice scent to potpourris and sachets.

TARRAGON

About This Plant

Botanical name:	*Artemisia dracunculus*
Also known as:	Estragon, Frech tarragon
Native to:	North America, U.S.S.R. (Siberia)
Parts used as herb:	Leaves
Medicinal properties:	(—)
Other uses:	Perfumery

About This Herb as Food and Flavoring

Tarragon is a tall weedy plant whose name is an anglicization of the Spanish word "tarragon" and the French word "estragon," both derived from the Greek word for "little dragon," a reference to tarragon's snakelike roots. Tarragon has slender stems and narrow dark blue green leaves. Because tarragon's flavoring oil evaporates when the leaves are dried, fresh tarragon is much more flavorful than dried.

The main flavoring ingredient in oil of tarragon is *estragole*, which tastes and smells like licorice. Oil of tarragon is used as a food flavoring, particularly in vinegar and pickles, and as a perfume. Tarragon is also an important source of *rutin*, the yellow flavonoid (pigment) that is included in the group of chemicals sometimes known collectively as "vitamin P."

Nutritional profile. One teaspoon (1.6 g) ground tarragon has 5 calories. It provides 0.4 g protein, 0.1 g fat, 0.8 g carbohydrates, 18 mg calcium, 0.5 mg iron and 67 IU vitamin A.

How This Herb Affects Your Body

In laboratory animals flavonoids such as rutin seem to work like vitamin C and to protect the strength of the capillaries, small blood vessels just under the skin. But these effects have not been demonstrated in human beings.

Estragole has been reported to produce tumors in laboratory mice. No such effect has been reported in human beings.

Benefits. (—)

Adverse effects. (—)

How to Use This Herb

In cooking: To preserve the flavor of fresh tarragon leaves, freeze the leaves in an airtight container. Unlike drying, which evaporates the flavoring oils, freezing protects them; frozen tarragon leaves will hold their flavor for as long as three to five months. Use the leaves right out of the freezer; there's no need to defrost them first.

For a flavorful tarragon vinegar, add a sprig of clean, freshly cut tarragon to a bottle of distilled white vinegar. Let it steep for three to four days, and then taste the vinegar. If necessary, continue steeping until the flavor meets your preference.

THYME

ABOUT THIS PLANT

Botanical name: *Thymus vulgaris*
Also known as: Common thyme,
garden thyme
Native to: Southern Europe
Parts used as herb: Leaves
Medicinal properties: Carminative
Other uses: Insect repellent

ABOUT THIS HERB AS FOOD AND FLAVORING

Thyme (pronounced "time") is a member of the mint family, a relative of basil, marjoram and oregano, with woody stems, clusters of small lavender flowers and ¼-inch long oval, gray green leaves.

There are more than 100 varieties of thyme—each looks slightly different and has a slightly different flavor and aroma. Thyme from England has broad leaves; French thyme has narrow leaves; and winter thyme from Germany stays green all winter. There are also thymes that taste and smell like lemon, mint, pine, licorice, caraway or nutmeg. The whole or ground thyme you get at the grocery store is dried *Thymus vulgaris*.

The most important flavor and aroma chemical in thyme is *thymol*. Oil of thyme, a colorless to reddish brown liquid, also contains sharp tasting, peppery scented *borneol, carvacrol* (which smells like thymol), *linalool* (which smells like French lavender) and *pinene* (which smells like turpentine).

Nutritional profile. One teaspoon (1.4 g) ground thyme has 4 calories. It provides 0.1 g protein, 0.1 g fat, 0.9 g carbohydrates, 26 mg calcium, 1.7 mg iron and 53 IU vitamin A.

HOW THIS HERB AFFECTS YOUR BODY

Thymol is an expectorant, an agent that causes the mucous membranes lining your respiratory tract to "weep" watery secretions, making it easier for you to cough up mucus. It is also an antiseptic that kills mildew and mold and is used for preserving anatomical and urine specimens.

Thymol has been widely used in patent medicines, but modern research questions its safety and effectiveness. Borneol, linalool, pinene and thymol are irritants that may cause contact dermatitis (itching, burning, stinging, reddened or blistered skin). Cosmetics such as bath oils or soaps that are perfumed with oil of thyme may be irritating. Toothpastes flavored with oil of thyme may cause cheilitis (cracked and bleeding lips) and glossitis (irritation of the tongue).

Benefits. (—)

Adverse effects. (—)

How to Use This Herb

In cooking: One sprig fresh thyme equals the flavoring power of ½ teaspoon ground dried thyme.

Thyme leaves are sweetest if picked just as the flowers appear.

To dry the leaves, hang them upside down in an airy room for 10 days; thyme leaves hold their flavor better than most herbs when dried.

To release the flavor of thyme leaves, crush or crumble them before using.

Around the house: Scatter dried thyme leaves or flowers in your linen closet. They will scent the closet, sheets and towels and are reputed to repel insects as well.

In the garden: Lemon-scented plants such as lemon thyme (*Thymus citriodorus*) seem to repel insects in the garden and may act as safe, natural pest repellents, keeping the bugs away without being poisonous to people or pets.

TURMERIC

About This Plant

Botanical name: *Curcuma longa*
Also known as: Indian saffron
Native to: India, China, the East Indies
Parts used as spice: Rhizome
Medicinal properties: Cholagogue, choleretic
Other uses: Fabric dye

ABOUT THIS SPICE AS FOOD AND FLAVORING

Turmeric is a member of the ginger family. Its thick rhizomes (underground stems) are ground to make an aromatic yellow powder used as a flavoring and to color a wide variety of foods including butter, cheese, margarine, fruit drinks and liqueurs, curry powders, mustards and mustard pickles. The pigment in turmeric is *curcumin*, also known as "turmeric yellow." Turmeric yellow was once used as a fabric dye, but it has since been replaced by synthetic colors derived from coal tar.

Turmeric has a mild, slightly bitter, peppery flavor and aroma that comes from oil of turmeric, which contains peppery-scented, mint-flavored *borneol*; spicy *eucalyptol*, which smells like camphor; and *zingerone*, the spicy sweet flavoring in ginger.

Nutritional profile. One teaspoon (2.2 g) ground turmeric has 8 calories. It provides 0.2 g protein, 0.2 g fat, 1.4 g carbohydrates, 4 mg calcium, 0.9 mg iron and 0.6 mg vitamin C.

HOW THIS SPICE AFFECTS YOUR BODY

The Food and Drug Administration is currently investigating the long-term metabolic effects of curcumin, including its effects on reproduction and the fetus. Although its safety has not yet been definitely established, the amounts used in food are currently considered unlikely to be hazardous.

Borneol and eucalyptol are irritants.

Benefits. (—)

Adverse effects. Turmeric is a choleretic, an agent that stimulates the liver to increase its production of bile. This yellow brown or green fluid helps emulsify fats in your duodenum and increases peristalsis, the rhythmic contractions that move food through your gastrointestinal tract.

Turmeric is also a cholagogue, an agent that stimulates the gallbladder and biliary duct to discharge bile and increases your body's excretion of cholesterol. Choleretics and cholagogues are ordinarily beneficial for healthy people but may pose some problems for people with gallbladder or liver disease. Some other choleretic herbs are ginger, oregano and peppermint.

HOW TO USE THIS SPICE

In cooking: Curcumin's color is very sensitive to light. Protect your turmeric by storing it in a cool, dark cabinet.

Turmeric is a cheap substitute for saffron, the world's most expensive spice and food coloring. Turmeric's flavor is stronger than saffron's, so use it with a light hand.

VANILLA

ABOUT THIS PLANT

Botanical name:	*Vanilla planifolia, Vanilla tahitunsis*
Also known as:	(—)
Native to:	Mexico, East Indies
Parts used as spice:	Unripe fruits ("beans")
Medicinal properties:	(—)
Other uses:	(—)

ABOUT THIS SPICE AS FOOD AND FLAVORING

Vanilla is the only member of the orchid family used as a food. The part used as a spice is the unripe fruit, which looks like a pod and is known as a "bean." The most flavorful vanilla beans are Bourbon beans, native to Mexico but now imported primarily from Madagascar.

The most important flavoring and aroma chemical in vanilla is *vanillin*, a white or slightly yellow substance whose pleasant taste and smell develop when vanilla beans are allowed to dry and ferment ("cure") after picking. In unripe beans the vanillin is bound to a sugar molecule. While the beans ferment, their enzymes separate the vanillin from the sugar molecule, creating the characteristic vanilla flavor and aroma. The cured beans are then chopped and covered with a warm alcohol/water solution that draws out the flavor. When the flavor is strong enough, the liquid ("extract") is drawn off, strained and aged for about a month to polish the flavor.

Vanilla beans are not the only source of vanilla flavoring. *Synthetic vanillin* can be made from *eugenol* (the flavoring ingredient in oil of cloves), *guaiacol* (white or yellow crystals isolated from resin in hardwoods) or *lignin* (a woody fiber in plants). *Ethyl vanillin* is a synthetic flavoring whose flavor and aroma are stronger than vanillin's. The only ingredients in a product labeled Vanilla Extract are vanilla and alcohol. A typical "imitation vanilla" flavoring contains water, propylene glycol (a solvent), alcohol, artificial and natural flavorings that may include as much as 20% pure vanilla extract, sugar, caramel color, dextrose and sodium benzoate (a preservative).

Nutritional profile. (—)

How This Spice Affects Your Body

Vanillin is an irritant that may cause contact dermatitis (itching, burning, stinging, reddened or blistered skin).

Benefits. (—)

Adverse effects. Prolonged handling of vanilla beans may cause vanillism, whose symptoms include contact dermatitis and headaches. Vanillism is most commonly found among food workers who sort and process vanilla beans.

Vanillin is a choleretic, an agent that stimulates the liver to increase its production of bile. This yellow brown or green fluid helps emulsify fats in your duodenum and increases peristalsis, the rhythmic contractions that move food through your gastrointestinal tract. Choleretics are ordinarily beneficial for healthy people but may pose some problems for people with gallbladder or liver disease. However, vanillin is not very active in the amounts normally used in food. Some other choleretic herbs are ginger, oregano and peppermint.

How to Use This Spice

In cooking: As a general rule, the better the vanilla extract or beans, the more they cost. To protect your investment from air and light, store vanilla extract in a dark bottle and vanilla beans in an airtight container in a cool, dark cabinet.

A 1-inch vanilla bean, scraped, equals the flavor of 1 teaspoon vanilla extract.

To make vanilla sugar, put a whole vanilla bean into an airtight container with 2 cups white granulated sugar. You can reuse the same bean until its odor fades.

To make your own vanilla extract, put one vanilla bean into a 350 milliliter bottle of vodka or brandy. (If necessary, break the bean into two or three pieces.) Close the bottle tightly, and let it stand for at least three weeks; then use the vodka or brandy as a substitute for commercial vanilla extract. Remember, the longer the bean is left in the bottle the stronger the vanilla flavor will be.

As a cosmetic: The scent of vanilla is a delicious perfume. Pour a few drops of vanilla extract on a small piece of absorbent cotton and tuck it in your bra. (Don't put the vanilla extract on your skin; it may be irritating.)

Around the house: A vanilla-scented cotton ball will serve as a sachet to perfume a dresser drawer.

VINEGAR

ABOUT THIS CONDIMENT

Chemical name:	Acetic acid
Also known as:	(—)
Native to:	(—)
Parts used as condiment:	(—)
Medicinal properties:	Acidifier
Other uses:	Household cleanser, hair rinse

ABOUT THIS CONDIMENT AS FOOD AND FLAVORING

Vinegar is a solution of *acetic acid* (a chemical that occurs naturally when bacteria metabolize alcohols) and water. *White vinegar* contains acetic acid derived from ethyl alcohol, the alcohol used in alcohol beverages. *Cider vinegar*, which is amber colored and has a "fruity" aroma, contains acetic acid made from the bacterial fermentation of apple juice. *Malt vinegars* are made with acetic acid derived from the fermentation of a barley or other cereal solution. *Herb vinegars* are made by adding herbs to any of the above. *Wine vinegars* are made with acetic acid derived from wine, usually red wine.

Nutritional profile. Vinegar contains minute amounts of calcium and phosphorus, plus iron and potassium. One tablespoon cider vinegar has 1 g carbohydrates, 1 mg calcium, 1 mg phosphorus, 0.1 mg iron, 15 mg potassium and a trace of sodium. Vinegar has no vitamins.

HOW THIS CONDIMENT AFFECTS YOUR BODY

Acetic acid is an acidifier (a chemical used to make solutions or tissues more acid) and a mild urinary irritant.

Benefits. The natural acid pH of the vagina usually prevents the overgrowth of yeast infections. To increase this protective acidity, distilled white vinegar is often used as an ingredient in vaginal douches, commercial as well as homemade. According to the FDA's Advisory Review Panel on OTC (Over-the-Counter) Contraceptives and Other Vaginal Drug products, a dilute solution of vinegar and water (1 ½ teaspoon distilled white vinegar in a quart of warm water) is a safe acid douche. However, there are no scientifically controlled studies showing that it is actually effective in preventing or curing a yeast infection.

Adverse effects. Eating foods marinated in vinegar may cause you to urinate more frequently, an adverse effect turned to an advantage in folk medicine, which generally considers frequent urination as being a way to "clean out the body."

A more serious adverse effect is the possible interaction of wine- or malt-based vinegars with monoamine oxidase (MAO) inhibitors, drugs used to treat depression or hypertension. Vinegars made from wine or malt may contain small amounts of *tyramine*, a natural chemical produced when bacteria digest the proteins in grapes or grains in making beer or wine. Tyramine is a *pressor amine*, a chemical that constricts blood vessels and raises blood pressure. Under ordinary circumstances tyramine is broken down by enzymes in the body and then harmlessly excreted. However, MAO inhibitors interfere with the action of these enzymes. If you eat a food rich in tyramine while you are taking an MAO inhibitor, the tyramine cannot be eliminated from your body. The result may be sustained high blood pressure.

How to Use This Condiment

In cooking: Because acetic acid breaks down protein fibers on the surface of meat, vinegar is a useful tenderizing marinade.

As an acid, vinegar reacts with metal ions from the surface of aluminum, copper, iron or zinc-lined dishes or pots, producing dark compounds that discolor the pot or the food. To prevent this, dishes made with vinegar should be cooked and stored in an enameled or glass vessel.

Vinegar can be used as a substitute for lemon juice. If you are out of lemon juice or are allergic to citrus fruit, try a drop or two of vinegar in your sweetened tea. You'd swear the tart taste matches that of lemons. You can also use a little vinegar in place of lemon juice to give a tart taste to fruit pies (especially apple pies).

As a home remedy: See *Benefits*.

Around the house: Vinegar is a natural acid that can shine chromium, copper and aluminum. To remove stains inside an aluminum pot, for example, fill the pot with 2 cups water plus ¼ cup white distilled vinegar; bring the solution to a boil; and continue boiling until the stains disappear.

After washing glass tumblers or dishes, dip them in a solution of warm water plus a tablespoon of white distilled vinegar, then rinse with cool water and dry thoroughly.

To clean a coffee pot, fill it with water plus a tablespoon of white distilled vinegar, and then run the pot through its cycle to remove coffee oils. Pour out the vinegar/water solution, fill the pot with plain water and repeat the cycle, then dry the pot.

As a cosmetic: Vinegar, which is acidic, will neutralize the alkaline residue left by a soap shampoo, leaving your hair smooth and shiny.

VIOLETS

ABOUT THIS PLANT

Botanical name: *Viola odorata*
Also known as: Garden violet, sweet violet
Native to: Europe
Parts used as herb: Leaves, flowers
Medicinal properties: (—)
Other uses: Perfume, flavoring

ABOUT THIS HERB AS FOOD AND FLAVORING

Sweet violet, which has heart-shaped leaves and root stalks that creep along the ground, is one of the most fragrant of the more than 600 species of violets. Its purple flowers can be candied or used fresh as a garnish in salads. Violets are also a source of an extract used as a flavoring or in perfumes, but many "violet" perfumes—used for scenting shampoos, soaps and other cosmetics—are actually derived from orris root.

Nutritional profile. (—)

HOW THIS HERB AFFECTS YOUR BODY

Benefits. (—)

Adverse effects. Violet flowers are nonpoisonous, but the rhizomes (underground stems), roots and seeds are *purgatives* (strong laxatives) and *emetics* agents that induce vomiting). They may cause severe gastric upset including nausea and vomiting, as well as breathing difficulties and depression of the circulatory system. The larger the dose, the more serious the potential problems.

HOW TO USE THIS HERB

In cooking: **Use only violets that have never been sprayed with any insecticidal chemicals. The safest rule: When in doubt, pass the flowers by.**

For candying, use *Viola odorata*, one of the few violets whose petals are strong enough to hold their shape when candied.

WATERCRESS

ABOUT THIS PLANT

Botanical name: *Nasturtium officinale*
Also known as: Cress, scurvy grass
Native to: Europe
Parts used as herb: Leaves, stems
Medicinal properties: Antiscorbutic
Other uses: (—)

ABOUT THIS HERB AS FOOD AND FLAVORING

Watercress is a cruciferous vegetable, related to broccoli, Brussel sprouts, cabbage, cauliflower and horseradish. It has dark green leaves whose spicy, peppery flavor comes from sulfur compounds similar to *allyl isothiocyanate*, a pungent chemical found in many members of the mustard family and, perhaps, in black pepper, onions and garlic.

Nutritional profile. One-half cup (17 g) chopped raw watercress has 2 calories. It provides 0.4 g protein, a trace of fat, 0.2 g carbohydrates, 20 mg calcium, a trace of iron, 799 IU vitamin A and 7.3 mg vitamin C.

HOW THIS HERB AFFECTS YOUR BODY

Benefits. Watercress is a good source of *beta*-carotene, the vitamin A precursor in deep yellow fruits and vegetables. According to the American Cancer Society, a diet rich in these foods may lower the risk of some forms of cancer.

Vitamin A also protects your eyes. In your body, the vitamin A precursor from watercress is converted to 11-cis retinol, the most important constituent of *rhodopsin*, a protein in the rods in your retina (the cells that enable you to see in dim light and protect your night vision). One-half cup chopped fresh watercress provides 20% of the vitamin A required each day by a healthy woman and 16% of the requirement for a healthy man.

Watercress is rich in vitamin C. One-half cup chopped fresh watercress provides 12% of the daily requirement for a healthy adult.

Adverse effects. Cruciferous vegetables contain chemicals known collectively as "goitrogens." (The goitrogen in watercress is *gluconasturtiin*.) These sulfur compounds slow the thyroid gland's production of thyroid hormones, causing the gland to swell in an effort to produce more hormones. The swollen gland is known as "goiter." Cruciferous vegetables are unlikely to be hazardous for healthy people who eat them in moderation, but they may be troublesome for people who have a thyroid disorder or are using thyroid medication.

CAUTION: Wild watercress may be contaminated by polluted waters and thus hazardous to your health.

How to Use This Herb

Do not tear or cut watercress until you are ready to use it. When you cut into a food rich in vitamin C, its cells release an enzyme called ascorbic acid oxidase. This enzyme destroys vitamin C and reduces the nutritional value of the food.

Chlorophyll, the green coloring in plants, is sensitive to acids. If you heat watercress, its chlorophyll reacts with natural acids in the leaves or in the cooking water, forming a brown compound called *pheophytin.* The pheophytin then reacts with the yellow carotene pigments in the leaves, turning the cooked watercress bronze. To prevent this color change, you must keep the chlorophyll from reacting with the acids in one of these ways: cook the watercress in lots of water to dilute the acids, leave the lid off the pot so the acids can dissipate into the air, or steam the watercress leaves very quickly so there is no time for the reaction to occur. Preparing watercress quickly has an extra benefit: It keeps the cress from turning stringy, which is what happens when it's overcooked.

WORCESTERSHIRE SAUCE

About This Condiment

Chemical name:	(—)
Also known as:	(—)
Native to:	England
Parts used as condiment:	(—)
Medicinal properties:	(—)
Other uses:	(—)

About This Condiment as Food and Flavoring

Worcestershire sauce is an anchovy-based condiment, a British adaptation of *garum,* an ancient Roman seasoning made of rotted fish. A typical modern Worcestershire sauce contains water, vinegar, sweeteners (molasses, corn sweeteners), anchovies, natural flavorings (perhaps including asafetida), and spices such as onions, salt, fresh garlic, cloves, chili peppers and shallots.

Nutritional profile. One teaspoon Worcestershire sauce has 55 mg sodium. One tablespoon has 206 mg sodium.

How This Condiment Affects Your Body

Benefits. (—)

Adverse effects. Because Worcestershire sauce contains anchovies, people sensitive to anchovies (or other fish) may be sensitive to the condiment.

Worcestershire sauce, which is high in sodium, is usually prohibited on a sodium-restricted diet.

Anchovies are preserved (salted) fish. They are high in *tyramine*, a chemical formed naturally when proteins break down during the preservation process. Tyramine is a pressor amine, a chemical that constricts blood vessels and may trigger an increase in blood pressure. Monoamine oxidase (MAO) inhibitors, drugs used to treat hypertension, interfere with the action of the enzymes that break down tyramine. If you eat a food high in tyramine while you are taking an MAO inhibitor, the tyramine cannot be eliminated from your body. The result may be a hypertensive crisis (sustained high blood pressure).

YEAST

About This Plant

Botanical name:	*Saccharomyces* spp.
Also known as:	(—)
Native to:	(—)
Parts used as herb:	(—)
Medicinal properties:	Nutrient, diet supplement
Other uses:	(—)

About This Herb as Food and Flavoring

Yeasts are living organisms with as many as 100 billion cells per ounce. They metabolize (digest) sugars, producing alcohols and carbon dioxide as by-products.

Baker's yeast is used to make bread and yeast cakes. When you mix flour and water and beat the batter, the long protein molecules in the flour relax and unfold, breaking internal bonds (bonds between atoms on the same molecule) and forming new external bonds between atoms in adjoining molecules. The result is a network of elastic *gluten* (protein) that stretches ("rises") as it is filled with the carbon dioxide released when baker's yeast digests sugars in the flour. When the batter or dough is heated, the stretched protein network is baked into place.

Brewer's yeast is a by-product of beer production, yeast cells that are rinsed, dried and sold as a nutritional supplement.

Smoked yeast, a flavoring agent used in prepared foods, including cheese spreads, is made by exposing dry yeast to wood smoke.

Nutritional profile. One packet active dry baker's yeast has 20 calories. It provides 3 g protein, a trace of fat, 3 g carbohydrates, 3 g calcium, 1.1 mg iron, a trace of vitamin C and vitamin A.

One tablespoon brewer's yeast has 25 calories. It provides 3 g protein, a trace of fat, 3 g carbohydrates, 17 mg calcium, 1.4 mg iron, a trace of vitamin C and vitamin A.

How This Herb Affects Your Body

Benefits. Baker's yeast is a good source of folacin. About 50% of the folacin in breads made at home comes from yeast. One packet of baker's yeast has 286 micrograms (0.286 mg) folacin, 72% of the daily requirement (400 micrograms/0.4 mg) for a healthy adult. One tablespoon Brewer's yeast has 313 micrograms (0.313 mg) folacin, 78% of the RDA.

Yeast is also a good source of proteins. It is particularly useful in bread, because the proteins in cereal grains do not contain sufficient amounts of the essential amino acid lysine, which is plentiful in yeast. Combining yeast with flour increases the value of the protein in the bread or cake.

Brewer's yeast is a useful nutritional supplement, providing a variety of B vitamins, plus protein. Yeast approved as a nutritional supplement must be at least 40% protein and contain not less than 0.12 mg thiamine, 0.04 mg riboflavin and 0.25 mg nicotinic acid per gram. (Baker's yeast is *not* a nutritional supplement; it is used only in baking.)

Adverse effects. Consuming large amounts of yeast (as a supplement, for example) may cause nausea and diarrhea. These symptoms have been reported in people who took as little as 20 grams (⅔ oz.) yeast.

Yeast extracts such as Marmite and Bovril may interact with monoamine oxidase (MAO) inhibitors, drugs used to treat hypertension and depression. The beef-flavored extracts, made by breaking down the proteins in beef, contain *tyramine,* a natural by-product of protein degradation. Tyramine—which is also found in aged cheeses and meats—is a *pressor amine,* a chemical that constricts blood vessels and may trigger an increase in blood pressure. MAO inhibitors interfere with the action of the enzymes that break down tyramine. If you eat a food high in tyramine while taking an MAO inhibitor, the tyramine cannot be eliminated from your body. The result may be a hypertensive crisis (sustained high blood pressure). The yeast used in baking bread does not pose this problem.

Yeasts are high in nucleic acids, which are converted to uric acid when metabolized by the human body. Uric acid consists of sharp crystals that may cause gout if they collect in your joints or kidney stones if they collect in your urine. Although controlling the amount of uric acid in your diet may not necessarily control gout (which is most effectively treated with *allopurinol,* a medicine that inhibits the formation of uric acid), limiting foods high in uric acid is still part of many gout regimes.

How to Use This Herb

In cooking: Baker's yeast comes in two forms: compressed yeast cakes and packets of active dry yeast. Compressed yeast becomes active at about 50 degrees F, releases carbon dioxide most effectively at 78 to 82 degrees F and dies at 120 degrees F. It must be kept in the refrigerator, where it will stay fresh for about two weeks. For longer storage (up to two months), freeze the yeast. Packets of active dry yeast are much more popular. They are easy to store. The packets, which are dated, have a life span of about a year. Active dry yeast goes to work at temperatures of about 120 to 130 degrees F.

One packet (one tablespoon) active dry yeast equals the leavening power of one 3.5 oz or 100 g cake of compressed moist yeast.

YELLOW DOCK

About This Plant

Botanical name: *Rumex crispus*
Also known as: Curly dock
Native to: Europe

Parts used as herb: Leaves
Medicinal properties: (—)
Other uses: (—)

About This Herb as Food and Flavoring

Yellow dock is a member of the *Rumex* genus, a group of plants that includes sorrel (*Rumex acetosa*). Yellow dock's slender, curly leaves are used as a vegetable and "pot herb" (an herb used to flavor soups and stews). The leaves have a sharp, bitter flavor similar to that of spinach. The astringency is due to a high *tannin* content, plus *oxalates* (calcium oxalate, oxalic acid and potassium oxalate) and vitamin C (ascorbic acid).

Nutritional profile. One-half cup (67 g) chopped fresh yellow dock leaves has 15 calories. It provides 1.3 g protein, 2.1 g carbohydrates, 0.5 g fiber, 29 mg calcium, 1.6 mg iron, 32.2 mg vitamin C and 2,680 IU vitamin A.

How This Herb Affects Your Body

Tannins are astringents. They coagulate the proteins on the surface of your skin, the mucous membrane lining of your mouth and the lining of your gut, making the tissues pucker.

Benefits. Yellow dock leaves are high in vitamin C. One-half cup chopped fresh leaves provides 54% of the daily requirement for a healthy adult.

The leaves are also a good source of the yellow carotenoid pigment, *beta*-carotene, the vitamin A precursor in deep yellow fruits and vegetables. According to the American Cancer Society, a diet rich in these foods may lower the risk of some forms of cancer.

Vitamin A also protects your eyes. In your body, the vitamin A precursor in yellow dock is converted to 11-cis retinol, the most important constituent of *rhodopsin*, a protein in the rods in your retina (the cells that enable you to see in dim light). One-half cup chopped fresh yellow dock leaves provides 67% of the vitamin A a healthy woman needs each day and 54% of the requirement for a healthy man.

Adverse effects. Yellow dock's pollen is a potential respiratory allergen that may trigger allergic rhinitis (hay fever) and bronchial asthma in sensitive people.

Foods such as spinach and yellow dock leaves, which are high in calcium and oxalates, are prohibited on a low-calcium, low-oxalate diet for people who form calcium-oxalate kidney stones. They may also be prohibited for people with arthritis or gout.

Because the yellow dock plant contains a number of irritants including the oxalates and rumicin, handling may cause contact dermatits (itching, burning, stinging, reddened or blistered skin).

The root of the yellow dock plant contains strong anthraquinone cathartics such as emodin. Anthraquinones, which are found in many plants, act by severely irritating the lining of the gut. They are used in over-the-counter medicines, but many physicians prefer a more gentle laxative such as bulk-forming fiber. **The yellow dock root is no longer considered safe for use as food.**

How to Use This Herb

In cooking: Do not tear or cut yellow dock leaves until you are ready to use them. When you cut into a food rich in vitamin C, its cells release an enzyme called ascorbic acid oxidase. This enzyme destroys vitamin C. **Use only unsprayed leaves.**

To reduce the oxalic acid content of yellow dock leaves, blanch them and discard the cooking water three times before using as directed in your recipe for a vegetable dish or green sauce.

Chlorophyll, the green coloring in plants, is sensitive to acids. When you heat yellow dock leaves, their chlorophyll reacts with natural acids in the leaves or in the cooking water, forming a brown compound called *pheophytin.* The pheophytin then reacts with the yellow carotene pigments in the leaves, turning the cooked yellow dock bronze.

Yellow dock, like spinach, is high in tannins, which react with metals to form dark pigments. If you cook yellow dock or spinach in an aluminum or iron pot, these pigments will discolor the pot and the leaves as well. To keep yellow dock and spinach from darkening, cook them in a glass pot or a pot with an enameled surface.

HAZARDOUS HERBS

A representative list of plants once
used in cooking or as medicines but now
considered unsafe for use
as either food or
home remedy.

ARNICA (*Arnica montana*)

Arnica, also known as bane or mountain tobacco, is an allergen. If you
get it on your skin, it may cause contact dermatitis (itching, burning,
stinging, reddened or blistered skin). If you eat it, it may cause serious
gastroenteritis. In addition, it contains chemicals not identified that may
affect your pulse rate, cause intense muscular weakness and interfere
with your central nervous system, ultimately causing collapse and
death.

AUTUMN CROCUS (*Colchicum autumnale*)

Autumn crocus, also known as meadow saffron, is not a crocus nor is it
closely related to saffron, the yellow spice used in Eastern cuisine. The
plant is the source of colchicine, a drug used to treat gout. Colchicine is
considered safe and effective when prescribed by a doctor who monitors
its use, but the plant itself is poisonous and may cause serious side
effects, including numbness in the throat followed by vomiting, kidney
and respiratory failure.

BELLADONNA (*Atropa belladonna*)

Belladonna, also known as deadly nightshade, contains *hyoscyamine*,
atropein and *hyoscine*, three anticholinergics (drugs that affect the
parasympathetic nervous system, which controls functions such as
breathing and the widening of the pupils of your eyes). They are also
antispasmodics (drugs that relax smooth muscle), extraordinarily useful
in medicine, for example, in drops ophthalmologists use to dilate your
pupils so your eyes can be examined. The plant is poisonous; even small
doses may cause coma or death.

Bittersweet (*Solanum dulcamara*)

Bittersweet, also known as bitter nightshade and felonwood, contains solanine and solanidine, narcotic poisons also found in the green parts (leaves and stems) of the potato and tomato plants, as well as the green spots that sometimes show up on the skin of a potato exposed to light. Solanine and solanidine may cause headache, upset stomach (pain, vomiting, diarrhea), disturbances of the central nervous system (dizziness, dilated pupils, difficulty in breathing and speaking), coma and death.

Black Cohosh (*Cimicifuga racemosa*)

Black cohosh, also known as black snakeroot, is classified by the Food and Drug Administration as an herb of undefined safety. It is known to lower blood pressure in laboratory cats and rabbits (but not dogs). In human beings, black cohosh may cause upset stomach (nausea and vomiting), dizziness, slow heartbeat and excess perspiration. Because it may trigger contractions of smooth muscle, including the muscle of the uterus, the herb is especially hazardous for pregnant women.

Bloodroot (*Sanguinaria canadensis*)

Bloodroot is a member of the poppy family also known as Indian paint because it yields a red juice that Indians once used as war paint. It contains *protopine* (which can make your heartbeat irregular) and *sanguinarine* (which causes glaucoma in laboratory animals). The plant's juice is so caustic that it can destroy skin and mucous membranes. If swallowed, it is a violent poison that causes disturbances in vision, produces opiumlike residues in your urine and, in high doses, causes a burning pain in your stomach, intense thirst, faintness, dizziness, paralysis and collapse.

Blue Flag (*Iris versicolor*)

Blue flag, also known as liver lily and water flag, has poisonous rhizomes (underground stems) that contain *iridin* (irisin), a potent diuretic that is also a liver poison. The plant is a cathartic (violent laxative) and an *emetic* (an agent that causes vomiting). Large amounts may cause nausea and collapse.

Broom (*Cytisus scoparius*)

Broom, also known as broom tops, Scotch broom, and Irish broom, contains *sparteine, isosparteine* and *hydroxytyramine*. All three are diuretics, cathartics (laxatives) and oxytocics (chemicals that induce uterine contractions). The symptoms of broom poisoning are similar to those of nicotine poisoning: headache and dizziness, rapid heartbeat, upset stomach (nausea and diarrhea) and circulatory collapse.

Caper Spurge (*Euphorbia lathyris*)

Caper spurge's buds are sometimes mistaken for true capers, the buds of the spiny shrub *capparis spinosa*. The buds of caper spurge may cause a burning in your mouth, upset your stomach and make you dizzy, and cause irregular heartbeat, delirium and, ultimately, collapse.

Castor Bean (*Ricinus communis*)

Castor beans contain ricin, a chemical that may make your mouth burn, increase your thirst, upset your stomach (pain, nausea and vomiting), blur your vision, make you dizzy and trigger convulsions. As little as one castor bean may be lethal for a child; two to 25 may be fatal for an adult. The oil from castor beans (castor oil), which is used as a laxative, is considered safe because it is extracted from the beans at temperatures lower than 100 degrees F, allowing the beans to release their oil without ricin. The active chemical in castor oil laxative is *ricinolein*, which works by irritating the intestines.

Cherry Laurel (*Prunus laurocerasus*)

Cherry laurel leaves should never be used as a substitute for the leaves of *Lauris nobilis*, which are commonly known as bay leaves. The cherry laurel leaves contain *prularasin*, a chemical that releases hydrogen cyanide in the presence of stomach acid.

Comfrey (*Symphytum peregrinum*)

Comfrey was once cooked and served as a vegetable or added fresh to salads, but it is no longer considered safe to eat. It causes cancer when fed to laboratory rats in concentrations as small as 0.5% to 8% of the diet and contains liver toxins (*pyrrolizidines*) whose effects in human beings are unknown.

FOXGLOVE (*Digitalis purpurea*)

Foxglove is the herb that gave us *digitalis*, the first effective drug for heart disease. Digitalis increases the heart muscle's effectiveness and acts as a diuretic, lowering blood pressure by eliminating excess water from the body. It is considered safe as used in medicine, but the foxglove plant is poisonous. Chewing even one leaf may cause paralysis or sudden heart failure, and fatalities have been reported in people who drank a tea brewed from foxglove. Symptoms of digitalis poisoning include visual disturbances such as a yellow cast over your field of vision, upset stomach (pain, nausea, diarrhea), severe headache, irregular heartbeat and pulse, tremors, convulsions and death.

HENBANE (*Hyoscyamus niger*)

Henbane, also known as poison tobacco, contains the anticholinergics *hyoscyamine, hyoscine (scopolamine)* and *atropine* (see Belladonna). Because henbane may be mistaken for chicory roots or parsnips, people have been poisoned by eating the roots. The symptoms include a red cast over your field of vision, excess salivation, headache, increased pulse rate and convulsions. Henbane may also cause coma and death.

HORSECHESTNUT (*Aesculus hippocastanum*)

Horsechestnuts are the source of a coumarin compound called *aesculin*. This substance is effective in medicine as an antiinflammatory but may cause muscle weakness, nerve damage, dilated pupils, upset stomach (vomiting and diarrhea). Very large doses of the fruit may cause paralysis and coma.

JALAP (*Ipomoea purga*)

Jalap (jalap root), which was once used as a strong cathartic (laxative), contains strongly irritant resins. Large doses may cause dangerous purging and collapse.

JIMSON WEED (*Datura stramonium*)

Jimson weed, also known as mad apple, is a member of the nightshade family. Like belladonna, it contains the anticholinergics *atropine, hyoscyamine* and *hyoscine (scopolamine)*, which are useful in medicine but dangerous in herbs (see Belladonna). Symptoms of jimson weed poisoning include dim vision, dilated pupils (which may occur if you simply handle the plant and then touch your eyes), reddened face and neck, abnormal heartbeat and delirium.

LILY OF THE VALLEY (*Convallaria majalis*)

Lily of the valley contains *convallatoxin, convallarin* and *canvallamarin*, chemicals that increase the effectiveness of the heart muscle. While they are useful in medicines, the plant itself can be poisonous. It is similar to foxglove in that it may cause death by sudden cardiac failure.

LOBELIA (*Lobelia inflata*)

Lobelia, also known as Indian tobacco or wild tobacco because it was once smoked by the Indians to relieve asthma, is a poisonous plant that contains *lobeline,* a respiratory stimulant. Swallowing the plant or drinking a tea made from its leaves or fruit may cause vomiting, profuse perspiration, paralysis, pain, lowered temperatures, rapid pulse, collapse, coma and death.

MANDRAKE (*Mandragora officinarum*)

Mandrake, also known as love apple, contains *atropine* and *hyoscyamine,* the anticholinergics found in belladonna, plus *mandragorine,* which is similar in effect (see Belladonna). Once thought to make a man more fertile, mandrake is now known to cause symptoms of poisoning that include profuse perspiration, paralysis of the gastrointestinal tract, increased heartbeat, dilated pupils and an extreme sensitivity to light.

MAY APPLE (*Podophyllum peltatum*)

Mayapple, also known as American mandrake, contains poisonous *podophyllotoxins.* All parts of the plant except its ripe fruit are considered hazardous and may cause nausea, potentially fatal inflammation of the stomach and intestines and, occasionally, vascular collapse. People who handle the underground stems of the plant and then touch their eyes may develop inflamed eyes or ulcers of the skin. The Food and Drug Administration lists this plant as "unsafe."

MISTLETOE (*Phoradendron serotinum* or *Phoradendron flavescens* or *Viscum flavescens*)

Mistletoe berries are poisonous. They may cause gastroenteritis or contact dermatitis (itching, burning, stinging, reddened or blistered skin);

there has been at least one fatality reported due to acute gastroenteritis and heart failure after drinking a tea brewed of mistletoe berries.

Mountain Laurel (*Kalmia latifolia*)

Unlike *Lauris nobilis*, which produces the bay leaves we use in food, the mountain laurel's leaves and flowers are poisonous. They contain narcotic chemicals that may cause excess salivation and watering of the eyes, vomiting, convulsions and paralysis of your arms and legs and respiratory system. The mountain laurel is hazardous for animals that forage on its leaves, shoots and fruits; people may be poisoned by honey made from its flowers.

Pennyroyal (*Mentha pulegium*)

Pennyroyal's oil contains *pulegone*, a toxin known to cause severe liver damage even in relatively small amounts. Eating pennyroyal may cause convulsions and coma. As little as one-half teaspoon of the pure oil may cause delirium, muscle spasms, shock and loss of consciousness. Two tablespoons have proved fatal. Pennyroyal may also cause contact dermatitis (itching, burning, stinging, reddened or blistered skin).

Peony (*Paeonia officinalis*)

Peony flowers and seeds are known to cause serious stomach upset (nausea, cramps and diarrhea). The root contains *peonal* (or "paeonol") and peregrinine, which can narrow the small blood vessels in your kidneys, decreasing the amount of fluid you excrete as urine.

Poison Hemlock (*Conium maculatum*)

Poison hemlock, also known as fool's parsley, is a poisonous plant containing *coniine*, a colorless liquid that turns dark when exposed to air. Touching the plant may cause contact dermatitis (itching, burning, stinging, reddened or blistered skin); eating it may cause muscle weakness, drowsiness, nausea, breathing difficulties and death.

Rue (*Ruta graveolens*)

Rue's silvery blue green leaves contain oil of rue, a pale yellow, odorous liquid that is 90% *methyl nonyl ketone* and *methyl heptyl ketone*, two smelly chemicals occasionally used in dog and cat repellents. Oil of rue also contains the bitter furocoumarins *bergapten*, *psoralen* and *xanthotoxin*, all of which are used by the plant to repel insects and fungi.

Rue is an internal and external irritant. Eating rue may cause flushed skin, irritation of the lungs, vomiting and collapse in sensitive people. Handling the plant may cause severe contact dermatitis (itching, burning, stinging, reddened or blistered skin), as well as severe sensitivity to sunlight. **Pregnant women should avoid this herb because it contains chemicals reputed to relax smooth muscles, such as the uterus, and may trigger premature labor.**

SASSAFRAS (*Sassafras albidum*)

Sassafras, the original flavoring for root beer and chicle chewing gum, is now banned from use in food in this country because the root and rootbark contain *safrole,* which causes liver tumors in laboratory animals. File, the herbal seasoning made from sassafras, is made from the leaves (which do not contain safrole).

SENNA (*Cassia senna*),
WILD SENNA (*Cassia marilandica*)

Despite their botanical names, these plants bear no relationship to cassia (*Cinnamomun cassia*), the cinnamon-flavored spice. The senna plants contain *anthraquinones,* strong cathartics (laxatives) that work by severely irritating the gastrointestinal tract, and may cause violent purging.

SHAVE GRASS (*Equisetum hyemale*)

Shave grass, classified by the Food and Drug Administration as an herb of undefined safety, contains the nerve poison *equisetine,* as well as nicotine. Eating shave grass will cause loss of appetite, followed eventually by loss of muscular control and, in serious cases, breathing difficulties, a weakened pulse rate, convulsions, coma and death. Shave grass has one practical benefit, however. Because it contains large amounts of silicon oxide, an abrasive, it is sometimes used to shine metals, particularly copper.

SWEET FLAG (*Acorus calamus*)

Sweet flag, also known as calamus and flagroot, is used in the Near East as a candy and breath sweetener. Its leaves and roots contain oil of calamus, a yellow aromatic volatile oil used in hair powders, perfumery and to flavor alcoholic beverages. In 1968 the Food and Drug Administration announced that a variety of oil calamus from Asia (Oil of calamus, Jammu) caused cancers in laboratory rats. The effect may be due primarily to asarone or to safrole (which is known to cause liver tumors in laboratory animals). The FDA has now declared this species unsafe.

SWEET WOODRUFF (*Galium odoratum*)

Sweet woodruff, also known as waldmeister, is the herb used to flavor German May wine. It contains bitter tasting, vanilla-scented *coumarin*, a liver toxin that has caused extensive liver damage when fed to laboratory animals. Coumarin is also a vitamin K antagonist. Vitamin K, which is made naturally by the bacteria that live in our intestines, enables the liver to produce prothrombin, the blood plasma protein that makes blood clot. Coumarin derivatives such as dicoumarol and warfarin (Coumadin, Panwarfin) are used in medicine as anticoagulants. They are also used as a rat poison, which kills by causing the animal to hemorrhage. If used during the first trimester of pregnancy, these drugs may cause birth defects including blindness and damage to the central nervous system. Large amounts of a tea made from sweet woodruff may cause dizziness and vomiting. The Food and Drug Administration has approved the use of coumarin as a flavor only in alcoholic beverages (bitters, May wine and vermouth); it is no longer allowed in food.

TANSY (*Tanacetum vulgare* or *Chrysanthemum vulgare*)

Tansy, also known as bitter buttons, is a member of the chrysanthemum family, a strongly aromatic herb with bright yellow flowers. Once used to give foods a bitter flavor, tansy is no longer used in cooking because its oil contains *thujone*, a toxin also found in sage and wormwood. Thujone may cause thirst, restlessness, dizziness, a tingling in your ears, trembling and numbness in your arms, hands, legs and feet, loss of muscular power, delirium, general paralysis and death. Tansy also contains *arbusculin-A* and *tanacetin*, two irritants that may cause contact dermatitis (itching, burning, stinging, reddened or blistered skin) if you handle the plant.

TONKA BEAN (*Dipteryx odorata*)

Tonka bean contains *coumarin*, a vanilla-scented chemical that is an anticoagulant (see Sweet woodruff). Laboratory rats and dogs fed the tonka bean have suffered liver damage, retarded growth and testicular atrophy.

VIRGINIA SHAKEROOT (*Aristolochia serpentaria*)

Virginia snakeroot, also known as snakeweed because it was once used to treat snakebite, contains aristolochine, a chemical that can violently irritate the gastrointestinal tract and kidneys and may cause coma and death from respiratory paralysis. The plant is also a mutagen and suspected carcinogen.

WAHOO (*Euonymus atropurpureus*)

Wahoo, also known as burning bush, contains a resin called euonymin, a cathartic (strong laxative) that works by irritating the lining of the stomach. Eating wahoo may cause severe gastric upset (vomiting and diarrhea), plus weakness, chills, convulsions and loss of consciousness.

WHITE SNAKEROOT (*Eupatorium rugosum*)

White snakeroot, also known simply as snakeroot, contains a poison that may cause an effect called "trembles" in cattle and other livestock who forage on any part of the plant. Human beings who drink milk or eat meat or butter taken from these animals may be poisoned by the plant.

WINTERGREEN (*Gaultheria procumbens*)

Wintergreen, also known as teaberry, is native to North America. Its leaves contain methyl salicylate (wintergreen oil), an oily liquid that smells and tastes like wintergreen. Swallowing even small amounts of wintergreen oil may cause severe poisoning: nausea, vomiting, acidosis, pulmonary edema, pneumonia, convulsions and death. Most modern "wintergreen oil" is a synthetic methyl salicylate.

WORMWOOD (*Artemisia absinthium*)

Wormwood, also known as absinthe, contains oil of wormwood, which may be as much as 13% *thujone*, a narcotic poison that can damage the nervous system and cause mental deterioration. Oil of wormwood, which tastes like licorice, was once used to flavor absinthe, a licorice liqueur that is now illegal in the United States. The symptoms of wormwood poisoning include thirst, restlessness, dizziness, a tingling in your ears, trembling and numbness in your arms, hands, legs and feet, loss of muscular power, delirium, general paralysis and death. The Food and Drug Administration has approved some thujone-free derivatives of oil of wormwood.

BIBLIOGRAPHY

BOOKS

AMA Drug Evaluations. 5th ed. Chicago: American Medical Association, 1983.

The American Dietetic Association. *Handbook of Clinical Dietetics.* New Haven: Yale University Press, 1981.

Berkow, Robert, ed. *The Merck Manual,* 15th ed. Rahway, N.J.: Sharp & Dohme Research Laboratory, 1987.

Briggs, George M., and Calloway, Doris Howes. *Nutrition and Physical Fitness.* New York: Holt, Rinehart and Winston, 1984.

Duke, James A. *Handbook of Medicinal Herbs.* Boca Raton, Florida: CRC Press, 1988.

Freydberg, Nicholas, and Gortner, Willis. *The Food Additive Book.* New York: Bantam Books, 1982.

Gilman, Alfred Goodman; Goodman, Louis S.; Gilman, Alfred. *The Pharmacological Basis of Therapeutics,* 6th ed. New York: Macmillan, 1980.

Gosselin, Robert E.; Hodge, Harold C.; Smith, Roger P.; and Gleason, Marion N., eds. *Clinical Toxicology of Commercial Products,* 4th ed. Baltimore: Williams & Wilkins, 1977.

Handbook of Nonprescription Drugs, 8th ed. (The American Pharmaceutical Association, the National Professional Society of Pharmacists, Washington, D.C., 1986)

Jaffrey, Madjur. *World-of-the-East Vegetarian Cooking.* New York: Alfred A. Knopf, 1981.

Krupp, Marcus A.; Chatton, Milton J.; and Tierney, Lawrence M. *Current Medical Diagnosis and Treatment 1986.* Los Altos, California: Lange Medical Publications, 1986.

Lewis, Walter H., and Elvin-Lewis, Memory P.F. *Medical Botany.* New York: John Wiley & Sons, 1977.

Long, James W. *The Essential Guide to Prescription Drugs.* New York: Harper & Row, 1987.

Lust, John. *The Herb Book.* New York: Bantam Books, 1983.

Magic and Medicine of Plants. Pleasantville, New York: The Reader's Digest Association, 1986.

McGee, Harold. *On Food and Cooking.* New York: Charles Scribner's Sons, 1984.

Rombauer, Irma S., and Becker, Marion Rombauer. *Joy of Cooking.* Indianapolis: Bobbs-Merrill Company, 1984.

Rosengarten, Frederic Jr. *The Book of Spices.* New York: Jove Publications, 1981.

Steiner, Richard P. *Folk Medicine.* Washington, D.C.: American Chemical Society, 1986.

Taylor's Guide to Vegetables & Herbs. Boston: Houghton Mifflin, 1987.

The Way Things Work. 2 vols. New York: Simon and Schuster, 1967.

Toxicants Occurring Naturally in Foods. 2d ed. Washington, D.C.: National Academy of Sciences, 1973.

Tyler, Varro E. *Hoosier Home Remedies.* West Lafayette, Indiana: Purdue University Press, 1985.

————*The New Honest Herbal.* Philadelphia: George F. Stickley Co., 1987.

Windholz, Martha, ed. *The Merck Index,* 10th ed. Rahway, N.J.: Merck & Co., 1987.

Zapsalis, Charles, and Beck, R. Anderle. *Food Chemistry and Nutritional Biochemistry.* New York: John Wiley & Sons, 1985.

Zimmerman, David R. *The Essential Guide to Nonprescription Drugs.* New York: Harper & Row, 1983.

PAMPHLETS & PERIODICALS

Ames, Bruce N. "Dietary carcinogens and anticarcinogens," *Science* (Sept. 21, 1983).

"Aspartame not linked to headaches," *Calorie Control Commentary* (Spring, 1988).

"Beware the bay leaf," *British Medical Journal* (December 20–27, 1980).

Composition of Foods, Spices and Herbs. Agriculture Handbook no. 8-2. Washington, D.C.: Government Printing Office, 1977.

Does Nature Know Best? Natural Carcinogens in American Food. New York: American Council on Science and Health, October, 1985.

Duke, James. "The Joy of Ginger," *American Health*, May 1988.

Enjoy Your Plants ... But Protect Your Family. Public Information Bulletin, National Poison Center Network, Children's Hospital of Pittsburgh (n.d.).

"Folk Cure for the Seasick," *The New York Times*, April 13, 1982.

"Food and Drug Interactions," *FDA Consumer*, March 1978

"Food Preservative Made from Rosemary," *The New York Times*, Jan. 24, 1987.

Gastrointestinal Disease Symposium Issues & Answers. Dallas: Texas Health Sciences Center, (n.d.).

Gebhardt, Susan E., and Matthews, Ruth H. *Nutritive Value of Foods.* USDA Home and Garden Bulletin no. 72, 1985.

A Glossary of Spices. Englewood Cliffs, N.J.: American Spice Trade Association, 1982.

Gossel, Thomas A. "A review of aspartame: Characteristics, safety and uses," *U.S. Pharmacist* (Jan. 1984).

Health News Tips. New York: Empire Blue Cross and Blue Shield, (Fall 1985).

"Healthwise," *U.S. Pharmacist* (May 1984, April 1987)

Hold the mayo questions. Cooperative Extension Service, Michigan State University & USDA, July 18, 1979.

"Horseradish Horrors," *Newssearch*, vol. 5 (Oct. 3, 1988).

"Hot Pepper and Pain," *The New York Times*, June 28, 1983.

"The hot side of chiles," *Science News*, July 16, 1988.

"If supping on sushi, watch that wasabi." *Science News*, January 16, 1988.

Jacknowitz, Arthur I., "Artificial sweeteners: How safe are they?" *U.S. Pharmacist* (January 1988)

Kiesel, Marcia. "From the Herb Garden," *Food & Wine*, March 1987, July 1987.

Larkin, Tim, "Herbs Are Often More Toxic Than Magical," *FDA Consumer* (October 1983).

"Low calorie allergy," *Science News*, June 18, 1986.

The McCormick/Schilling Guide to Gourmet Spices. (Baltimore, Md: Mc-Cormick & Company, Inc.) n.d.

Moffatt, Anne Simon, and Sears, Cathy, "Plant Power," *American Health,* April 1987.

"Questions of Taste," *Food & Wine,* September 1986, October 1987.

"Red pepper eases pain of cutaneous nerve disorders," *Medical World News,* January 11, 1988

"Salt sensitive genes," *Science News,* November 29, 1986.

Schneider, Elizabeth. "The Era of the Edible Blossoms: Innovation and Rediscovery," *The New York Times,* August 24, 1988.

The Sodium Content of Your Food. U.S.D.A. Home and Garden Bulletin 233. Washington, D.C.: Government Printing Office, 1980.

"Study Finds that Mayonnaise Can Inhibit Spoilage of Food," *The New York Times,* May 12, 1982.

"The Sweet and Sour History of Saccharin, Cyclamate, Aspartame," *FDA Consumer.* February 1980.

Sweetener Fact Sheet. Atlanta, Ga.: Calorie Control Council (April 1983).

Thomas, Patricia. "Chinese data base may shed light on diet, heart disease," *Medical World News* (May 23, 1988).

"Toxic Reactions to Plant Products Sold in Health Food Stores," *The Medical Letter,* April 6, 1979.

Tropp, Barbara, "All About Peppercorns," *Food & Wine,* May 1985.

Tufts University Diet & Nutritional Letter. ("An Expert Answers Questions on Herbal Teas," June 1986; "More Evidence on the Safety of Aspartame," February 1988).

Watt, Bernice K., and Merrill, Annabel L. *Composition of Foods.* Agriculture Handbook no. 8. Washington, D.C.: Government Printing Office: 1975.

What You Should Know About ... (Allspice, Basil, Capcisum Spices, Celery Seed, Cinnamon, Cloves, Coriander, Cumin Seed, Dehydrated Garlic, Dehydrated Onion, Dill, Fennel Seed, Mustard Seed, Nutmeg & Mace, Oregano, Paprika, Pepper, Sage, Sesame Seed, Thyme, Turmeric). Englewood Cliffs, N.J.: American Spice Trade Association, (n.d.).

"When hot may be anticarcinogenic," *Science News,* July 16, 1988.

INDEX

*Nutrients in herbs, spices and
condiments*
(Note: For information about the
nutritional values of specific seasonings,
please see the Nutritional Profile in each
entry.)

Recipes